SECOND EDITION

MOBILE & SOCIAL
GAME DESIGN

MONETIZATION METHODS AND MECHANICS

SECOND EDITION

MOBILE & SOCIAL GAME DESIGN

MONETIZATION METHODS AND MECHANICS

TIM FIELDS

CRC Press
Taylor & Francis Group

CRC Press is an imprint of the
Taylor & Francis Group, an **informa** business

AN A K PETERS BOOK

CRC Press
Taylor & Francis Group
6000 Broken Sound Parkway NW, Suite 300
Boca Raton, FL 33487-2742

© 2014 by Taylor & Francis Group, LLC
CRC Press is an imprint of Taylor & Francis Group, an Informa business

No claim to original U.S. Government works

Printed on acid-free paper
Version Date: 20130827

International Standard Book Number-13: 978-1-4665-9868-3 (Paperback)

Library of Congress Cataloging-in-Publication Data

Fields, Tim.
  [Social game design]
  Mobile and social game design : monetization methods and mechanics / Tim Fields. -Second edition.
      pages cm
  "An A K Peters book."
  "First Edition published as Social Game Design: Monetization Methods and Mechanics by Morgan Kaufmann in 2011."
  Previous edition by Tim Fields and Brandon Cotton.
  Includes index.
  ISBN 978-1-4665-9868-3 (alk. paper)
  1. Computer games--Design. I. Title.

QA76.76.C672F553 2014
794.8'1536--dc23   2013034564

Visit the Taylor & Francis Web site at
http://www.taylorandfrancis.com

and the CRC Press Web site at
http://www.crcpress.com

Tim would like to dedicate this book to the new generation of gaming mentors Hill, Cogburn, Mobley, Decker, Cotton, Maddin, Crow, Klier, and Barton, once passionate young men, now the grizzled veterans. And always, RS.

Contents

About the Author

Tim Fields has been playing and designing games since the Commodore 64. He has built text adventures, board games, card games, pen-and-paper games, drinking games, RPGs, shooters, 3D engines, squad-based tactical games, sports games, racing games, mobile games, and a few others besides. Tim has been lucky enough to get paid for making games and software since 1995 as a designer, producer, team leader, marketer, and business developer.

He has been involved with several of the top franchises of the last few decades, such as *Halo, Need for Speed, Call of Duty, Brute Force, SSX*, and others. In addition to leading teams who make great games and helping companies and teams find partners, Tim is active in the game development and financial community as a consultant, writer, and speaker. He rambles about the world with his wife, cats, and way too many books, trying to help brilliant people make games that will delight millions.

CHAPTER 1

Introduction

1.1 THE CHANGING TIDE

A few years ago the war looked like it had been won. Microsoft and Sony had divided up the gaming public into two hostile camps. Nintendo's Wii managed to widen the traditional audience of core gamers to include families, expanding the target audience to both younger and older prospective players. Instead of accepting a third-place to Sony and Microsoft's superior hardware, Nintendo took simpler game mechanics and cheaper hardware and proved that they could expand gaming into a more mainstream market.

In the meantime, while the three console manufacturers continued to focus on living-room experiences, fans lamented the supposed death of PC gaming. Games like *Halo* and *Call of Duty* had moved the traditional first-person shooter (FPS) and action markets toward the consoles, but millions of new players flocked to PC-based online experiences. In particular, thirteen million of them happily shelled out fifteen dollars a month to Blizzard to play *World of Warcraft*, and hundreds of thousands more subscribed to a half dozen or so of the less-successful massively multiplayer online (MMO) games. Most of these MMOs danced happily in the wake of early innovators like *Ultima Online*, *Meridian 59*, and *EverQuest*, and even more ancient MUDs (multi-user dungeons), MOOs (MUD, object oriented), and BBS (bulletin board system) games, forgotten by all but the old sages of game design. The death of PC gaming turned out to have been exaggerated, and the PC remained a viable platform for game development—albeit one that now needed to offer a different type of product, with a different business model. The war for the hearts, minds, and, more importantly, the pocketbooks of gamers seemed likely to settle into a comfortable four-way victory, in which console manufacturers competed with one another for an expanding market, and PC gamers subscribed to one or two of the big MMOs.

However, a quiet, powerful new force was germinating, heralded by companies like PopCap Games, and led by a vanguard of strange, cheap, lo-fi experiences with names like *Habbo Hotel* and *Second Life*. Games like *Puzzle Pirates* and *Bejeweled* demonstrated that there was room for innovation in smaller, more casual games, games for gamers who didn't have hours each day to devote to their hobby. More and more Flash-based games, built to take advantage of the increasingly high bandwidth of the ever-expanding

World Wide Web, appeared on the scene, providing users with quick, cheap experiences just a click away from their favorite website. Yet few of these games made much money or attracted serious notice.

Then, in 2004, a brilliant misfit from Harvard named Mark Zuckerberg turned the geography of the battlefield upside down. A cynical loner, at least according to the award-winning biographical film *The Social Network*, Mr. Zuckerberg managed to take the principles first illustrated by sites like MySpace and transform them into a global empire that connected us all with first our fellow students, then our social circle, and eventually our long-lost friends, family, their neighbors, and even some pets. In so doing, Facebook manifested a new breed of platform that appealed to a new, much larger and diverse user base, rocketing the world of "gaming" far beyond the old console or MMO crowd, and even past the expanded living room audience the Wii commanded. The socially "sticky" elements of the platform made it easier to encourage friends to make connections, join in the fun, and eventually play the games. While first imagined as a platform for Harvard University students, Facebook quickly expanded to accommodate other college students, who signed up by the tens of thousands. In 2006, the network was opened to anyone over the age of thirteen. Within two years, the site had more than 100 million registered users.

Beyond just sending messages to friends and posting pictures, huge numbers of these Facebook users began to use the platform for gaming. More interesting still, many were not people who traditionally spent money on console, handheld, or MMO PC games. Online social networks made a whole new breed of gamer possible, a gamer who wanted to play in bite-sized chunks, in those brief moments while they were online, checking on their friends or updating their own statuses. Many would never have considered spending sixty dollars on a retail game but seemed quite comfortable parting with two or three dollars per day to play games like *Mafia Wars* or *FarmVille*. Facebook didn't just change the demographics of gamers; it changed the economics of gaming.

At the same time, the rapid adoption of smartphones, first Apple's staggeringly successful iPhone line, then Google's Android platform, gave hundreds of millions of users a new way to play online games, and a second, even handier mechanism through which they could "connect" with their friends. These devices let users make calls and text, sure, but they also accessed email, connected to the Internet, and allowed the user to purchase "apps," which, due to their low (or no) price and abundance of options, helped the user tailor their smart phone to their unique needs. More like tiny handheld PCs, these devices delivered thousands of games, dressed up like apps, which could be played on the phones themselves. More importantly, they swelled the number of users who interacted with Facebook, and the number of hours those users *spent* on Facebook, driving the site to over 600 million users by the beginning of 2011, and passing the one billion user mark in late 2012.

Once apps became games, devices like the iPhone began taking huge chunks of market share from traditional handheld gaming devices like the PlayStation Portable (PSP) and the Nintendo DS (NDS). Handheld devices manufacturers have countered this trend by introducing technological gimmicks like stereoscopic 3D (in the case of the Nintendo 3DS), or ever more full-featured interfaces and software suites (as with the PlayStation Vita), but it's unclear that these efforts will save the market for dedicated handheld gaming devices. Social gaming via full-featured smartphones has proven its power and increasingly appears to be the dominant mobile platform going forward. The integration of mobile devices and social networks continued; the Facebook Messenger application lets users call their friends using VOIP technology from their mobile devices. Many mobile games now offer matchmaking services, which allow users to find friends within their social networks to play with. And mobile devices themselves, smartphones are growing in terrific numbers. By the time you read this, there will likely be more mobile phones on Earth than people.[*] And the percentage of these which are smartphones is growing rapidly.[†]

By the beginning of 2013, the clearly defined battle lines in the console wars and the MMO dominance of PC games have become a fractured free-for-all, in which upstart companies like Zynga can go from unknown shops to media powerhouses having more than 250 million monthly users (in Zynga's case, a journey that took them less than one thousand days) and then founder on the rocks of Wall Street just as quickly. Most game designers are no longer able to focus on designing their game for just one system. Even console products are now expected to have social tie-ins, both on Facebook and on mobile platforms, in an effort to drive customer awareness and customer engagement. As Sony and Microsoft gear up for another revision of their home consoles, and Valve's Steam platform makes a play to move into the center of the living room, the mobile platform creators are eyeing the console gamers as well, with Android-based home consoles appearing on Kickstarter, and many tablets and phones offering advanced video output options that let users play a game on the go and then seamlessly connect and keep playing on their HDTV.

Beyond the particulars of the hardware and software that powers this panoply of devices, this kaleidoscope of gaming options all have this in common: All games on all devices can now make use of the interconnectedness of social networks to make stickier, more compelling games. This book will explore how.

This book will also explain how the gaming industry arrived where it is today by giving an overview of the major phases of the evolution of the gaming sector. We'll discuss the way early games were marketed and monetized. We'll talk about how early BBS games and MUDs evolved into the sophisticated subscription-model-based products that *World of Warcraft* and its competitors have become. We'll study the rise of free-to-play models in South Korea and China, brought about by an effort to circumvent rampant piracy. We'll learn how those games managed to retain their customer base by adopting Western designs but simultaneously fitting into the Internet café culture of rented PCs, where users pay a few RMB per hour to smoke cigarettes and while away the hours on first-person shooters, MMOs, and MOBAs (multiplayer online battle arenas). We'll look at how these games ended up paving the way for much of what the West currently understands about microtransaction models (in which users get the client software for free, or at very low cost, and are asked to pay small fees for in-game items, perks, or services), a model that is fast becoming dominant. We'll study the different generations of Facebook games in greater depth and devote a little time to looking at some of the other social media networks, both

---

[*] http://www.cisco.com/en/US/solutions/collateral/ns341/ns525/ns537/ns705/ns827/white_paper_c11-520862.html
[†] http://www.nielsen.com/us/en/newswire/2013/mobile-majority—u-s—smartphone-ownership-tops-60-.html

the all-but-forgotten and the up-and-comers. We'll look at early mobile games that succeeded due to their expert use of social network features, and we'll investigate some of the later waves of mobile and tablet game platforms, which have helped push the convergence of social and mobile gaming. We'll study popular mechanisms for acquiring users, popular dual currency models, and methods of monetizing users once you get them. We'll look at how to put the right kinds of hooks in your games, gather the right kinds of metrics, and evaluate that information to increase the game's overall stickiness and revenue per user. We'll look at games like *Magic: The Gathering*, and how it influenced a generation of online collectible card games, and at other games on platforms ranging from the iPhone and Android to Facebook, to help further illustrate some of our key lessons.

We'll spend time demystifying the alphabet soup of industry terms that have sprouted up around mobile and social game design and monetization like brambles around a castle; we'll teach you how to cut through the jargon to reach the treasures that await within. Confused by DAU, MAU, ARPU, PCU, ARPPU, and the rest? By the time you finish reading this book, you won't be. Would you like to know what social and mobile game designers mean when they talk about "whales" or "gold sinks"? We'll teach you. Whether you're a game designer trying to beat out *FarmVille*, a studio manager looking to take your company in a new direction, or an investor who wants to better understand the financial opportunities in this brave new space, we'll better prepare you to navigate the maze.

Next we'll dive deep into the different strategies for monetizing your games. This isn't a book about how to make "great" games; this is a book about how to make money through brilliant design, flawless execution, and painstaking iteration. As such, we'll spend a lot of time visiting about the different mechanisms for giving users the types of experiences they're willing to pay for. Different approaches can vary in effectiveness for different genres of games, so we'll look at a number of common types of games, both those that treat games as a service and more traditional, one-time purchase products. (If you're still in the console biz, there are ways to use these techniques and mobile companion applications to further monetize your retail customers…if you're clever!) We'll talk through episodic content, advertisement, and optional subscription models.

The sale of virtual goods made $15 billion in 2012.* Yeah, that was *billion* with a *b*. This amount has doubled since the first edition of this book. It's not a trend that is going away. So we'll spend a lot of time studying how your game can get a piece of that pie, from markets in Europe, North America, and Asia and even in emerging markets like Russia, Brazil, and Turkey. We'll talk about how to combat the illegal sale of virtual goods that you *don't* want freely traded and how to charge for those you *do*, with either single, dual, or more complex currency systems. We'll give examples of how to make use of instrumentation and analytics to hone these offerings for maximum player value. We'll investigate the challenges of dealing with the volume of "big data" that such analytics can generate and how to mine it for gold. Finally, we'll talk through some of the more interesting balancing issues associated with managing game economies.

---

* http://www.superdataresearch.com/monetization-is-a-four-letter-word/

Along the way, we'll consult industry thought-leaders, those who design and produce the games, run the shops, analyze the metrics, and make the deals that motivate these exciting new sectors of the market. Each of these luminaries will discuss one of the above topics, in a Q&A interview format.

At the end of this wild ride, you will know the history of game monetization, from the first cartridge-based games sold through retail in 1981 to the most innovative online mobile and social game monetization tricks from 2013. You'll have a superb working knowledge of industry terminology, both for retail products and for the new-language jargon of MMO and social, mobile, and tablet game metrics and user-tracking data. You'll have learned how more than fifty different games fit into the tapestry of the marketplace, how the companies that create and publish them have sought to innovate, and which have won (and lost) in this high-stakes business. You'll understand the overlap between console, mobile, handheld, PC, MMO, and social games and how to evaluate success in each of these market segments. You'll also understand the ways that the lines can be blurred between these types of products, as well as what design elements can be harvested from major successes in each area to be applied to other types of games. You'll understand the interplay between Asia and the West and why different types of design features work better in different territories. You'll know about the also-ran social networks that pioneered the model that Facebook currently owns, and you'll be familiar with the newcomers worth watching, both in North America and in emerging markets like Brazil and Turkey. You'll get to spend a little time thinking about the coming advancements in mobile and tablet gaming and how these fast-growing market segments all converge in the minds and living rooms of your users. Finally, you'll have been exposed to a dozen or more game design techniques for making your mobile and social games attract users; you'll know how to make money from them by providing superior play experiences and how to retain those players so they don't lose interest and go spend their dollars elsewhere. When you're done, we'll point you to a website and (of course) a Facebook page where you can visit with other designers, product managers, and investors interested in continuing this discussion in an online forum, so the conversation can continue to evolve as new trends and new games appear on the scene.

1.2 WHAT THIS BOOK IS NOT

This is not a book that will teach you how to program games. Even if you are already a skilled software engineer, this book will not teach you how to write code for social or mobile games. There are many fine books on the market that deal with these types of topics, and the SDKs and APIs you'll need to master to succeed in this endeavor evolve too quickly to be well served in print.

This is not a book about project management (though we have written those). To build high-quality mobile and social games you will need expert producers, knowledgeable development managers, and skilled team leads. You'll also need to find a process that works for your staff, be that Scrum, Lean, Kanban, Old-School Waterfall, or something altogether different. Of course, given the relatively low barrier to entry in the mobile space, you can likely use the lessons herein even if you are just a few good friends making your game out of a dorm room.

This book will not teach you how to lead teams effectively. (We've written a book on that topic, as well.) You'll need to know this—to have a blend of intelligence, charisma, and wisdom that would do a cleric proud—in order to successfully build social games. But we simply don't have the room to teach those skills here, and for mobile games, you may not need them—at least not until after your first hit.

This is not a book that pretends to teach you how to build a social game in three days or even three weeks. While such a feat may be possible, we doubt it and are skeptical of those books that claim to tell you how to do it. In any case, we believe the best games are built over time, by teams led by expert professionals who have a proven track record in making great games.

However, if you are new to game development, do not despair. This book will teach you a great deal about how to think about games as products, how to consider design choices as both a game designer and a businessperson, and how to evaluate your game against the market.

Finally, it's worth mentioning as a caveat that this is an incredibly rapidly evolving space. From the time we began writing this book and the second edition, there have been several major acquisitions of major players in the space, a few implosions, a roller-coaster stock offering and subsequent crash that shook the foundations of the social gaming sector, the introduction of a brand-new social network, and a massive rise in tablet devices. This new and revised edition was written quickly, because we know you need this information in early 2014, not early 2017. As a result, many topics may have only sufficient depth to give you an idea of what to look for; it is our hope that this volume will spark discussion and inspiration among the community and that we can all continue the conversation online in the coming months and years.

So let's dive in.

CHAPTER 2

What Is a Social Game?
Are Mobile Games Social?

2.1 MEET YOUR COMPETITION

There's a strong temptation to imagine that social games should be narrowly defined only to include those games that have infiltrated Facebook, mostly courtesy of Zynga and the like. Certainly, many of those games initially set the gold standard for massive user acquisition in online social gaming. And despite a cooling of the Facebook game sector, these games are played by over a hundred million users per day, according to various metrics-tracking websites. They make a fortune in microtransaction revenues every day. So in writing the first edition of this book, we wrestled with the question, Should we stick to an analysis of how to design Zynga-like games for Facebook and call it a day?

Even a few years ago, the answer was "no." Such a study would have limited utility and would cease to be topical the minute new social networks eclipsed Facebook, as undoubtedly will happen…eventually. Moreover, as many companies and investors are discovering the hard way, it is extremely difficult to succeed as a "fast-follower" in a space that already moves with a speed and agility that would make a falcon jealous, in an industry that seems to reinvent the "core experiences" it offers to the user every nine months. An intimate dissection of *FarmVille*, *Vampire Wars* (already moribund), *CityVille*, *Candy Crush*, or even *Clash of Clans* might remain current for the next year or two, but little more, and it would be extremely difficult for the lessons learned in such a narrow study to help guide the reader's steps over the next decade. Moreover, as we noted in the first edition of this book, the powerful effects that social games can have also exist quite outside "traditional" social networks. Many of the most successful mobile games have succeeded with designs that take advantage of the network effects that exist in so connected a world. Mobile and tablet games can be social games as well. So can console games.

Indeed, most or all of the really successful social game development companies out there have pivoted toward mobile and tablet gaming in recent years. Virality on the Facebook platform changed and can easily continue to change, ads got more expensive, and constant changes to the platform forced developers to regularly invest in reengineering parts of their games in ways that may not have paid dividends to the gamers.* Moreover, mobile devices and tablets are quickly taking over the mindshare for many gamers. Indeed, many analysts suggest that phones and tablet devices (or the so-called hybrid "ph-ablet" devices) will be the dominant gaming device within a few years.† And these devices all exist as part of online networks that allow them to take advantage of almost all of the features that once defined "social" games. At the same time, users seem to be showing some fatigue with Facebook games themselves,‡ while the mobile market continues to grow.

So then, let us define social games a bit more broadly, and hopefully in a less arbitrary fashion, in an effort to glean broad principles that will apply to game design and monetization over the next decade, across a variety of platforms. To do this, we'll look at a few "social games" from the last two decades (yes, there are some!) and hopefully offer an inclusive definition that is still sufficiently narrow that we won't end up talking about all games on all platforms throughout all of gaming time. Here's the definition we've agreed upon, based on our own understanding of the market and an analysis of the types of games that we believe will benefit you over the course of reading this book:

> A social game is one in which the user's interactions with other players help drive adoption of the game and help retain players and that uses an external social network of some type to facilitate these goals.

Let's indulge ourselves in a quick dissection of the definition. To be a social game, we believe you need to encourage users to interact with one another. This needn't necessarily be in a real-time, synchronous manner. In fact, in many of the games we'll study, user interactions are tangent to the core gameplay. But a purely single-player product without any way of communicating, assisting, or thwarting other players just isn't going to qualify as social. (Though we may still explore one or two in cases where they nicely illustrate elements of game design that we think can be applied the social and mobile gaming space.)

We believe that new player acquisition and retention are two of the most important things to consider for any game. This is even more critical in games where your users didn't have to pay you for the product initially. So-called *freemium* games, whose business model is almost synonymous with social and mobile gaming, only return money to the degree that they keep passing users through their funnel and keep them coming back.

Finally, we want to draw a distinction between games that create their own social ecosystem within the game and those that leverage external social networks to achieve their ends. As we'll discuss, there are many types of social networks, from those that explicitly so identify to far looser collections of communication features that simply help bring gamers together. Most modern smartphones, for example, provide the user with a rich array of tools for social communication but are not social networks in and of themselves. Some

---

* http://gamasutra.com/blogs/AndrewChen/20130422/190988/Why_developers_are_leaving_the_Facebook_platform. php

† http://techcrunch.com/2013/04/25/juniper-games-downloads-forecast/

‡ http://www.gamasutra.com/view/news/190679/Social_games_decline_is_holding_digital_market_back__report.php

games can create their own external social networks as forums, or through other types of community building, though for the most part, the most successful products in this space leverage the power of existing social networks to drive user throughput.

So armed with a definition that can at least serve as a field guide to identifying the types of games we're most interested in talking about, let's move on to an investigation of the history of social gaming.

2.2 BBS GAMES AND MUDS

A few early examples of social games can be found by digging through the histories of early BBSs (bulletin board systems). These were proto-websites, effectively text or ASCII graphics-based social networks hosted on individual machines or small computer clusters, typically accessed via dial-up modems. In the mid-1980s, before much of the world had even heard of email accounts, these BBS systems acted as basic mail servers, discussion forums, and central hubs for uploading and downloading files. They also had games. These were games that required a great deal of imagination but also took advantage of a new medium. Users could log in and play their turns at different times of day or night. (Since being online tied up a phone line, many early BBSs could have only one user online at a time.) In games like *Ole West* and *Legend of the Red Dragon*, users would log in, be given a fixed number of turns per day or hour, and take their turns in a world inhabited by other players (albeit asynchronously; see Figure 2.1).

For the few hundred thousand early adopters who happened to understand things like baud rate and the BBS concept of doors, these games offered a first glimpse at the world to come. They featured early leaderboards and even ways to taunt other players. By most standards, these were the first online social games, because they used interactions with

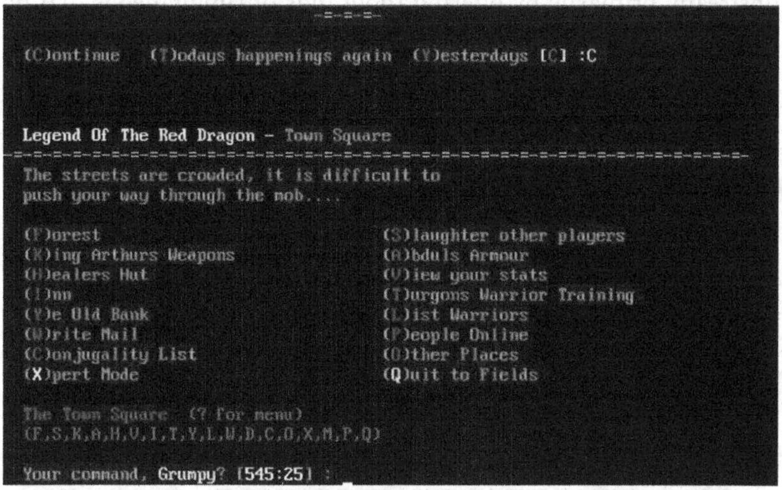

FIGURE 2.1 *Legend of the Red Dragon* by Seth Robinson gave users a limited number of turns per day during which they could fight their way to become powerful enough to face the Red Dragon that menaced the fictional town. Early BBS games presented entirely in text and allowed users to interact with one another asynchronously.

other players to drive adoption of the game (users showed up on the BBS to download a file or ask a technical question, then saw dozens of posts about in-game events and thus were enticed to begin playing). Players dialed in every day (sometimes "wardialing" with modem software that would automatically keep dialing the BBS phone number in the hopes of getting through the minute it stopped being busy) to get those precious ten or thirty turns, because that was the only way to stay ahead of your friends or help out your corporate team in venerable groundbreaking games like *Trade Wars*. The social element made the game "sticky"—users came back, again and again, to stare at those sixteen colors of text that transported them to fantasy worlds, to the old west, or to the depths of space. In many ways, these games were quite similar in design to some of the first wave of social games, like *Vampire Wars*.

Simultaneously, MUDs (multi-user dungeons) pushed these concepts further, allowing simultaneous play in which dozens or hundreds of users could coexist in the game world, interacting with one another in real time. Many MUDs did away with the concept of limited numbers of moves or turns per day. MUDs typically featured turn-based play, in which turns passed at a fixed rate (called "ticks"). The MUDs required access to university mainframes or networks or to private servers, which users would pay for access and connect to using Telnet clients and later custom MUD clients, which enhanced the experience by parsing information from the MUD server, translating the information into more user-accessible user interface (UI) elements, and automatically running scripts that helped perform tedious gameplay tasks. TinyMUD, LPMud, and DikuMUD were popular pieces of back-end server software that were customized into hundreds or thousands of different individual games, some of which still run today, usually with World Wide Web main pages that let users discuss the game world outside of the MUD itself. (See Figure 2.2.)

Early social networks like America Online (AOL) are responsible for taking the BBS concept mainstream, primarily by offering thousands of simultaneous dial-up lines and

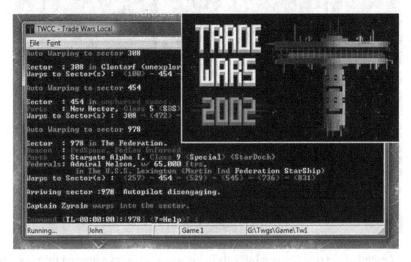

FIGURE 2.2 *Trade Wars* launched on BBS systems in 1984 and quickly sprouted up in many different versions. *Trade Wars* allowed users to compete for resources and form corporations with one another in epic galactic battles.

networks of computers capable of passing messages and other real-time chat functions. This new category of social network also offered social games. One of the most popular of these was a basic solitaire game embedded in a chat room channel. While not technically a social game (the name gives it away!), *AOL Solitaire* claimed millions and millions of hours of play. People were content to "play cards" by themselves, in a way that offered no social interaction, because the social network itself—the ability to "hang out" online and chat with friends or strangers—was such a powerful draw that people were willing to indulge in games that took almost no advantage of the social nature of the network just to be together. This leads us to what seems to be a basic truism of social and mobile game design: *People like to play together even if they aren't really interacting with one another.* Often it's not what you're doing together; it's the concept of being part of a community that excites people. AOL, CompuServe, and the like first popularized the sorts of interactions we now see reaching true mainstream fruition in social networks like Facebook. And many of the game design principles that were first proven out there are still important today.

2.3 MMOS

These types of games led the way for the modern MMO (massively multiplayer online) juggernauts like *World of Warcraft* or *ZT Online*, which have attained such a huge number of users and such a powerful gravitational pull that they are, in effect, their own social networks. These MMOs, the majority of which are third-person role-playing games (RPGs), which explore traditional sword and sorcery or science fiction themes, are played almost exclusively on the PC. They require an Internet connection at all times, and the game simulation code runs on a collection of game world servers hosted by the development or publishing company that created the game. Some of these games have been extremely successful, though many more have also floundered on rocky shores that are hard to navigate. Modern MMOs tend to be extremely expensive to build; they can easily cost upwards of $80 million just to build a product that can begin to compete against the best-of-class games in this sector. (And those that are trying to truly take market share from *World of Warcraft* can end up costing several times more than that to create and market.) Many social features tend to be built into games like this. For example, users can typically message one another using in-game client mail, can chat in real time, can form clans and guilds and other types of social organizations, and so on.

These types of games achieved great success by effectively creating a large number of features that make them end up acting a bit like social networks themselves. This is a tempting proposition for many developers, since it allows the developer or publisher a great deal of control over the users and the revenue from the product.

And while it is possible to create a social infrastructure inside your game itself that serves the same function as being tied into a traditional social network, it is challenging.

First, you need to have sufficient scale of users to create a "network" in the first place. It takes more than a few hundred thousand players to create an ecosystem. This is doable if you have a marketing budget sufficient to raise awareness about your game. Otherwise, you run the risk of throwing a party no one attends; an empty MMO dies a sad, speedy death, as many have learned over the last fifteen years.

Second, your ability to attract those who aren't initially interested in your product is limited. Like waiters on a slow day, standing outside a restaurant holding menus, true social networks can lure in the uninitiated with various types of infectious ways of spreading the message. But enticing a novice gamer to try a stand-alone MMO like *World of Warcraft* takes a significant amount of energy; without the surrounding social network, there are no passersby for the waiters to appeal to, and MMO publishers are forced to spend heavily on raising awareness through traditional advertising. And even once users hear of the game, before they can try it out, they are asked to invest a significant amount of time and attention to learning about and procuring the software itself. There is a barrier to entry that has historically kept many of these sorts of games from being accessible to a true mass market.

Thirdly, creating the features necessary to a social network is hard work, requiring hundreds of man-years of engineering and user interface design; this probably isn't the core competency of most game development teams, and those are resources that could potentially be better used making the core game better. Do you really need to invent your own chat systems, mail systems, and so on?

Finally, when a user decides to quit *World of Warcraft*, or any other game with a self-contained social system not part of a larger social network, they are simply gone from the system. With games that exist inside a true external social network, users return to the host system even though they've tired of the particular game; it's much easier to lure them back in to the original game or into another of your similarly situated products. When I quit a Facebook game, I still come back to Facebook, because that's where my friends are. What they play next, I'll probably play next, and that shared space helps retention and reacquisition numbers greatly. Of course, stand-alone games like *League of Legends* that are sufficiently sticky are able to keep huge numbers of users engaged and returning for months, but even these would be better served if they offered other types of products inside the social network they have created.

However, spending five minutes in the "General Channel" of any MMO like *World of Warcraft* or on the online forums of any major retail game should make it clear that a social ecosystem can exist outside the context of the game itself…if the game is big enough. Like tailgaters outside a big football game, people show up just to participate in the social forum, and the time they spend at the event only tangentially relates to "playing" the game. If your game is popular enough, and you invest enough energy in social feature design, it can become a social network of its own.

2.4 JUST BEING MULTIPLAYER DOESN'T MAKE YOU SOCIAL

Other early online games, like Dan Bunten's classic *Modem Wars*, offered far more engaging interactions between users—direct synchronous gameplay between two humans—in what would end up being a precursor to modern RTS (real-time strategy) games like *Command and Conquer* or *StarCraft*. However, for our purposes here, *Modem Wars* was not a truly social game. Certainly it was far more interactive than solitaire, but the connection to another human was brief, and what little connection there was neither offered nor relied upon a social "network." (You had to know each other's phone numbers and direct dial in, let your modems "handshake," then play the game…praying that line noise or your mom

FIGURE 2.3   Blizzard Entertainment's *StarCraft 2* is an intense real-time strategy game from 2010. With *StarCraft 2*, Blizzard released Battle.net 2.0, which offered many features of a social network, as well as integration with Facebook.

picking up a phone in another room didn't kill the connection and the game.) There was no concept of a larger, socially networked structure driving players to try out the game. (You had to learn about the game from an existing friend, read about it in a magazine or learn about it from a user's group, and then go buy a copy at a retailer like Babbage's.) There was also no element of stickiness; each game was self-contained, over when you lost connection or one player won. There were no leaderboards, no achievements, nor anything else to keep a player coming back the next hour or the next day (except whatever fun there was in playing the game itself). This example illustrates an important point: just being a head-to-head or multiplayer game doesn't make something a "social" game and misses out on many of the advantages of user attraction and retention. Some modern *Modem Wars* descendants like *StarCraft* have addressed this shortcoming by creating their own homegrown social networks (like Blizzard's Battle.net) to become social games in their own right. Just being multiplayer doesn't make a game a social game. (See Figure 2.3.)

2.5 GREAT MOBILE GAMES *ARE* SOCIAL

The rapid rise of smartphones and connected tablet or pad devices has created a new type of hardware platform for social gaming. While these games may not be launched from within a social networking website, many of them, such as *Words With Friends* (now owned by Zynga), do meet our definition. While at its heart *Words With Friends* is a straightforward

FIGURE 2.4 *Words With Friends* by Newtoy allows players to compete in a familiar word game over their mobile phones or tablets. *Words With Friends'* attention to social networking features has made it a top seller on iOS.

word game for mobile devices, the characteristics it shares with other social games have helped catapult it to success, leading the way for many clever followers. Mobile games exist on inherently socially connected devices. This means they can almost all benefit from social game design techniques. (See Figure 2.4.)

First, the game makes it very easy for players to invite their friends to play. By using the platform and social network integration (with Facebook), the game was able to rapidly acquire a large number of users. (See Figure 2.5.)

Second, a few elements of the game design make excellent use of the platform to make the game very socially sticky. The asynchronous nature of the game, the ability to have multiple games going at once, and the constant notifications when a friend is waiting for you to take your turn have made the game very sticky and helped user retention. As anyone who has ever received a text message demanding that they "hurry up and take their turn" can attest, *Words With Friends* is hard to put down.

So mobile games can be social games too, if they incorporate certain key elements of social networks to propagate and thrive. To qualify under our definition, they need to actively make use of features that allow users to help the game spread itself and remain sticky.

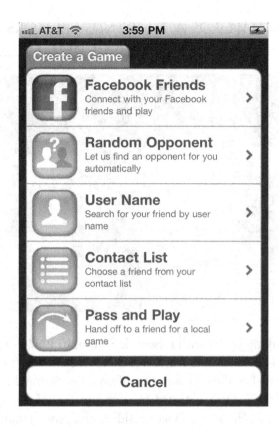

FIGURE 2.5 *Words With Friends* makes it easy for players to invite their friends. By integrating Facebook and other types of existing connections, games can acquire new users rapidly.

A social game is one in which the user's interactions with other players help drive adoption of the game and help retain players and that uses an external social network of some type to facilitate these goals.

Throughout the coming chapters, we'll stick with this definition, but we'll apply it generously. We'll try to evaluate game features, pricing, content, and other components in the light cast by these three principles:

1. The game must provide a way (and a motivation) for users to help grow the game's user base.

2. The game must be socially sticky, using social interaction to motivate users to regularly return to the game platform, if not to the game itself.

3. The game must interact with (or create) some sort of social ecosystem or framework so that users can be entertained beyond simply the core mechanics of "playing the game."

2.6 INTERVIEW WITH *WORDS WITH FRIENDS* CREATORS PAUL BETTNER AND DAVID BETTNER OF NEWTOY

Paul Bettner began making games with Ensemble Studios in 1997 as a game developer. He spent eleven years with Ensemble and Microsoft Game Studios building the *Age of Empires* and *Halo Wars* series and has shipped over 22 million units during the course of his career. In 2008 he and his brother, David, started Newtoy, creators of the incredibly successful *Words With Friends* game. He is now a vice president and general manager at Zynga.

David Bettner earned a BS in Computer Science from the University of Central Florida before joining Ensemble Studios as a game developer in 2003. He founded Newtoy in 2008, created *Words With Friends*, and is currently a studio director for Zynga in Dallas, Texas.

Q: After your work at Ensemble, you guys got in on the ground floor of the mobile game phenomenon with Chess With Friends. *What made you want to focus on mobile multiplayer games instead of retail products?*

PB: I've always been drawn to multiplayer game development. Interacting with another person (or people) in a game raises the experience to another level, and I've always been fascinated by those dynamics. Also, we knew we wanted to create products that leveraged mobile, products that could *only* exist on a mobile device. That led to exploring the unique capabilities of the platform, and what stood out to us was the always-on, always-connected, always-with-you nature of these devices. They are communications platforms, first and foremost. So we wanted to create a new type of game franchise that was built around this always-connected experience. At the time we called it "text messaging meets gaming."

Q: With Words With Friends, *you took a traditional game concept and made it socially sticky. What can you tell us about the power of connected devices that allows players to play old games in new ways?*

DB: The smartphone revolution sparked by the release of the iPhone has changed everything about the way we think about games. Looking at the iPhone, we thought there was an amazing opportunity to create a game that takes advantage of the always-on, always-connected, and always-with-you nature of the device. There really wasn't anything like that before. Additionally, we wanted to have a personal connection with our friends through games. Coming from a multiplayer background at Ensemble Studios, single-player games weren't very exciting to me. They felt less alive, less fun. *Chess With Friends* and *Words With Friends* was our attempt to create a game that tapped into those unique capabilities. Also, as simple as it sounds, we just imagined it would be really fun to play.

Q: *In the wake of the incredible success of* Words With Friends, *what lessons did you learn? What would you do differently if you were going to do it all over again?*

DB: It's been an incredibly fun, difficult, and rewarding journey with many lessons learned over the past few years. The biggest lesson that first comes to mind is "keep it simple."

When we first launched *Chess With Friends* I thought we were keeping it simple. A chess game with a "your turn" and "their turn" move list. That's it, right? It wasn't simple enough. For one, it was chess. That right there I think is too complicated. If you don't know the rules of chess, you're out of luck. A user isn't going to stumble through a game with a live opponent and learn the rules as they go. We also had this arduous sign-up process we forced everyone to go through before allowing them to play with their friends. At one point we even were asking for their mother's maiden name. Looking back, it's amazing we were caught by surprise when that didn't go over well. In the mobile social space people are looking for a quick, painless few minutes of fun, and in order to deliver that you need a keen eye on how to keep things as simple as possible. As game developers we always naturally gravitate toward more complex designs. Always putting yourself in your users' shoes, knowing your audience, is key and something I've learned to always remind myself of.

Q: *Where do you see the convergence of social network games and mobile games in the next few years?*

PB: Mobile *is* the convergence. In a few years, we won't look at social and mobile as two separate things; we will all expect our game experiences to follow us wherever we go. That's the future we're building towards.

Q: *What advice do you have for mobile game developers who want to tap into the power of social connections with their games?*

PB: Don't add social as an afterthought! The most successful mobile social titles are built with social play at the core of the game loop, not something that's bolted on after the fact. That's not to say that all successful mobile games require a social component, but I believe that the most successful social games on mobile will be the ones that implement fresh, unique, and simple social dynamics that mirror interactions we have with each other in the real world.

Q: *Last year, you were acquired by Zynga. What kinds of things did you learn about game design and production by joining forces with them?*

PB: Zynga sometimes gets a bad rap in the traditional games industry, but the reality is that Zynga is more passionate about good game design and creating fun for our players than any game company I've ever worked at. Zynga studies its players and how they play, relentlessly. This drives a deep level of insight into game design through analytics and a metrics-driven approach. The opportunity to learn and apply these skills across the *With Friends* games has already had a noticeable impact on our "player delight."

Q: How have your successes changed things at your studio?

PB: Our success has allowed us to grow, hire more of our friends, and build towards the creative powerhouse that we've always hoped our studio would become. Success has also had a very positive impact on morale. There's nothing like wearing our *Words With Friends* T-shirts and being stopped in a mall or an airport by someone who wants to tell us how much they love the game. That fuels the fire for all of us—it's why we do what we do!

Q: As mobile phones and tablets advance, what sort of new game design challenges and opportunities do you see?

DB: Looking to the future of mobile game development, I see increasing game complexity as a challenge. We're able to make hit games right now with relatively small teams, compared to the console world I came from. As handheld phones become more and more powerful, I hope we can stay true to the mentality we have now where a fun, well-designed user experience is at the core of the game. With more power comes the potential for more complexity, bigger teams, bigger budgets, longer dev cycles. As an industry, I'm optimistic we've learned our lessons and we'll be able to strike the right balance between eye candy and innovative design.

As to what opportunities will present themselves? I think we're still only beginning to scratch the surface of utilizing the current feature set of our phones. Who would have thought I would one day use the same device to play games with my friends, track my jogging route, and make a phone call? Smartphones are integrating themselves into every part of our life and what defines a "game" is becoming more loosely defined all the time. So, I guess that's a long-winded way of saying I think the opportunities are almost endless, and I can't wait to explore them.

Q: Tell us a little more about the goal of Indie Fridays and how they make the Newtoy culture unique?

DB: Indie Fridays started as a result of the Google 20 percent idea. I'm actually not entirely sure what the Google policy is, but the way we phrased it was "Do whatever you want, so long as it contributes something back to the studio in the end." That could be anything from learning a new programming language to working on a new game prototype you've had bouncing around your head for a while. It sounded cool, so we decided to give it a try and change it if it didn't work out. It was pretty tough the first few weeks. I remember Paul sending me an email one Friday saying "this doesn't feel right, I think 20% is too much." I suggested we wait a couple of weeks and reevaluate, and I'm glad we did.

Indie Fridays have become a place where many of our new game ideas are generated and allowed to incubate. Both *Hanging With Friends* and our next still unannounced title both were born out of Indie Fridays. Developing new game ideas is an extremely difficult and highly creative process. Often what you need is time for an idea to bake, in between iterations. Fridays allow us to take an idea and get it up and running in a rough prototype very quickly, often just a pen-and-paper prototype at first. During the rest of the week the game sits in the back of your mind, or if it's far enough along it's already in prototype on our phone and we're playing each other all week. By the time next Friday rolls around, we have a solid idea of what's working and what's not, and a list of new ideas we'd like to try.

It continues to be a difficult practice to embrace. Folks here often want to work on their mainline projects all week. It can be hard to switch from the game you're working on Monday through Thursday, but we continue to encourage it. It wasn't obvious at first, but now that we've seen the output it's become apparent how valuable and important it is to our studio and its success.

Q: *Any other advice you'd like to share with game designers who are moving from the world of AAA retail game development into the mobile/social space?*

PB: There's nothing quite like the thrill of working on a game that *everyone* plays, from your wife to your mother-in-law, to your kids. Fast development cycles, small, tight teams, cutting-edge game design challenges—it's the most fun any of us have had making games.

In other words: come on in, the water's warm!

CHAPTER 3

History of Game Monetization

3.1 WHAT DO WE MEAN BY MONETIZATION?

Throughout this book we'll be talking freely about ways to monetize users. What do we mean? We're talking about the ways you can get users to pay you. That simple.

The ways you can go about trying to accomplish this goal are numerous, and the strategies that you can use can become quite involved. But at its heart, we're looking at games as a business, designed to provide entertainment to customers in exchange for revenue. Throughout this chapter, we'll look at the ways games have traditionally been monetized and how the industry has evolved to its current point.

Along the way, keep an eye out for the major types of monetization:

- Retail purchase

- In-game microtransactions

- Digital download

- Subscription model

- Indirect monetization

3.2 A BRIEF HISTORY OF GAME MONETIZATION

Originally, games were free. They were simple programs like *Space War* (though writing them was anything but simple at that time!) that were passed around mainframe labs, then later college Computer Science departments. Within a few years these games were being sold on floppy disks packaged in Ziploc baggies at small specialty software stores, then on cartridges in retail outlets. Most of this software was sold first at specialty computer stores that sold hardware and software, and then, a few years later, in more mainstream retail outlets like Sears and Babbage's. The transaction was straightforward; you paid your money and you took your chances. This model continues to hold strong in traditional retail game markets today.

When MMOs appeared in something approaching their modern form, they needed to offset server and maintenance costs so they started charging subscription fees. Early games such as *Island of Kesmai* for CompuServe charged as much as $12 per hour to play. *Neverwinter Nights* for America Online reduced this price to $6 an hour, an amount still prohibitively expensive by today's standards. Joe Ybarra's *Shadow of Yserbius* followed, along with Kesmai's *Air Warrior* and a handful of other titles with similar hourly or monthly service fees. Bandwidth and server time were relatively expensive then compared to what they cost now, and the number of total users was fairly small, so companies were forced to charge higher prices because they lacked a significant volume of customers.

As home PCs grew more powerful, and more people became connected to the Internet, new games appeared that took advantage of better graphics and online connectivity and refined the pay-for-play business model. The first of the modern wave of MMOs were games like *Meridian 59* and *Ultima Online*. These cemented the practice of charging a monthly fee for unlimited play time, a pricing model that provided a more regular income stream and greater predictability for game operators. These and other games like them attracted hundreds of thousands of new users to the space. *Asheron's Call*, *EverQuest*, *Dark Age of Camelot*, and eventually Blizzard's *World of Warcraft* followed. They expanded the user base by an order of magnitude and cemented the basic MMO pricing model, which involved a boxed purchase through retail, followed by a monthly subscription fee for unlimited access. This model dominated most paid online gaming in North America and Europe until almost 2009.

Users were enchanted by the interactivity with other players, the ability to explore large virtual worlds, to assume roles as craftsmen and merchants, as well as the more traditional fighters and wizards. Stories of online relationships and marriages flourished. Sony Online Entertainment, Electronic Arts, and other publishers became hooked on the high yield of games that could monetize users every month and rushed to build more of them. Attracted by the promise of riches, and the exciting design challenges associated with creating pervasive worlds for millions of users, development studios flocked into the space, creating something of a gold rush. Unfortunately, for every success like *World of Warcraft* or *Eve Online*, there were a spate of failures, from *Anarchy Online* to NCSoft's doomed *Tabula Rasa*. Development costs continued to rise, and the quality bar set by the successes made it very difficult to pull users away from whichever of these games they were already playing. These products made fortunes (and some continue to), but the space also generated a number of spectacularly expensive failures, which made investors and developers gun-shy. They are a great type of game for us to understand because they usually feature very advanced social features but are not typically social networks unto themselves; secondly, because many of these games were early leaders in user-behavior metrics gathering and analysis, and their techniques are widely emulated within many social games; finally, because many of the less successful MMOs were forced to adopt alternate mechanisms for monetization, some of which borrowed from their successful brethren overseas.

In South Korea and China, the rules were different. First, very few people owned home PCs or consoles. Instead, millions rented time at Internet cafes, a highly social setting that set the tone for the way games in general, and online games in particular, would be played. Rampant piracy of PC games in these territories meant that traditional retail models simply didn't work; for each game sold, tens of thousands of copies were pirated. Developers were forced to extract money from their users in other ways. Subscription fees worked to offset this problem, and Western-influenced MMO games like *Lineage* attracted huge numbers of users in South Korea and Taiwan.

Many Eastern companies adopted Western game design ideas, particularly the highly popular MMOs, but, by necessity, found ways to distribute the client software for free, instead selling the users peripheral equipment and gear. This focus on selling virtual items for avatar-based games (perfect for the MMORPG genre) worked and generated significant revenues by extracting small amounts at regular intervals (often every day, for avid players) from a very large number of users. Before long, the modern microtransaction model was born. There have been a near infinite number of minor refinements to this practice, from offering non-gear types of services (transferring or renaming characters for a small fee, and the like) to offering users ways to save time in the game by obviating the need for tedious tasks, and so on. For the most part, this microtransaction model carried forward directly into the realm of social games. The Internet cafes of Asia formed the petri dish in which the freemium microtransaction model was born.

This is the world that Facebook stepped into, initially with no games and no real plan for monetization of its users. Fairly early on, they allowed third-party developers to create games and apps for the rapidly expanding platform. By 2007, Zynga was making significant revenue from its players by offering free games where play could be upgraded through microtransactions. Such microtransactions operated in an abstract form within the meta-world of the game, initially as opportunities offered to players to purchase a type of in-game currency that could be used to speed up the completion of tedious in-game tasks or let users keep playing when their daily or hourly allotment of turns had been expended. Though it took this model several years to become profitable, with a number of refinements, Zynga, Digital Chocolate, and a few other social game companies have managed to reap huge rewards and attract a number of daily users that dwarfs the numbers seen on almost all console or MMO games. These successes have led to a second, more recent gold rush, this time into the social free-to-play game space.

Facebook itself entered into the microtransaction game in 2009 with the alpha release of Facebook Credits, a system that sought to provide a common currency for all games played on Facebook (and in so doing, guarantee that Facebook would take a piece of Zynga's ever-expanding pie). Facebook Credits became the official currency of all games on Facebook as of July 1, 2011, and it is currently used in hundreds of different games. Facebook offers game developers various incentives to make use of their currency system, some liability protection, and a number of tools to facilitate integration into the game economy. For these privileges, Facebook takes 30 percent of the transaction. This fee is transparent to the users, such that if a player spends 9 Facebook Credits in your game, which they bought for $9, you get $6. While many social game developers decried Facebook's greed in taking such a significant cut of each microtransaction, the introduction of a universal currency on the platform is good for both users and developers on balance. However, it has caused many social development companies to attempt to shift users to company-hosted portal sites instead, in an effort to avoid the "Facebook tax."

Gamers are provided a consistent, secure, trustworthy marketplace for purchasing credits. They can work to resolve any disputes with a major brand, rather than with individual vendors. The credits can be purchased and given as gifts to friends and relatives, even if the purchaser isn't certain what game the recipient likes. Since they can be used at point-of-purchase in any Facebook game, the credits themselves also have more value than tokens that have currency in only one game or one family of games.

Developers ended up getting easy-to-implement application programming interfaces (APIs), which save them a great deal of work creating their own systems for getting money from users. Developers and publishers are freed up from the expensive dispute resolution and customer service headaches that go along with the transactions themselves and can benefit from a unified currency that has far more legitimacy than did the previous host of different currency types. Best of all, by selling Facebook Credits, Facebook has made clear the rules of customer engagement on their platform, and developers no longer have to fear that their game could simply be taken offline by the platform for an unwitting violation or due to a change in platform policy.

Other social networks have followed Facebook's lead. For example, the online gaming website hi5 offers a similar currency, which they call hi5 Coins. They augmented this system with a comprehensive suite of tools called SocioPay, which uses player metrics to tailor microtransaction offers to particular players, in an effort to increase their average revenue per user (ARPU). For example, a customer who seldom buys anything is more likely to be served up general advertisements, while a user who regularly buys items in a certain price range is more likely to be offered items targeted around that particular price point. By offering a unified currency model, and taking a piece of the action, social networks become more likely to invest in creating tools like SocioPay which in turn help developers make more profitable games.

Around the same time as Facebook's rise to dominance, Apple's iPhone division took off like a rocket. Apple sold millions and millions of mobile devices that offered users power, connectivity, and visuals that were beyond the reach of most home PCs only ten years earlier. Google followed with their more open Android platform, and game developers flocked to the "app stores" these providers offered. The app store model allowed almost any small development team to create software, subject only to a fairly lightweight approval process, and then release their program or game into a marketplace flooded with consumers, many of whom started playing games for the first time. iPads and other tablets by manufacturers like Samsung, Toshiba, and Amazon followed, offering similar types of connectivity and touch-screen interface, all using the app store model. The economics of this new model for game distribution have continued to push down prices for applications, such that somewhere between $5 and free has now become a near-standard price for most games. But since it's hard to make money on free, the microtransaction models we first saw in Asian MMO games are quickly rising to dominate the mobile and tablet games market. Over the coming chapters, we'll discuss how these models work and why many industry gurus believe they represent the future of almost all forms of electronic gaming.

The history of game monetization is far from complete. As of this writing, a player can get great games ranging in price from completely free, to upwards of $70, and there is no limit to the amount of money that can be spent on "upgrades," both in-game and as hardware, add-ons, accessories, and the like. The market has fragmented such that there is currently no standard monetization paradigm, though free-to-play microtransactions are quickly moving toward dominance. It's anyone's guess if a single standard will emerge (though with such a vast array of products available, and such a broadly expanding and diversifying group of "gamers," this seems unlikely). By understanding the history we've just discussed, and the types of different models that have worked (or failed) in the past, we'll be better armed to react quickly to future changes in the marketplace, like the emergence of new platforms, and the continued increase in players.

The way games were monetized changed as the gamer population of the Earth increased from a few hundred thousand in the mid-1980s, into the millions by the 1990s, and into the hundreds of millions by the first decade of the twenty-first century. We've observed a general trend for games to get cheaper as they reach larger economies of scale. What types of business models might begin to emerge or become feasible in a world of three billion gamers? Such a world isn't here yet, but given population and connectivity trends, one can imagine that it might not be so far off.

The rest of this book will seek to give you a view of the types of game, feature, and UI design that can be broadly applied to many of the different hybrid game models out there, as well as to those new models that have not yet come to light. Going forward, we'll look at some of the reasons to create social and mobile games, why they have become so popular, and how they are changing the marketplace for all other forms of entertainment.

3.3 INTERVIEW WITH RICHARD GARRIOTT: "THE THREE GRAND ERAS OF GAMING"

Richard Garriott, AKA Lord British, is one of the best-known figures in the history of computer gaming. He published his first game, *Akalabeth*, in 1980, then went on to create the beloved *Ultima* series. He cofounded Origin Systems in 1983 and published the first major MMO, *Ultima Online*, in 1997 as part of Electronic Arts. His second company, Destination Games, was sold to Korean MMO developer NCSoft in 2001. He holds a lifetime achievement award from the Game Developer Hall of Fame. Richard has traveled to the International Space Station, owns a small part of the Moon, and has visited the wreck of the *Titanic*. He currently runs Portalarium, a social game development company in Austin, Texas.

Q: How did you monetize your first game, Akalabeth?

A: In the very beginning I had a summer job at a ComputerLand store. The owner of the store noted this game *Akalabeth* I was working on was better than any of the games he could buy from the handful of the first companies that came into existence. He encouraged me to self-publish because self-publishing was just as high quality as formal publishing. All games at that moment were sold in Ziploc bags hanging on the peg board on the wall of the store. When I spent $200 on Ziploc bags, Xerox coversheets, hand-stapled little manuals that I made at a print shop two doors down, and hung them on the peg board, it looked every bit as good as any other game being published from a quality of packaging standpoint. It probably was better that most other games being sold that could be purchased but that is only one store. In that first week I sold somewhere between five and ten. This was infinitely better than the zero from the week before.

One of those copies found its way to California, and California Pacific was the company that happened to see it. Back in the very earliest days there were only a couple of people you would describe as distributors. These were people who had a relationship with the handful of computer stores that existed around the country, which was maybe a hundred stores. One of those was the company California Pacific and they were the publisher of my mentor, a guy named Bill Budge, whose work I admired. They called me on the phone and said they would like to distribute this nationally. We signed contracts and the first summer in 1980, they sold 30,000 copies. Back at that time all games were sold as a royalty contract very much like a book. There were no games that took more than one person to build. There were no teams for games. I was paid 30 percent royalties in this case, which now seems incredibly high. I was selling them for $20 and the reseller sold them for $35. My royalties were 30 percent of the wholesale price. That was about half of the $35, which net means I made about $5 a unit. You do 30,000 times five and that's $150,000 for what took me about seven weeks of time in my evenings after school. My cost was really zero. Cost basis was zero and it generated about $150,000, which paid for a few years of college. There really was no competition back at this time so the return on investment was obviously exceptional.

Q: Talk a little bit about the "Three Grand Eras of Gaming" and why the current one is so important.

A: First let us look at why each of what I call the "Three Grand Eras of Gaming," which are solo player games, massively multiplayer games, and now social and mobile games, are both interesting and important. Social and mobile are really two areas and not the same but they are both happening at this moment.

Solo player games were obviously a very good business from the beginning but small. A top-selling solo player game, starting with things like *Akalabeth*, immediately sold in the hundreds of thousands and over twenty years moved up into the millions. Between 1980 and 2000 a top-selling solo player game might sell in the six, eight, or ten million unit range for a true top seller. Those games by the definition were solo player games that you bought at a retail store and brought home to play alone on your computer. At this time computers as a percentage of your personal income were fairly expensive and the instructions required to install these games on your personal computer were fairly sophisticated. The combination of having to go to a retail store to buy it, bringing it home to install it with a fairly complex install, along with fairly complex instructions, on an expensive home computer, meant that the marketplace was limited to relatively wealthy teenage male nerds. This was really the total market. It was still a great business. The business grew very rapidly and even before that era ended the games industry exceeded the movie industry as far as scale is concerned, if you compared box office revenue to revenue from games at retail.

The second grand era came with the release of the first massively multi-player games. Even back before the Apple II people were networking computers together. As soon as there was a computer people began to hook them together and try and do things. There were multi-user dungeons and the AOL dial-up RPGs like *Neverwinter Nights*. They were multiplayer but I do not know if you would qualify it strictly speaking as massively multiplayer. *Ultima Online* was the first one that went past the 100,000 user mark and sold in the millions. What is interesting about shipping *Ultima Online* is our publisher, EA, had no expectations for its sales. It was going to demand that not only did you have to go to a retail store, you also had to pay $50 up front. It was a complicated game to install, a complicated game to play, and the kicker was before you could even play for one minute, you had to agree with a credit card to subscribe for $10 or $15 a month. The barrier to entry was dramatically higher even than for solo player games. It also required an Internet connection and this was still the early days of the Internet. The deck in many ways was stacked against the success of *Ultima Online* according to the analysis of the sales department. It clearly demonstrated that the ability to play with other real people through the Internet and the human motivation to connect to other people were so strong that they radically outweighed those additional barriers.

The market increased from a million units being a great success, into the tens of millions. Between 2000 and 2010 *Ultima Online* sold to single digits millions of people. If you look at the biggest U.S. success, *World of Warcraft*, it has sold to probably close to 100 million players in its history. It has easily sold in the high tens of millions. That is a lot people that were not solo player gamers that have become gamers during the massively multiplayer era. It is important to realize a lot of these gamers did not have previous experience with games. They did not call themselves gamers and probably really were not gamers until the massive multiplayer era. They came in during a fairly complex period. Computers by this time were a little bit cheaper compared to your base income. The market for MMOs is still about 80 to 90 percent male. MMOs did attract some females but not a large percentage. A gamer was no longer required to be a wealthy hard-core nerd, but it was still a mostly male, fairly broad age group, with a few females. Even though the economics of the deal obviously got much bigger during the MMO era, the computer game industry exceeded not only movies at the box office and home DVDs and television but also books and all other creative media combined. This was when video games took the absolute clear lead over all other mediums economically. Compare how many people have seen a TV show or know the name of a movie star to how many know the name of a game. Games are still selling to a dramatically smaller percentage of humanity for no other reason than we left out all the women on Earth, and a good chunk of men. They were not into games even though everyone goes to movies periodically and most everyone watches television periodically.

This is what is exciting about the third and final grand era that we are in now. In my mind the key attribute of this new era is that instead of going to the retail store and paying $50, you find games through the Internet or app store and pay somewhere between zero and an impulse purchase price. That is the main functional difference. The game feature main differences are instead of going through a complex install and complex instructions you auto-install without any concern. I do not know any of these games that have instructions. They teach you through an in-game tutorial without any other form of instructions.

The final kicker is that while the MMO era determined that playing with anyone online (including strangers you meet) was far more compelling than playing alone, in this new social era the people you are connected to are not strangers when you bump into them online, which was already pretty damn compelling. These are the people you already have a relationship with in the real world. They are the people who you do go to the movies with, the people you do have dinner with, and some of them you might have met in an MMO. The point is these are people you already built a relationship with and therefore you care a lot more about sharing and tracking. Sharing what you do and tracking what they do and maybe interacting in real time.

The last thing that I would throw in there about this new era that is really compelling is the discovery of the power of asynchronous game features. In the MMO era for us to play together we had to always be online at the same time. The great new feature discovered during this new era in my mind is the way to let us give each other benefit without necessarily having to be online at precisely the same time. If I need some help on my farm I can send you a request for help. If I see you have been asking me for help, I can lob over the fence to your farm the help you need. When you log back on, you will have seen my help and provide me my help for the next time I log in.

The result of not having to pay retail, not having to go to a store and pay any large amount of money up front, the fact that it's on the app store for free or an impulse purchase, the fact that it has no install or instructions, combine that with the asynchronous feature set to augment what other features it has, the result of that is that the scale of the market has yet again grown ten times. We are only two or three years into it and the top-selling games are about to cross 100 million users. That is generally going to continue to grow and most importantly we now have men and women of all ages and of all walks of life playing.

The good news is that you can create a game that is capable of capturing all those people in theory. I personally believe what is now going to evolve is just like television and movies. There are going to be the chick flicks and there are going to be the action movies. Chick flicks for the women, action movies for the guys, and now and then a rare and special game that captures everyone that could be a chick flick or an action movie. It could be *Star Wars* that will capture everybody, or *The Notebook*.

I think it is very clear that casual and mobile are already dominant and if you are a designer or investor, if you want to make the games or invest in this business, this is the opportunity. I would still enjoy making a solo player *Ultima*. I would enjoy writing the story for it, but there's no business opportunity there. There's no reason to support it. MMOs are more of the same thing. I enjoy making MMOs. I love the craft that goes into the worlds. I love the scale of the reality of what we are building, but the creative challenge and business opportunity is clearly now in this new space.

Q: *With this expanded audience, how do you see the face of the average gamer changing moving forward?*

A: If you look at the skills and taste of the new wave of gamers, it is already evolving very quickly. If you look at the first games that were astonishingly popular with tens of millions of players, they were not particularly well-written games. I do not mean from their fun-factor but from their user interface and other usability factors that you would think would be very important. These are especially important to a new user and they were not really done that well. It feels very much like a reflection of when *Ultima Online* came out. The graphics were not that great. It was pretty buggy and the user interface was inconsistent. People were very critical of it and it succeeded dramatically in spite of all that because of the power of the new features. The early social and mobile games, primarily social games really, had that same kind of problem. UIs were terrible. Graphics were terrible but they succeeded dramatically in spite of that because playing with your real friends is so much more powerful than playing with strangers or by yourself.

Harder-core games have shown to port over to this medium without much success. It is very important to realize that when we were in the era of hard-core nerds, the install was so hard to figure out that some UI was no big deal compared to just installing the game. Their ability to embrace and figure out complex screen arrangements was acceptable.

There is a stereo maker, Bang and Olufsen, whose architectural beauty of their equipment is always first-rate. They look really cool. But if you buy one, they have the worst user interface. It's complex. It is different. Even if it is consistent to their own product line, it is not the same as everyone else's product line. Most washers and dryers you can just walk up to and use. There is an occasion I have ended up with one that has left me scratching my head. They tried to make it too high-tech with too many options. Everything is pretty standard on automobiles, other than your turn signals and windshield wipers. These seem to vary universally from car model to car model. It is one of the things you look for when you sit down in the car. Maybe adjusting the mirrors is also a discovery item, but most people can eventually handle it because it is such a limited list. The real important challenge for us designers now is the hard-core people that say, "I've got to dumb it down for the masses." That is not the right way to look at it. Do you think a Ferrari has been dumbed down for the masses? No. It is just good UI design to make sure that when you sit down in a Ferrari and you have just been driving your Lamborghini that you know how to make the thing go.

I do not personally find those things overly restrictive although they are occasionally challenging to what we want to accomplish. In our game we are already having the problem of how do you scroll through more than one screen full of items to select. Do you turn pages or do you use the scroll bar? Both have their problems. You have to communicate, "Don't forget there's something on the next page." As we have discovered, and other companies' research has shown, people buy everything on the first page because a huge swath of people do not realize there is a second or third page of stuff.

Q: Do you think the game industry veterans have been slow to come around to social games?
A: Absolutely, and by the way, I think that's changing. I think this is the year that everyone is getting it. I have to sadly confess that I was kind of resistant and was slow to get it too. Fortunately I got over that resistance earlier than many others. Right as we formed Portalarium in 2009, I went to DICE and to give a talk about this space. It was very clear I was talking to deaf ears. When I would sit down with the press and say we are going to go build this online social company their response was "You've got to be kidding." I would ask them if they are interested in this space and the press people and developers all answered, "No."

"Maybe I've tried one but I thought the game stunk." Or, "Why would I want to go make games in a field where there is not one game I would be interested in?" Or, "I wouldn't want to create any on that limited platform." Or, "I don't like the games that are there."

That was my attitude at first. Even if some of them had begun to sell somewhat well, I would have not been convinced. As soon as one is selling ten times better than any game that has ever existed, you are an idiot if you do not pay some attention. This was the time for me when I was thinking, "Better pay attention."

Upon closer examination, you have to look at it the same way we do with *Ultima Online*. There really is nothing fundamentally limited about the platform. A new player prefers to have nice graphics and nice sound. Everyone would prefer elegant user interface. Everyone would prefer a deeper *Lord of the Rings*-style ultimate experience, but they're not willing to tolerate going to the store to pay $50, a complex install, complex instructions, subscribe before I learn if it's any fun, then spend five hours creating my character and getting the first quest cycle loop before I know if this game is interesting. I do not think the things that were bad about MMOs and solo player games are something that we should worry about having gotten rid of. Those are good things to get rid of and so ultimately I believe we will be able to make just as high-quality games in this new era as we did in any other era.

Q: *When* Ultima Online *was released, how controversial was the monthly fee? Did you know from day one that you would have to charge a subscription fee?*

A: It was clear we were going to have to find a way to make money on the backside. What was not clear is that previously to *Ultima Online* there were not too many examples of subscriptions. There were examples of pay by the hour on AOL, but that was dying off as the Internet was coming up. Pay by the hour was dying and there really were not any subscription services. Plenty of retail games, but there was not a good model. It was very clear we could not have supported it just on the retail sale. We made the decision to go subscription, which we thought was fair for compensating ourselves for the service we provided.

I do not remember there being too much debate on whether that would be the hurdle that killed the game. We already had so many people thinking the game was dead for so many other reasons that would have been one of many. When the game finally did launch, very few people complained about the subscription fee. Afterward it seems like the obviously right thing to do because it sold so well. People subscribed for a short amount of time, but the churn rate in these games that are popular is about nine months. People are willing to pay six months to a year to sustain these characters in these MMOs.

Q: *As eras of gaming have evolved, how has the role of the designer as it relates to game monetization evolved as well?*

A: I look at it as a natural evolution to quality continuous engagement. You look at the difference between a good book and bad book and a good movie and bad movie. You can imagine the story of *Lord of the Rings* could have easily been made into a longer movie. First off, it was a phenomenally long movie, but you could have easily made it two or three times longer and it could have been very draggy. Some people that are not as big of fans could argue that it was still very draggy or that the director's cut is draggy and carries on for too long. Any story can be told in a way that continuously keeps you engaged or fails to completely continuously keep you engaged. The same story but told by two different directors. The director that is keeping you engaged constantly is doing a better job. That game, movie, or book will do better even though they are telling a similar story.

If each of us is going to write the same *Lord of the Rings* solo player game, the one that did a better job of continuous engagement would ultimately sell better and dwarf the others. All this new era of continuous microtransactions does is it lets us know you have continually kept someone engaged. It is a better feedback loop into the same result. I believe it is giving the designer better tools to understand engagement, which, as a result, is closer to the monetization path. You have better visibility on user engagement.

What I find most interesting about this data-driven era is when you talk about engagement, there is no question that these tools are all better. When I hear people critical of our thinking or challenging us on our thinking, they are almost universally challenging us on "Good game design no longer matters; all that matters is doing A/B testing of using pink cows instead of brown cows." Then you have a great monetizing game. There is clearly a science to what I will call slot machines. You want to use every trick in the book in order to maximize your engagement and ultimately monetization, but I would argue that the same science influences a filmmaker. You must have your correct crescendo of highs and lows to keep your audience captivated and keep them wanting to come back. Let's make you watch the sequel and the next sequel. Their monetization events are longer periods. You see franchises die because someone does a bad movie. No one will touch it and it comes back a decade later because someone is doing a good job with it. The property has not gotten any better or worse. It's the same property.

And so yes, I do think the designer has greater responsibility and is closer to understanding what it takes to create good game design, but fundamentally it is just another tool in his arsenal.

Q: *How do you see the eras of gaming evolving as we move forward? What do you see as the next game era?*

A: I think we will eventually get to a true virtual reality. If not "The Matrix," at the very least the personal pod or headset motorcycle helmet that plugs in pretty darn deeply in virtual reality and allows you to live there. That is ultimately a future that I believe we will see. The question is: How many steps and how far away is that? It could be pretty darn far away as far as I'm concerned. It is not around the corner but there will be another iteration. I would not have foreseen this one, so I do not think I have any insight into the next one; what I can tell you is how quickly this one is going to shake out. This has happened before. We are in our third era.

If you look at the first era, it took twenty years. Solo play started in 1980 and ended really in about 2000. For the first five years, tons of new companies were created. For the second five years the second quarter of that, lots of those companies flourished. Any of those that did a good job of producing top-quality product and were marketing and distributing it in a top-quality way got their fair market share based upon their quality.

After about ten years, halfway into it, the consolidation began to happen. The big retailers, whether it's Target, Electronics Boutique, or specialty retailers, they do not want to talk to twenty, thirty, or forty individual publishers because it's too many relationships to manage. They really only wanted to talk to a few major distributors. They would talk to some of the biggest companies like EA and the biggest aggregators of other products. That meant a relatively small company, like Origin, was always in the top ten but usually at number ten. Target would say, "We don't want to talk to the tenth-largest company; if you want us to carry your product, you have to sell it through one of these other distributors." Suddenly that was the writing on the wall for, "We're in trouble." That means margins start getting cut. EA and others try and muscle you out and start buying end-caps making it harder and harder to let the small people in on purpose. It's just business. Ten years of growth of opportunities, then ten years of squashing that down into a handful of key distributors.

Now you look at the MMO space from around 2000 to around 2010. It is only ten years but the same cycle, first five years lots of new companies. Origin was one of the very first. Blizzard did not come out with their first MMO until five or six years after *Ultima Online*. They are the last big company that joined the fray and after that began the consolidation. A lot of companies were either bought up or pushed out of the distribution capability. We started in about 2010 at the start of this new social and mobile phase. We're already a few years into it.

An argument can be made that if the second era took half as long as the first, this era might take half as long as the last in which case we are already halfway there. We are already at the beginning of the consolidation phase. You look at it and the earliest movers, like the Zynga's and Playfish's of the world that started a little before 2010, many of them have seen billion-dollar evaluations, which no MMO company has ever seen. A lot of them have already been bought up. Playfish was bought by EA and now newer companies like ours are looking at a distribution pinch. A user might say, "The Internet is the great equalizer; all you have to do is put something up on the app store and it'll do great." This is not true. The ability to be in front of the user's eyeballs is still a foundationally limiting problem that requires marketing or distribution. It's a different form of marketing and distribution just like the previous era, but we're already now at the point where we are trying to scale quickly.

When people talk about the great new open field, compared to MMOs and solo player games there's certainly tons of opportunity in this space, but compared to three years ago, it's already reducing quickly.

CHAPTER 4

Why Create a Social or Mobile Game?

4.1 SOCIAL AND MOBILE GAMES PUT A LOT OF POWER IN THE HANDS OF THE DEVELOPERS

Making games for social and mobile platforms and monetizing them using new techniques can restore a great deal of power to your development teams. However, as the cliché goes, with great power comes great responsibility. Modern social and mobile game design and monetization can free you from the tyranny of top-tier publishers. And since these games typically are built for much less money up front, they can also liberate teams from unwieldy budgets that, paradoxically, as often as not end up restricting creativity. Yet the freedom that comes with mass-market social and mobile game development and in-game monetization has its own type of price. The monetization techniques themselves, as well as the unique nature of the audience you're courting, will force traditional game designers to think about game design differently and react much, much more quickly than they would with traditional retail console or MMO games. If you set your prices incorrectly, or try to charge for the wrong types of "products," you'll lose sales. But luckily, there are no rules on what you can, must, or even should charge for! Perhaps you charge to play as different types of characters in your game. Or maybe characters are free but equipment costs. The flexibility about which features and content your users can be asked to pay for gives you huge latitude, but also puts a heavy onus on you to get it right or to change things quickly if you turn out to be wrong.

The same philosophy must guide other elements of the game design and implementation. If part of your UI is clumsy or opaque or generates friction for your users, they'll leave you for a shinier, better-designed game. They've got much less investment in your inexpensive social or mobile game than they do in a boxed product that they had to go buy. So embrace the power that comes with the speed and flexibility of developing social games. Delight in your ability to get products out for hundreds of thousands instead of tens of millions of dollars, treasure your ability to gather metrics from users to an unprecedented degree, and most of all, appreciate the creative freedom that comes with quick and frequent iteration on platforms that allow for fast deployment of new versions. But beware, because there's no safety net here; if you make mistakes with your game design and don't notice and fix them very quickly, you'll be left with an empty shell of a game that makes no money.

What are some of the advantages to developing social and mobile games? Let's investigate.

4.1.1 Smaller Development Teams and Shorter Development Cycles

Unless you've worked on a 300-person development team for one of the really big studios, building an *Assassin's Creed*, a *Need for Speed*, or some other huge multiplatform project, you can't properly appreciate the complexities and pressures that accumulate at that sort of scale. The initial investment required puts competing at the AAA level beyond the reach of most companies outside of the Fortune 500 at this point. The ability to create a game with a few dozen people, and in the process regaining that bygone sense of nimble, garage-band esprit de corps that attracted so many of us to the business in the first place, is seductive. Working on huge teams can make it very easy to feel like an insignificant cog in a vast machine and can often bear little resemblance to the dreams of creative freedom that attract so many to the games industry. Then, on those happy occasions when you find you've got a monster hit, you don't have to share the revenue so many hundreds of ways. Additionally, a game that needs to run, must be playable, and can hopefully be profitable, all within a six-month or a year development timeline, is a wonderful breath of fresh air for developers who have worked for two or three years (or often more) on projects (projects that often never actually cross the finish line). It's true that costs in the social and mobile space are both mounting; we've moved past the era of the $50,000 social game, and many mobile games cost more to build now too. Right now, a medium-quality entry into the social space tends to cost a few hundred thousand dollars to build, as do many phone and tablet products. First-generation Zynga games like *FarmVille* are reported to have cost between $500,000 and $1 million to develop. The bar has simply been raised since the first round of social games hit the marketplace, and to compete with the newest offerings, the design, graphics, and engineering that go into the product require a larger number of specialists than in years past. Beyond this, the cost to acquire users on both Facebook and in the app stores is ever increasing. But compared to the $50 to $100 million price tags on many AAA retail products, or the $100 million or more investment required to build an MMO to compete with *World of Warcraft*, development budgets for social and mobile games are still cheap. It's possible to make ten to a hundred bets on mobile games for every AAA product that finishes production.

4.1.2 No Need to Ship a Boxed Product

Have you ever waited with your fingers crossed while someone on your team boarded a plane with a physical copy of a "Gold Master" DVD? Have you been the one on that plane, hoping that you land in time to get to the manufacturing plant and hand off the disc for printing? Ever had to deal with creating box art for a dozen different territories, each with their own sales reps and laws about what can (and must) be on the cover of a product sold in stores? For many with a stake in the retail sales game, these sorts of problems were commonplace. But you won't have to deal with them when building social or mobile games. And more importantly, you won't have COGS (cost of goods and services) to worry about in your P&L (profit and loss) calculations for the game. No need to budget for fuel to power delivery trucks sent to drop off your product; no paying FedEx to ship your game to hundreds of different retail outlets in a desperate attempt to honor a street date. Digitally sold and released games bypass a thousand complications of a physical supply chain and can allow you to save a great deal of money when it comes time to get your game into the hands of your customer. And since social and mobile games are digitally distributed, they benefit from this far simplified process. (However, as we'll see, updating "live" games that have active users twenty-four hours a day presents its own set of difficulties.)

4.1.3 Ability to Be Your Own Publisher

Ask a thousand game developers who've worked in the industry for less than five years what the worst part of making games is (aside from the hours) and they'll likely start complaining about their publisher: their seemingly arbitrary deadlines, the endless stream of know-nothing production types showing up from L.A. or London to tell you what you already know how to do, marketing d-bags with unreasonable feature requests and a job description that sounds a lot like a party…milestone failures…predatory contracts…canceled projects…withheld royalties, and so on.

Those who have been around a bit longer may still smile wryly when asked about the relationship between developers and publishers; they might even point you to a picture of one of those birds that lives in the mouths of crocodiles, feeding on the rotten meat stuck between the predator's giant teeth. Sure, those birds eat well, but they earn their grey feathers—that kind of power differential is never stress free.

So congratulations. Building social and mobile games could free you from the tyranny of the powerful publisher/developer relationship by letting you take on the role of the publisher yourself. All it takes is money, a skilled staff, facilities, a testing mechanism, a marketing department, partnerships, a recruiting team, strong game development skills, and the stamina to stay in the ring until the revenue starts rolling in.

4.1.4 Faster Payments

One reason that traditional "deep pockets" publishers are still essential to the retail games industry is that the cash outlay to produce boxed products is large, and the time it takes to get a return back from retailers can be substantial. With social and mobile games, the chain of people with a hand out between the developer and the customer can be shorter. Depending on the payment scheme used (most social sites and application stores have a required method now), you can be paid weekly, or even receive daily direct deposits of your revenue, minus the cut of the digital storefront, of course. This quick return on investment can be of critical importance, especially to a small developer who doesn't necessarily have the financial cushion to wait a full calendar quarter or longer before the revenue-train pulls into the station.

4.1.5 No Need to Own Your Own Servers

For a long time, running online games carried the additional expense of owning and maintaining server farms. Paying for the electricity and cooling for the warehouses full of server gear necessary for these types of games places them out of reach of most smaller developers. But with the advent of cloud computing, social and most game designers now have dozens of options for purchasing server usage from cloud service providers like Google, particularly since the types of games that work well on social and mobile platforms tend not to require the massive database back ends needed by MMOs. This is far less expensive than owning your own servers, it gives you the flexibility to choose the OS you want your code to run on (Linux or Windows), and best of all, you can dynamically throttle up or down the amount of computing power you need to purchase, based on user demand. As you game gets more popular, you can automatically scale up to get the servers you need, and you don't need to cultivate (and pay) a team of high-priced server experts to keep them running. This logical division of labor between companies who provide cloud computing and the developers who build and maintain online games has helped drive prices down and quality up.

4.1.6 Immediate Feedback from Players

Long ago, players who hoped to be "heard" by the developers of the games they purchased mailed in comment cards contained in many boxed products. More recently, gamers submitted feedback on forums, on websites, via email, or by calling customer support. For online games, users could email or instant message a game master directly to get help with their problems or to have their questions answered. However, with social and connected mobile games, feedback can be harvested more proactively. Every time users stop playing your game, they have, in effect, given you feedback. Every time they don't buy something you offered, they are telling you that they do not see the value in your proposition. While these kinds of marketplace decisions similarly inform every other type of consumer product, the ability to instantly evaluate data about what your users have bought, rather than having to wait months for that information to come back from individual retailers, changes the speed at which online service providers can react. Since every social and mobile game exists as part of an online service, they should all be taking advantage of this ability. To best employ this great power you must harvest, understand, and adjust your game based on the available metrics. Your adjustments can't just be haphazard either; they must be founded upon careful study of the data, from which you formulate theories on why the users are behaving as they are and then rapidly test those theories with changes to the live product, followed by additional careful study of the new metrics that result. This requires a new type of design skill that relies more heavily on volume data analysis and rapid software iteration far beyond that of most traditional game development companies. In fact, many game development studios are creating a new breed of business analytics trained designers who are proficient at making sense of all the data that can be easily mined from customers.

4.2 SOCIAL GAMES MAKE THE DEVELOPER RESPONSIBLE

All of the responsibility of pleasing your customers is yours. We talked about the phenomenal cosmic power afforded a social or mobile game development studio. Now let's emphasize the responsibilities:

You're on your own. The low initial investment required of players who try your game means they don't have any real financial incentive (sunk cost) to stick around. If your customers don't like your game, they move on, and you're paid very little, if anything. If this happens often enough, you go out of business. There is no crack team of marketers, poised to make a silk purse out of a sow's ear.

You can never rest. Your worries don't disappear if your game turns out to be great. If your competitors like what you're doing, they'll copy you mercilessly, and within a month or three they'll have a reskinned replica of your game, perhaps even better (since they've had the opportunity to watch your successes and failures for whatever time you've been active). And if you don't adapt to these kinds of changing market conditions, your game will sink beneath the waves.

You're never done. And let's say you do produce a great game, and you do manage to fend off your competitors. Your worries still aren't over. If you don't immediately begin building up a portfolio of games, users who get bored of your first offering (and eventually they always do) will transition away from you…to a competitor's product. All it takes is a small migration of their friends, and then you've lost even your most die-hard fans. The games are built to be social, after all. This migration is worse on social networks like Facebook than it is for mobile games, because the barrier to getting a new game is slightly higher, but the problem exists in both places.

Nothing's free to you. If you don't monetize cleverly, you'll be paying server-cloud costs and CPI marketing for hitchhikers who play your game without ever giving you a penny. Free to play is great if you're the customer; if you're the creator or owner, it's only great insofar as it gives you a chance to monetize more users.

Cheaters sometimes win. If you don't safeguard against cheaters and exploits, your game economy will fall apart and the currency you hoped would translate into money in your pocket will suddenly become worthless. It requires constant maintenance to prevent the latest exploits, and users flee a game filled with cheaters very quickly.

You now live to please. If you don't have a responsive customer service department who can help players when they have trouble, they'll leave you. And remember too that the audience you are courting doesn't have to be technically savvy; they don't even have to have had the technical sophistication to hook up an Xbox or a PlayStation. So your user-education bar is much higher, and your game probably needs to be much simpler than traditional retail games.

You get the point. Developing social and mobile games puts great power into the hands of the developer and can even turn developers into direct publishers. But publishing games, it turns out, is hard work. Luckily, in modern social and mobile gaming environments, where the virality of the platform and the massive install base can generate millions and millions of users in just a few months, the rewards can be majestic and make all this hard work worthwhile.

4.3 SOCIAL GAMES GIVE POWER TO THE USERS

There's a reason why Zynga's number of daily users is still larger than the population of many small countries. And there are several reasons that the number of users playing mobile games at this exact second is so large. Social and mobile games have done an excellent job of creating games based on a far wider variety of themes than traditional retail games and thus appeal to a far broader audience. For most web-driven social games, users don't have to buy or install anything to try the games out. And mobile platforms make checking out new games cheap and easy. Once users start playing, many gamers find these games compelling, even addictive, due to their intuitive gameplay, tight reward-loops, and the social interaction between users. These games have opened up a whole new market by attracting those who were never interested in computer or console gaming before. Let's take a closer look at some of the high-level design philosophies that have contributed to some of the successful products in the social and mobile space.

4.3.1 Make It Easy to Start Playing

One of the truisms of web design is that "you lose 50 percent of your users for every additional click it takes them to find what they're looking for." It's possible that this statement is just one of the many urban legends of the dot-com era, but it's a useful premise for front-end and UI designers to keep in mind. Even if you're designing social games for a touch platform, like a tablet, where the user does not actually "click" to take action, the point still applies. Don't introduce barriers between your user and getting into the game. If you're an old-school gamer, you probably remember Origin Systems, whose slogan "We Create Worlds" was synonymous with epic, open-world experiences throughout the late 1980s and the 1990s. You probably also remember the terrific hoops gamers had to jump through to get their 386 and 486 machines to have enough free RAM to actually play any of those wonderful, genre-defining games. (Custom boot disks, anyone?) At that time, being a PC gamer required a level of technical sophistication that is typically reserved for the IT department these days. As computing and gaming became more mainstream, and as everyone got wired, the concept of accessibility and usability rose to the forefront. When a user had already paid $60 for a game, they were a lot more likely to spend an hour or five to set up and install before they were rewarded with a title screen. (Games like *Strike Commander* used to require a user to install from more than fifteen disks, a process that could take hours.) It's not that gamers were more dedicated to their hobbies then than they are now, but instead that the marketplace offers so many more options that gamers are no longer required to be willing to jump through such hoops. Users have a plethora of choices now,

FIGURE 4.1   *FarmVille* by Zynga features a streamlined front-end flow, with only four to five clicks before a user is playing. Make it as easy as possible for your users to start playing and you'll have more users.

and they won't tolerate lengthy setups and time-consuming UI. And even if they would be willing, it is likely that their friends wouldn't. And without their friends, you don't have a social game. Thus, every additional click you require from your users is an opportunity for them to lose interest and go do something different. And then you don't get paid.

Let's look at the steps users have to go through to play Zynga's megahit, *FarmVille*, on Facebook (see Figure 4.1):

1. Have a computer with a web browser installed.
2. Have a Facebook account.
3. Go to the *FarmVille* Facebook page by searching for it or by following a friend's link.
4. Click through the splash page by selecting "Play Now."
5. Allow access to *FarmVille* so it can use your social network to spread its message.
6. Wait for *FarmVille* to load (about fifteen to thirty seconds, depending on connection speed).
7. Play.

While it's possible that Zynga could have streamlined this process further (perhaps waiting with the somewhat alarming "Allow Access" page until after I'd played a bit?), this is, overall, a very smooth and streamlined process. You should be wary of any front-end design flow that takes longer or involves any more steps than this. We're not going to pick on some of the games that have introduced more tangled initial user experiences, but they should be easy enough for you to find. If you still aren't playing one minute after you first saw an ad for the game, the process for funneling users into the game isn't good enough. Make it easy for users to start playing and you'll get more users. This is even more true on mobile devices, which have the additional disadvantage of forcing users to install the games before they are able to start playing.

4.3.2 Make It Easy to Stop Playing

It may sound counterintuitive, but sometimes players avoid games that require too great a time commitment. If you're a hard-core gamer—or have ever dated one—then you know what it's like to end up delaying bedtime so you can go on "just one more" corpse-run in *EverQuest,* or to wait for a raid to finish in *World of Warcraft,* to wait for a *League of Legends* match to finish, or to have to go find your body in *Demon Souls* before you can finally put down the controller. By way of comparison, watch the way people play a turn-based game on a mobile phone, playing a quick turn at a stoplight, then another turn at the next stoplight. Watch an iPad player casually flip shut the case, returning their attention to real life, confident that the game will be waiting for them, just where they left it, when they return. What can we learn from this? Also, many users play social games at work, where they may either be distracted at a moment's notice and have to stop playing, or where they aren't really supposed to be playing in the first place, and may need to be able to instantly close their browser or shut the case on their mobile device. Make sure your game lets users stop playing instantly and they'll find it easier to integrate your game into their busy lives.

Many users are reluctant to make a substantial time commitment, or commit to any gameplay, the endpoint of which they cannot control. A game that might make me late to dinner, or penalize me for having to stop playing without having time to "make camp," or somehow force me to go through a time-consuming logout process, may dissuade users from starting up a session. On the other hand, a game that allows players to suspend play instantly—anytime, with one click—then return to a game that is exactly like they left it, the minute they have time to return to it… That's a game that millions of users can play at home while waiting for the kids to get ready for school, or on the subway while traveling to a friend's house, or in line at the grocery store, between classes, or at work when the boss isn't looking. Think about how users quit playing, and how you can offer them tiny, bite-sized chunks of gameplay that can be resumed at any time, without having lost the thread. Make it easy to quit your game, and users will return more often.

For a great example of this mechanic, play Infinite Interactive's wonderful *Puzzle Quest* (any version). (See Figure 4.2.) While it is not a social game, it offers several lessons that illustrate the above point. First, notice that no matter what happens, when users pick up the game, they know what to do: Match three like gems. That's it. No matter how long it's been, no matter how drunk or distracted your players, they know how to play. True, it might take some time to remember second-order strategies (saving up certain types of mana for certain spell combinations, etc. And maybe even longer before they recall the maze of whatever dungeon they are exploring, where to proceed next, etc.) But when they face these issues, *they'll already be playing the game.* Their first move is always crystal clear. Second, any time spent playing equates to forward progress. Even if they lose a match, they gain XP and are rewarded for their time investment. Finally, the game offers the player a stopping point after every single user action. Match three, and you can quit. Move to the next battle, and you can quit. Add a new spell to your repertoire, and you can quit. And guess what? Players will still stay up way past their bedtimes—not because the game design impedes them from stopping when real life calls, but because the core mechanic lets you stop at any time, making it easier to play just one more turn, and then just one more turn, and then just one *last* turn, and so on.

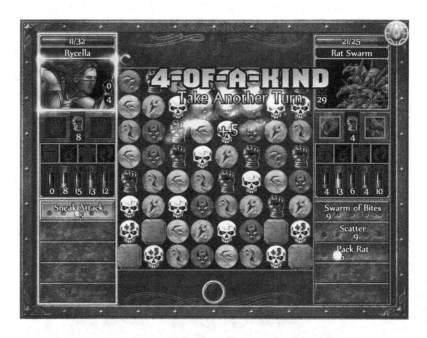

FIGURE 4.2 *Puzzle Quest 2* is a great example of game design that delivers simple, addictive game-play, with a compelling level of depth. It allows a user to easily play for three seconds at a time…all night long. By making your game easy to start and stop, you'll make it more accessible to your users who have other demands on their time.

4.3.3 Make It Easy to Play with Friends

Don't forget the social part. If your game is online on the web or available on mobile devices, you'll have to specifically design social features to get the real value of the platform. And the features you design need to be intuitive and streamlined. Your users need to understand how easily their existing social connections can tie into their games. There are a terrific array of features you can use to reward them for interacting with their friends in some way, but none of that is worth much if they don't know the friends are there or can't figure out how to invite, play, and otherwise interact with them. Much of the rest of this book will address the details of how to incorporate these sorts of features smoothly.

Zynga's *CityVille* is a fine example of a game that makes it easy for users to "find" their friends (see Figure 4.3). Immediately upon starting the game, you'll find a populated "friend" bar running across the bottom of the main screen. This list is presented as a collection of photos and names of users who are in the player's Friend's List, who have also played *CityVille*. Clicking on your friends will give you various options of ways you and your friends can socially interact. Moreover, *CityVille* gives users a tab that allows them to see a more detailed breakdown of their friends' levels, experience points, and total cash. In *CityVille*, players regularly (every thirty clicks or so) get a pop-up encouraging them to share news of their progress (and money) with their friends, including those who have not

FIGURE 4.3 *CityVille*'s "My Neighbors" bar across the main window makes it easy to find friends. Every major event in the game can easily be shared with friends via a clean, pleasant user interface.

ever played the game. By making it easy to find and interact with friends, Zynga's *CityVille* makes it easier for users to play together—which makes them more likely to invest continued time in the game. And by making it easy for users to share news of their exploits in the game with friends who aren't yet playing, they can help "infect" new users and spread the game itself.

4.3.4 Let the User Decide How Much Is the Right Amount

With a retail game, the player has to shell out a set amount of money; that initial price often amounts to several hours' wage for many people, and this expenditure comes before they ever get to play the game. This is a huge leap of faith for a consumer to make, and usually only the established titles from well-recognized publishers can garner this kind of trust, at least with any regularity. With some subscription-based MMOs players have the same initial cash outlay for the "box" and still must agree to a fixed per-month cost. But with most social games and many free-to-play mobile games, the user has the power to decide just how much money they want to spend to improve their experience, and when they want to spend it. Obviously, then, a successful strategy might be to design your gameplay and flow such that users have numerous and varied opportunities to spend money, and are easily able to do so, when they make that choice. Some suggestions:

- Let them buy something at any time by always offering a vendor button; have one on every screen. This allows users to always opt in if they wish, though if executed poorly it can end up creating the perception that your product is "greedy."

- Give them options to purchase enhancements at a variety of price points to appeal to users with different economic resources. Donald Trump might be happy to drop $1000 on a powerful item in your game, but one of your high school players might think a $1 purchase was quite extravagant enough, thank you.

- Don't penalize users for buying things; particularly don't penalize them socially by attaching a stigma to bought items. Specifically, this means you should be very careful offering items that can only be bought with real money transaction, since these will stand out and may be the equivalent of wearing a scarlet *A* to some users, particularly in the West, where the idea of "buying your way ahead" is still frowned upon in some circles. There's a concept, particularly among more traditional or hard-core gamers, that buying items that give the user an advantage is "cheating" and that games that are "pay to win" are fundamentally shady. So ensure that users aren't stigmatized socially by having paid you.

- Remind players early and often that while they can always play for free, they can also purchase items to make their game experience even better, and that it'll be a bargain! So remind your users regularly that they can buy something that will make them squeal, and it'll be a screamin' deal. Of course, you'll have to walk a fine line between interrupting gameplay regularly like a panhandler rattling a tin cup and making sure that the extra delight they can purchase is never more than a few clicks or presses away. (See Figure 4.4.)

FIGURE 4.4 *CityVille* offers users the chance to purchase a special "deal" whenever they return to the game. Remind your users often that they can spend only a little money to vastly improve their game experience.

4.3.5 Make It Easy to Return to the Game

This serves as a corollary to the point about making it easy to stop playing. Store and automate as much return user login information as you can without overly compromising security. When users come back, make sure that you automatically load their progress to the last saved spot. This runs counter to many console front-end designs over the last few decades, so watch for designs that violate this principle by first asking users which of their "saved games" they want to load, or similar. Moreover, make sure that players know exactly what they should do next. Remember the *Puzzle Quest* example, where the user may always default to matching three gems? This kind of simple mechanic makes it easy for users to resume playing your game after hours, months, or even years. If your game mechanics are a bit more complex, consider using tooltips that will remind users of what they should click on next, or a graduated form of reentry into the game, so players can comfortably get their "game legs" back. Never underestimate the degree to which friction between the customer and getting back to playing the game can make them give up and move on to a different form of entertainment. Streamline everything associated with reentry to your mobile or social game and customers will return more often.

Always keep these straightforward design concepts in mind when designing or evaluating the user interface and flow of your social and mobile games. Run usability tests and pay close attention to the early live metric data you get back after the game's launch. Then go back through each of these points and streamline your product, wherever possible.

4.4 USED RETAIL GAME SALES: FRIEND TO SOCIAL AND MOBILE GAME DEVELOPERS

Ask any professional game developer (who has been paying attention) which evil entity had a bigger negative impact on their pocketbooks in the last five years: GameStop or Somali pirates. I can guarantee you the truthful answer is GameStop. To be fair, the Somali pirates have yet to begin trading in software, but their hacker brethren, while capable of doing serious damage, have still likely done less to reduce the money in developers' pockets than GameStop's aggressive move into the resold games market. (At least this was true until Sony's PSN was compromised in 2011.) Why? Simple: People who pirate games on consoles must do so on "modded" or hacked hardware. This is difficult enough that it limits the number of people out there actively stealing and copying code. Moreover, many of those who "pirate" these games would likely never have purchased more than a few titles a year, in any case. (The number is roughly in line with the rest of the game-buying population.) But customers who walk into GameStop and pick up a used game think they are doing the morally and fiscally right thing. They walk to the register, pull out and swipe a credit card, pick up their free copy of *Game Informer*, and head home happy—content that they have bought and paid for a game they are excited to play. But lo! The developer and publisher of the product get no money from GameStop.

This type of used trade accounted for 48 percent of GameStop's total revenue in 2010. In fact, the practice of buying and reselling used games proved so successful and popular that GameStop has introduced a "PowerUp Rewards" program, giving users points for trading in their used systems and games—points that can then be converted into additional discounts for future purchases…at GameStop.

PC games developed subscription fees and in-game purchasing via microtransactions in an effort to beat piracy. They largely overcome the trading of "used" games in the same way. (No reputable store will take a used PC product, as they are too easily copied.)

But social and mobile games have no similar problem. Retailers are cut completely out of the loop when your game is on Facebook or available directly from an app store, and you make all of your money through the various advanced monetization methods we've discussed.

However, GameStop didn't get to the top of the highly competitive retail games trade by sitting back and resting on their laurels or by being fools. Recognizing that social and online games were beginning to take a bite out of their market, they bought Kongregate, an online gaming service, in 2010. Kongregate is a fledgling social network and a portal for small Flash-based games. Players win points for playing games on Kongregate, for rating games, or for referring friends. These points are converted to PowerUp Rewards points, which are then redeemable at GameStop stores or online.

In May of 2011, GameStop continued this move into the digital download space by acquiring Impulse, software written by developer Stardock, which allows users to purchase and download games directly from GameStop. Because games purchased through Impulse are not eligible for resale (they are all PC products), many publishers of traditional retail games have supported this move.

Around the same time, GameStop opened a digital storefront on Facebook. However, as of this writing, GameStop has not yet moved into the social or mobile games space per se. (Though they have dabbled in Android tablets.) Indeed, their deleterious effects on the retail sector have likely helped drive the movement of many game developers and publishers into experimenting with social and mobile games and are encouraging traditional publishers and console manufacturers to accelerate the arrival of direct-digital-download AAA console titles.

Why should you care about all this? Because GameStop is and will continue to affect the social and mobile gaming scene. Their attention has turned to digital downloads and their move to create a Facebook storefront means that they are very clearly paying attention to the digital gaming dollars that are currently slipping through their fingers. As bandwidth continues to increase and as the distance in production values between retail products and social and mobile games continues to narrow, GameStop will become a greater threat to companies like Zynga and to game designers like you. Either figure out how to beat them or figure out how to join them, but do not ignore them.

4.5 INTERVIEW WITH JASON DECKER AND POCKET LEGENDS: "LOVE LETTERS FROM YOUR COMMUNITY"

Jason Decker has been making games for more than fifteen years. He's built console, PC, MMO, mobile, and social games. Currently the art director of Spacetime Studios, he has worked as an environment lead and technical art lead for Microsoft and Digital Anvil. Jason holds a BS in Computer Science from the University of Texas and currently resides in Austin, Texas.

Q: Tell us a little bit about who you are and what you do.

A: I'm Jason Decker. I've been in the games industry for a long time, about fifteen years. Currently I work at Spacetime Studios here in Austin as an art director on multiple projects. Last year we released *Pocket Legends*, which is an MMO for the iOS devices, Android, and will soon be released on Chrome and PC. We're currently working on a couple of new projects too.

Q: Was Pocket Legends *the first MMO on mobile?*

A: Yes, I think it was! We were able to put it on iPhone 3G, and even on Edge network. So you can play it at the airport, in line at the store, wherever. We were trying to get an old arcade game *Gauntlet*, mix it with some *Diablo*, add a little bit of *World of Warcraft* and make it so you could play it anywhere. There was some toilet humor around this idea: We joked that we wanted to let you play through an instance while in the john.

Q: So you built the first MMO I can play on the can?

A: Exactly. It was interesting because our company was into the big MMO, AAA development. A few years ago, when the economy tanked, we lost some contracts. Our big game got killed and we were forced to whittle the company down to just six or seven people. And we wondered, "What would it be like to take all those millions of dollars of research and development and squeeze it into the phone?" A few days later, Rick Delashmit, one of our great programmers, showed us some pink boxes walking around on a pink dungeon floor. That was half the battle right there. There was *Pocket Legends*.

Q: Pocket Legends *is an amazing product... How many people play at any given time together?*
A: When it first came out it was a pretty big deal. We weren't free to play at the time. And I can't remember exact concurrency numbers from then, but it was in the thousands.
Q: So you had thousands of people getting together in instances?
A: Well, the instances would hold between twenty and thirty people at a time, and you could go on dungeon runs with groups of five. So we'd have hundreds of people playing together at any time.
Q: And now?
A: Last E3 we started doing something called "Chase the Droid Flashmobs" where we would announce, "At various times in the day, look for the droid. If you wave to him, he'll give you some presents!" So on the big screen at E3, we'd have the droid character running around. And it was funny to see thirty or so people from inside the world running around chasing this guy to get the prizes. We've done a few of those "Flashmob" events in the gameworld.

We've learned in the past year how to go more social. We'd Twitter stuff, and use every avenue you can imagine to get the word out. Little sidebar ads, Facebook, friend us, like us, tell your friends. That's how you have to make it; you have to keep chipping away at delivering to new people and getting their friends to go viral with it.

It sounds cheesy on some level, but for social games, the customer is always in your face. Previously, in the retail world, someone would buy your game and spend $60 on it. Maybe they didn't like it, but you already had their $60. We're trying to get you to give us a nickel! A dime! A dollar would be great. But we're letting you have the game for free, and you can a la carte your way to be anywhere you want.

We rely on people who love the product to help us build the community. Some people spend more time on our forums than they do in the game. We're trying to create a network of people that love to live in the world, make friends there, and go to the forums to talk about where they go to school or where they live. It's not just the game—we've created a social space. And it's one that's big enough to include everyone, but still small enough that people know each other.

Q: When it comes to monetization... The game is free to download on all these various devices—every mobile device and soon on PC—so how does Spacetime get paid?

A: We joke that the game is free, but we make our money through volume. When I say you have to chip away, the reality is that you have to take every angle possible to monetize your game.

For one thing, we sell indirect advertising. It's a push/pull world out there. One aspect of how things work is by ranking. Advertising, marketing, getting on the shelf (in the app store)—you have to do some dastardly tricks to get seen. To expose a secret underbelly: In the app world there's a lot of noise. Anyone can make an app. That sounds great, really democratic, and I'm all for it. But the flip side is, there's tons of noise, so even getting people to know about your game is nearly impossible.

The whole scene is so new that the app stores on iOS and Android don't have a good grasp on how to handle all the choices. Should you sort by ratings, price, or number of downloads? It's so hard to tell what's really popular, because some apps will give you free stuff if you download a different app—which means one app will get popular because it'll reward you in some other program.

Q: This is stuff like TapJoy?

A: Exactly. Stuff like *TapJoy*. There are cheap ways to do it, like *iVampire*. And it's cool the way that all works, but it clouds the market. If you download this expansion, you'll get free hearts in this other game. It's very noisy with all these offers.

Q: Once people are playing your game, what things do you offer them in exchange for money?

A: We decided after launch to go free to play for all of our content. And we're design purists, in that we don't want people to be able to play to just be "better" at the game. We don't want you to spend $5 on this Sword of Dragon Breath that lets you kill everybody. That feels like cheating, if the rich man can come in and just dominate everyone else. So instead we monetize in ways that let you speed up your progress in the game. For example, maybe it takes someone who doesn't want to spend any money five hours to reach level 20 in the game. But if you don't have that much time, you can buy some elixirs that will give you double the experience for combat or give you more strength. Since you're fighting zombies or monsters, not other players, it doesn't feel like you're cheating to people. You advance faster if you enjoy the game and have the money, but not the time. We called it "value-added playing." If someone is in middle school they might have all day to play, while someone else might only have enough time to play for an hour a day, but still wants to see more of the game.

Q: What do you know about your average customer?

A: We've made an MMO, but it's an MMO-lite. For some of them, they've come from *WOW*, but for many of them, it's their first MMO. Our game is pretty deep, so we've been able to win over some hard-core players, but it's accessible, so we've also won a bunch of casual gamers, once they check it out. I think the most appealing thing is that it's always with them. We've gotten many letters from people who tell us that they love that when they're out of town they can still play with their friends.

So for us, if you're talking about how to be successful: We listen to our players. We haven't abandoned anything, we've always added. Adding new content, trickling it out a little at a time to provide a living world. And interacting with the community outside of the game world too.

Like, we'll have bake sales and hold a Facebook contest where people can send in pictures of cakes they've baked in the real world. And we'll give out super-unique rare items to people who win these competitions.

Q: You use Facebook for spreading the message, but the game isn't playable on Facebook, right?

A: Right. If you're making a social game, you have to approach every arena available to you to reach your players and your fan base. You have to nurture the people who enjoy your game. They're there because they feel like they're being heard. Our fans are a living system.

Q: They feel like they can talk to you and you'll listen, and make the game better for them?

A: Yes. We will respond. They will demand changes that we listen to, and we'll evolve the game over time for them. That's the most interesting thing about making a social game—it's a give-and-take between the fan and the developers.

Q: How do you get feedback and suggestions from your customers?

A: We have a really active forum, and we chart activity there. We have areas for bugs, improvement suggestions, and we have flame wars all the time.

Everyone will complain about everything, but if they weren't complaining, they wouldn't be there. If you're hearing about it, they're playing, and they're enjoying so much they want it to be even better. So having rabid fans may sound like a pain, but it's really a good indication that you're doing something right. They love your game enough to talk to you about it. They'll come back from other games that they've played and talk about other games and give us suggestions from other products. Your players want you to win. You've created a virtual world, and they want it to stay around forever. That's what real social gaming is about. These are people who send goodbye emails when they're leaving; they post it on the forums when they're going to be away on vacation and won't be around to help each other. We have a cast of game characters around the office that we know because they are regulars. And you need to nurture those people.

If you're talking about social games, nurturing the community is a big part of it. And by social games, I mean where people are actually in the world together. This doesn't really happen that much in most "social games."

People want to show off their characters. If you hold up a "Shield of Impossibility" in the game, the twelve people who manage to get it will be proud of that. As a developer, I've gone into the game world before with gear that I just made to test out. And within seconds I'll have twenty-five friend requests and a dozen messages from people asking me, "Where did you get that, and how do I get one?"

That's awesome and terrifying. Our customers know much more about our game than we do. They're in it more than we are. We created a game that we thought we'd get people to play in fifteen-minute bursts when they weren't playing *WOW* or other games. It turns out, they play it all day. They plug their phones into the wall. Almost as if being on a phone didn't matter at all.

You can't forget that at the root of a social game, it's a community. People are there to be heard. And it can be a nice thing to be a bigger fish in a smaller pond. When I play *Call of Duty*, I get killed every two seconds. It's inaccessible, because it's so mainstream in a way. Social games can be a sort of niche market, because players can be so fanatical about their small niche in the community.

Q: *Does* Pocket Legends *use a dual currency system? What's the economy of* Pocket Legends?

A: Platinum is our in-game currency. You can convert U.S. dollars into platinum, which is a pretty straight conversion. Platinum used to buy you access to different parts of the world map, stuff like that. Now that we're completely free, though, platinum buys you potions, vanity items, extra boosts that make you faster or stronger. But gold, which you earn in game by opening chests and killing monsters, can also buy you most of the same things. So if you want to grind up and play zero money, you can play for tons of hours and have a lot of fun; there's no limiting factor.

Q: *Can you tell me more about other ways that you can monetize your users or give them value for their money?*

A: In a lot of ways, people are paying for access to your users. If you have a game that is slightly popular, other people approach you, because you have "eyeballs" of a certain demographic that advertisers want to reach. Well, one way is that you can trade. Some other game will offer you a certain amount of money to give your users an offer that will let them get some in-game currency in exchange for them downloading that other game. If your player doesn't want to spend a dollar, but they want the value of it in our currency, and are willing to spend time to download that other game, then everyone wins.

It's a very noisy world out there. I don't have time to see everything out there, and I don't even know what I should see. I rely on friends to tell me. The virality of the game world is so important, because we're all built to ignore advertising right now. So our players who don't have money or don't want to spend money put in the extra effort. I used to be against this kind of thing, but I don't see any loss now. If player doesn't want to do it, they won't do it.

Q: *Some people would say that "social games" are just games available on Facebook and that's it. But I think you guys have built a truly social game. Do you think of* Pocket Legends *as a social game?*

A: I'm not gonna bad-mouth Facebook games—obviously a huge number of people play them in the world. But I don't know how social they really are. You're not necessarily chatting or even interacting. You just happen to be on a platform with millions of people on it. It's less that they are social games, and more that Facebook is a channel, a platform. It's great in that they've brought so many people together and can then provide them with games: *Pachinko*, arcade games, or *Pong*. But would *Pong* be a social game if you were playing it against an AI just because you're playing it on a social platform? I don't know.

But the social games I'm talking about are the ones that generate hundreds of pages of people giving us their real picture, introducing themselves to all the friends they've met in our game. These are people who live in the United States, in Russia, and all over the world!

We all live in a world where it's hard for people to establish a sense of unique identity, and community is very fractured. You probably know more people online than you do in your neighborhood. So for many people, it may be much more important what hairstyle their avatar on the Xbox 360 has than what car they drive to work each day. You're great, so long as you're the king of your forum, of your social space.

Q: When you think about things you'd do next, starting fresh on a new social game and wanting to explore different ways of monetizing the game, what would you do differently?

A: I'm always surprised that we're able to get money from people, because we're really laying it all out there for free. I think we would try to lend an air of exclusivity—maybe only create ten of a certain item. *EVE Online* has done something like this... Where you can buy a piece of clothing that will cost you as much as a battleship, but everyone else will know that you spent that much on it. It's a status symbol, just like in real life.

We've shied away from that so far—we prefer to give the super-duper prizes to people who are community leaders and really active in forming a community. We rely on these people to shape and police the community, because we don't have the money, time, and wherewithal to keep people from naming their character "Face Raper" or something like that.

Q: Uh, what's a Face Raper?

A: We forgot to turn on our profanity filter for names initially. So of course, some people named their character some horrible stuff. We had to spend a ton of time going through and renaming people like Face Raper to Happy Pony, and that kind of stuff. We use a name generator now, and lots of the names that are left are like "Iskitraaun"—some Serbian knight from the Middle Ages or something.

Q: What's the most fun thing about the development of social games?

A: For us, it was definitely when we were only six people. That ended up being a high point in my career. Because with six people and six tables, there's no stopping work for a meeting. You're developing all the time, and everyone knows what everyone else is doing. It's just "Go, go, go!" And I think that's an important lesson for anyone trying to do social games. Work lean and fast.

Put something out first, then fix it later. Because the big problem and joy of social games and having such a large market to deal with is churn. Churn is a huge factor.

Q: What do you mean by churn?

A: People download your game, they look at it for five minutes. Hell, maybe someone else *paid* them to come download it in the way I talked about. So maybe they aren't even really interested in the game. But I still have to try to hook them in the first few minutes, so they stick around long enough to buy something.

Q: How long do you let a user play for free? When do you start thinking about trying to monetize a user?

A: How long you let a player play? As long as they want! If they enjoy the game, and twenty days from now they decide to spend a dollar, well, that's a dollar I want. The key is that they are there for twenty days. If they are there for five minutes, and don't know what to do, you never got a thing out of them. You shouldn't be concerned about how long they play without paying you. You should be concerned when they quit playing.

Q: Any final thoughts for social game developers out there?

A: Steal from the best. That's the best advice I have. There's so much learning going on right now about what works and what doesn't. Don't waste your time trying to invent brand-new stuff. I believe in being original, but you have to look at what's done well and learn from it, then bring your own voice to it.

Don't hold on to stuff to a point of perfection either. Learn to fail fast. When you're making a game you can't be in the minds of the masses; so get it out there quickly, and react quickly to what they like and don't like.

You'll get fan letters if you do something right, sure. But you'll get a lot more complaints. And you should treat every hate mail as a love letter. They love your game so much that they care enough to write. They've invested so much somehow into your dream that they really care. Otherwise, you're just a commercial for them to ignore. They want the soul in everything that you do.

Two things that are happening—first, the chips that are waiting to come out on the phones now are about twenty times more powerful than what you're holding today. And the reality is that we're now all holding mega-PCs in our hands. Between the powerful phones and cloud computing, technology is going to be a big game changer in the mobile gaming market within the next few years.

Q: Tell me about the erosion of the AAA market.

A: The reality is, for any device that's polished and expensive, like a new big TV, you're going to always buy something to show it off. If you buy a 3D TV, you're going to buy a $30 *Avatar* 3D DVD that shows it off, even though you're still mostly going to be watching streamed movies off Netflix that don't look nearly as good. If you have a PS3, you're going to buy a $60 game. If I buy an iPhone 5, I'm probably going to buy that new *Unreal* tech demo that runs on it. Stuff like XBLA erodes that a bit, because you can get really great entertainment for a fraction of that price, but you're still going to occasionally buy those summer blockbusters that show off your hardware. So social and mobile games aren't going to kill the big AAA games—just give people another way to play.

CHAPTER 5

Industry Terms and Metrics

5.1 INDUSTRY TERMS AND METRICS

One of the most challenging things about coming into the social and mobile games space from another industry is the often bewildering array of acronyms dealing with users and monetization. Each publisher and developer seems to value slightly different key metrics, but almost without fail, the obsessive focus put on ARPU or DAU or more sophisticated DAU indices would do a baseball bookie proud. Anyone with a stake in the financial performance of social and mobile games needs to learn to live, sleep, and breathe metrics. This chapter will help explain what the most commonly referenced user metrics tend to be, why you should care, and how different groups evaluate these metrics to determine product health. At the end of this chapter, we'll take a look at John Romero's *Ravenwood Fair*, a game that has generously shared oodles of metrics with the community at large. We'll sift through the *Ravenwood Fair* data to see how a successful game has made use of user metrics to improve its offering and thus to become even more profitable.

5.2 MEASURING PLAYER POPULATION

Particularly when discussing free-to-play games, total number of users is often considered about the most important measure of success. Let's start with the two kings of the analytics world.

5.2.1 Daily Active Users

Daily active users (DAU) is a measure of the number of unique users per day, typically calculated over a floating seven-day period. Commonly, to qualify as a DAU a user need only start up the app or enter the game. There is no minimum play time or further interaction required. Specific definitions do, however, tend to vary in their details, beyond this initial basic premise.

Facebook defines[*] a user as active when they "view or engage with your application or your application's content."

---

[*] http://www.facebook.com/help/?faq=219375581424410

The following are actions that count toward DAU on Facebook:

- Users who visit your application's canvas page (enter your game)

- Users who view your application tab on a page

- Users who publish to news feeds (stream) through your application

- Users who "liked" a stream story from your applications

- Users who commented on a stream story from your application

5.2.2 Monthly Active Users

Monthly active users (MAU) is a measure of the number of active users in a given calendar month, typically calculated from the first to the last day of that month. MAU can also be shown as a current floating thirty-day average. Activity is evaluated as described above, such that effectively MAU is just an aggregate of the DAU over a month. Note that there is a pervasive lack of clarity in what constitutes a "unique" user, such that in many cases MAU numbers are drastically inflated by users who visit a site multiple times per day. A more accurate accounting would likely yield a far smaller number, as each user would only be counted once toward the total monthly count. (So, for example, if I cared only about unique users, then assuming only 1000 people played my game and each of them logged in once per day, every day of the month, my DAU and MAU would be identical. But if uniqueness wasn't important to me, my numbers might show 1000 DAU and, for example, 30,000 MAU depending on how often those users were active in my game.) Something to note: MAU and MAUU (monthly average unique users) are often conflated, but they are very different values and can give you very different types of useful information.

Several useful online resources now exist for tracking MAU and providing insight into each week's winners and losers. One of these is AppData (www.appdata.com), which makes it easy to study user online habits as measured by MAU, both for traditional social network applications, and for mobile apps.

So what can I do with these two numbers? First, I can look at the relationship between the two and draw some inferences about the stickiness of my game.

By calculating DAU/MAU, I get a measurement of how many of my players show up or log in to play each day. If I've got one million daily active users and three million monthly active users, then I have a DAU/MAU of 0.3 or 30 percent; a third of my players are checking in at least once per day.

This number measures the daily "addictiveness" of your game. The higher the ratio, the better; you want every user coming back for more and more gameplay, every single day. This number is of great value to you because it can be used to directly measure the impact of game design changes. Alter the way the user first interacts with your game—something crucial in the first few minutes, or something that affects the core gameplay loop—and then study how your DAU/MAU changes. Did you improve something about the accessibility or addictiveness of the game? This ratio will tell you.

To really properly measure the effect of a particular change on DAU/MAU, it can be wise to limit the change to a particular subset of your total number of users. The DAU/MAU ratio of this "cohort" can then be compared to the control group (the rest of your users, who did not receive the change) to isolate the effect of the change from any other factors that might affect DAU numbers (like a weekend, or a network outage, or a holiday).

As an indicator of overall success, this metric can be quite useful. If users are coming back to your game, then all you need to do is increase the total volume of users (and the percentage of those users who pay you), and you're on the road to profitability! And luckily, this ratio scales nicely. It seems to be as accurate a predictor of success for games with 20 million users as it is for games of a more modest size.

Without a high DAU/MAU, it likely doesn't make much sense to spend a significant portion of your budget to market your game. Why? Your problem isn't getting users to try the product. Your problem is getting them to come back. Many of the games that care about this statistic are "freemium," meaning that they let users play for free in the hopes of making their money on microtransactions. And the freemium model only works if the first taste the users get is so addictive that they can't help but come back for more. Until this number looks good for a thousand users, it doesn't help you much to increase to a million, because the hard reality is that most of them won't return.

5.2.3 Peak Concurrent Users

At any given second, how many users are playing the game? Those are your concurrent users. What's the largest this number has ever been? That's your number of peak concurrent users (PCU). For synchronous, real-time MMO-type games, this ends up being a big deal because it affects server loads, how many customer service people are required at peak times, and other planning details that affect operational costs. However, the rapidly expandable/contractible cloud of servers that are quickly becoming available on the cheap are reducing the importance of this type of statistic. Finally, since the DAU/MAU ratio ends up being a lot more informative than learning how many people are playing your game simultaneously, PCU is slowly falling into obscurity and may soon be little more than a vanity metric for many games.

However, as games grow in popularity, some have decided that their users represent a target-rich market for advertisers. As we'll examine a little later, some games endeavor to increase their profits through in-game advertising. (Indeed, this economy drives many free web games.) As this model evolves it is possible that PCU could end up being an important way of pricing advertising, much as viewership is for prime-time television (though the online game medium often has more precise ways to guarantee viewers to advertisers).

5.3 MEASURING MONETIZATION

Now let's look at some of the more important terms and metrics dealing with how your game monetizes. The overall notion to remember is that if your game is a typical freemium model, all the high DAU numbers in the world don't do you much good unless you're also converting these players into paying users. Ask yourself how many of your total users actually pay, expressed as a percentage, and how much each user gives you on average in a given time span. This is the only surefire way accurately to predict what your revenues will look like.

Conversion rate (CVR)—Of those users who try out your game, how many are converted into paying customers? The higher this rate is, the better. While this metric only directly applies to free-to-play games, in which many players may use the application without buying anything, it is also regularly used when speaking of "demo conversion rates" for more traditional games that offer a free demo on Steam, Xbox LIVE, or similar.

Average revenue per user (ARPU)—Take your total revenue for a given time period (say, a month) and divide it by the total number of users that month. The result is an average revenue per user, a number that tells you how much revenue you can expect, on average, for every person who plays your game. If you can get this number to be as high as a dollar per user, per month, you're probably doing quite well (assuming you can scale up the total number of users without significant added operational costs and then keep them around long enough to offset whatever you spent to acquire each user in the first place!)

Average revenue per paying user (ARPPU)—Take your total revenue for a given time period and divide it up among the total number of users who paid you any amount during that same time period. For a game like, say, *World of Warcraft*, in which all users have a fixed subscription price, this amount is quite easy to predict and should be identical to the ARPU (ignoring trial subscriptions). However, with microtransactions and other freemium-model games, this number will typically be much higher than your ARPU, as the vast majority of your users will never pay you anything, and this metric only tracks the average for those who do.

User acquisition cost (UAC)—How much money will you spend, on average, to get a new user to try your game? This is an aggregate of your development cost, advertising cost, back-end server costs, and so on. Your first user is by far the most expensive; the minute you acquire your second user, this cost is cut in half. Before long, this will level out to a point such that you can reasonably calculate what the cost of each additional user you attract is likely to be. (The additional cost is based almost entirely on the costs you pay to online advertisers, or other applications that can drive traffic to your game or encourage installs from the app store.) You can compare this info against the ARPU to determine if it makes sense for you to pump money into your advertising budget. The greater the virality of your product, the lower this cost can go, as your users "infect" others and turn them on to your product without you spending a penny. Unfortunately, social networking sites have so clamped down on viral channels in the last few years, and the number of apps on the iPhone and Android app stores has increased so rapidly, that UAC has risen dramatically in the last few years.

Lifetime value (LTV)—The LTV of a user represents the total amount of money you expect to be able to extract through the course of your relationship with them. For example, if an average user gives you $1 per month, and you expect to maintain each user for an average of twenty-four months before they move on, then you can estimate a LTV of $24 per user. If you compare this number against your UAC and determine that you can acquire a new user for only, say, $14, then you can anticipate your profits. Obviously, user retention is key to increasing your product's per-user LTV; the longer they play, the more they pay. It is worth cautioning against blind reliance on using LTV to justify slamming a foot down on the marketing accelerator once a game has shown some glimmer of promise. LTV has proven to be a useful metric, but in some cases, it has driven a fanatical devotion to marketing dollars and customer acquisition rather than providing enhanced value to customers. For a fuller discussion of this concern, I recommend reading Bill Gurley's excellent article on Above the Crowd.[*]

Lifetime network value (LTNV)—Your users have a dollar value to you beyond their own direct payments. The degree to which they are able to recruit friends to join them or enhance the play experience of their friends (thus adding stickiness to the game) both have a value to you as the game's creator. For each user you add, how many friends will he or she recruit? This value is very difficult to calculate with accuracy. However, despite being challenging to calculate accurately, understanding what this value approximates to for a particular game can help inform decisions about how to spend marketing money to attract new users. A satisfied customer can have far more value to your business than just the contents of his or her wallet, but quantifying that value may be difficult.

5.4 SOCIAL NETWORK ADVERTISING

Click-through rate (CTR)—An online ad, be it a banner ad, a direct Facebook ad, or one of those loathsome pop-ups, can be measured for efficacy by calculating the number of people who click on it divided by the number of people who see it. Theoretically at least, this value, usually expressed as a percentage, will describe how successful the ad is at converting awareness to interest. If users see it, they are suddenly aware of the offer. If they click on it, they have expressed interest. For example, if 100,000 people see an advertisement, and 400 of them click on it, the ad has a CTR of 0.4 percent.

Conversion rate (CVR)—When speaking of online advertising, CVR is a reflection of the number of users who respond to an ad favorably. After your potential users have expressed sufficient interest in an advertisement or a free-to-play trial, some of them decide to express their desire by either installing your game or paying you something. In either case, this conversion from interest to desire-driven action is described as a CVR. CVRs are typically expressed as a percentage and must be given context to make much sense. For example, if 400 people click on an ad for your game, and get

---

[*] http://abovethecrowd.com/2012/09/04/the-dangerous-seduction-of-the-lifetime-value-ltv-formula/

to the install screen, but only 20 of them end up actually installing the application, then your CVR is 5 percent.

Cost per install (CPI)—Getting users to install your game in the first place typically has costs, the vast majority of which are associated with the advertising you bought to drive initial awareness and interest in the product. (Usually development costs for the product itself are excluded from this value.) CPI measures the total marketing cost divided by the number of total installs. If you bought 10 million impressions at $1 each, and 1 million installed the game, then your total advertising cost would be $10 million, and your CPI would be $10.

5.5 MOBILE TERMS

In-app purchase (IAP)—When a game allows a user to spend money to purchase something from inside the game, be it new characters, new abilities, items, more power or turns, or anything else, this is considered an IAP. Typically, the purchase flow for buying these value-added goods requires that the user return to the application store on the mobile device, purchase something, download it, and then restart the application. Streamlining this flow to the minimum level of complexity required by the platform holder is strongly encouraged as a way of making monetizing users through IAPs as easy as possible.

5.6 GENERAL TERMS

Let's take a quick look at some of the common jargon used in the business.

Key performance indicators (KPI)—Broadly speaking, key performance indicators refer to whatever your company, studio, or organization cares about most. Almost any and all of the metrics described in this chapter are considered KPI for someone.

A/B testing—A/B testing is often also called split testing. This is a mechanism, first developed by print advertisers, who publish catalogs and the like, for determining which type of advertising is most effective on their customers. By releasing two versions of a catalog with the same products, advertisers could test how design changes affected consumer purchase interest. The same type of testing can be used in games to determine the viability of a particular feature, UI change, email reminder, or almost anything else.

Auditability—You may hear game designers talk about the auditability of their metrics. What this means is that any metric data you gather should be able to be sanity checked against other known valid sources, to ensure that your data is accurate. Google Analytics and Facebook's metrics both provide good places to cross-check your data for auditability. For mobile products, you can easily cross-check the information your application uploads against the information provided to you by the app stores, at least for auditing number of paid downloads and similar.

Entry event distribution (EED)—Put simply, this refers to the first action that users perform when they come to your game or to your site. By measuring and understanding this information, you can determine why users actually play your game. When users have a collection of choices upon entering a game, what do they select first? This tells you a lot about what draws them back to the game. For example, if 80 percent of your users always first check the leaderboards to see how their ranking has changed relative to their friends, you can deduce that social competition is a huge motivator to your players. On the other hand, if their first action is always to check their in-game mailbox to see what gifts friends have sent them, you can tell that they are playing for the cooperative social aspect. Each game will have different types of events and different EED measurements. But it's very helpful to learn to think in terms of common user actions and use cases.

Exit event distribution (XED)—What's the last action users perform before they stop playing? If you've got an event that commonly occurs to a majority of users just before they stop playing, you'd be well served to investigate that event. What do users come to your game to do? What makes them want to leave? If you can understand what they are doing just before they leave, then you can begin to ask the next important question: Are they leaving because that event is unpleasant or dull and needs to be fixed, or is there something about the game flow and progression that naturally makes users save a particular action until they are ready to stop playing? By understanding why your users quit a session, you can work to extend their session length and frequency. If they've left the game, they can't possibly pay you.

Outbound messages per user—This number is used to study the events that cause users to commonly send out messages to friends. It is directly related to the virality of your product (as in when your players contact friends who don't yet play) and the stickiness of your product (as in when your players contact other players in-game or about the game). Understanding this type of information can help you tweak your design to be more infectious and stickier. If your game exists as part of a web-based social network, are there more opportunities for you to add value to your users by letting them interact with their friends? For mobile games, are there other ways you could allow users to contact, taunt, or invite their friends?

Message conversion rates—When users receive a message, how likely are they to either return to your game or start playing it for the first time? Studying this information can allow you to better tailor your outbound messages. Outbound messages generally come in two forms. The first of these is a message generated by the game (or instigated by the user) that posts a news item to that user's wall or social profile. ("Jimmy just found a lonely sheep in *FarmVille*.") The second type is a message the game sends directly to its users, reminding them to come back. ("Play *FarmVille* today and collect 20 cash and an English Hen!")

Virality—When you talk about the virality of your game, you're discussing the ways in which it attracts new users and the rate at which the users who hear of it, are messaged about it, or are in some other way exposed to the product become converts. The theme, the artwork, the messaging, and the word-of-mouth surrounding your product all affect its virality.

Engagement—Studies of user engagement are a way of measuring the amount of time a user spends, per session, interacting with your product. As a rule of thumb, the longer players remain engaged, the more likely they are to spend money. Your game design mechanics greatly affect your goals here. This can be measured in minutes and seconds, but since users can sit on some pages for hours without interacting, it may be more useful to measure the average number of page views per user, the total number of clicks, or something similar. Depending on the mobile device you are authoring a particular version of a game for, you may have a way to measure actual playtime or "focus" time as opposed to just how long the application is left running.

Engagement currency—When a game gives away currency, like gold for slaying monsters or Coins in *Empires and Allies* as a reward for the user doing whatever they are supposed to be doing in the game, this is called an engagement currency. Typically, this is also used to explicitly distinguish between the in-game reward money and the actual virtual currency derived from cold cash. Engagement currency is also often called "soft currency."

Hard currency—When users translate real money into a virtual currency that can be used to play games or buy things within games, this is called a hard currency. Imagine the "tokens" players used to get from those dollar bill machines in arcades, but gone digital.

Retention rate—How many of your users return after their first visit? This can be measured by the DAU/MAU calculation described above. Retention rate is also synonymous with the "stickiness" of your game.

Casual gamer—Most Facebook and mobile gamers fall into this category. Typically, these gamers play games occasionally but aren't into the gamer "lifestyle." They likely only play on one or two platforms (mobile phone and Facebook, for instance), and they aren't particularly interested in the technology. These gamers don't typically track release dates or follow the game industry press.

Hard-core gamer—Hard-core gamers are ones who are much closer to the traditional demographic (twenty-three years old and male). They often are involved in the gaming culture, read websites and gaming magazines, typically track and discuss new releases, usually own one or more gaming consoles, and typically devote several times more hours per week and many more dollars per year to their hobby than do casual gamers.

Unity—Unity is a 3D engine, editor, pipeline, and toolset that is commonly used to create multiplatform browser and mobile games. While it might seem a bit peculiar to explicitly call out one engine, but not the hundreds or thousands of others that exist, the pervasive use of Unity for developing mobile games and its accessibility and affordability for developers of all skill levels have catapulted Unity into a unique position in the gaming business. Moreover, the company provides public information on the types of devices that run Unity software every day.* This page ends up providing quite valuable insight into usage by device (Samsung Galaxy II versus Kindle Fire, for example) as well as specific hardware statistics that can answer many types of important questions. ("How much RAM is common for mobile phone gamers these days?") Knowledge of this engine, toolset, and the handy reference the Unity site provides can prove invaluable to almost any developer.

Whales—We promised we'd tell you, so here it is: Whales are users who are disproportionately monetized. For example, the ones who give you a thousand dollars a month when your average user gives you $3. Spending time thinking about the way your whales behave, what their social group looks like, and what it is about your game that keeps them coming back and spending is extremely valuable. After all, you certainly don't want to make a change to your game design that inadvertently disenfranchises your best customers.

5.7 WHY THESE METRICS MATTER

You need to understand the health of your product, and you need to be able to react quickly to changes in your user base. Because most social and mobile games are working to extract money from players in tiny increments, on a minute-by-minute basis, they are well served to massage the details of your game mechanics and content over time to improve profitability. While PC-based MMO games have understood and harvested user engagement metrics like those described above for years, this model is often quite alien to traditional console developers, who may be more familiar with a "release and forget" approach. Simply put, in the modern era of social and mobile game development, such an approach is doomed (as it likely is for console products as well). Your competition is excellent at tracking every detail of how users interact with their products, and they often iterate on their games on a daily basis. You need to cultivate a similar mentality.

Studying metrics like these won't, by themselves, make a game successful. You still need to have an appealing theme, great mechanics, attractive art, and all the rest. But careful study and regular iteration based on metric data can act as a force multiplier, transforming your "good" game into a huge hit.

The relevance of some of these metrics is obvious; you already understand why you care about the ARPU, for example. The relevance of other types of data may be less obvious. For example, why do you really care about the cost to acquire a new user? Won't existing on a social network automatically make your game "go viral"? Won't users just find your great game on the app store and tell their friends about it? The answer, sadly, is "not anymore." Social networks and app stores alike have been flooded with products, many of which are of low quality or which alienate users by spamming their friends, or worse, compromising

---

* http://gamasutra.com/blogs/ArasPranckevicius/20130408/190055/Mobile_and_more_Hardware_Statistics.php

sensitive user data. This has led to a noisy market in which gathering new users is difficult. Typically, you will be forced to rely on advertising to reach an initial critical mass of players. The number of users you can attract tends to be directly related to the amount of advertising sugar you have to spread around. But since these users don't actually pay you unless they decide they love your game, the only way to really know how big a bet you should place is to evaluate the LTNV of your users against your UAC. At the simplest level, the formula you care about is

$$(\text{LTNV} - \text{UAC}) \times \text{Number of Users} = \text{Total Profit.}$$

Using a formula like this, you can determine which games deserve the big bets. A high LTV justifies spending marketing dollars to acquire new customers. It represents the net present value of your customer base (and in some ways, when viewed as an aggregate of all of your users across all games you operate, reflects the total value of your company).

When considering your metrics, here are a few things to keep in mind:

- It's easy to track and gather metrics, but it's famously difficult to interpret them. So be sure to become, or hire, people with superb minds for analytics and understanding statistical data. A whole class of business analytics experts and game designers who are proficient in this type of numeromancy has emerged in the last few years.[*] Either become one or hire one if you are serious about playing in the social or mobile space. As the amount of information we collect from customers grows, and as we build up ever more massive volumes of historical data on customer behavior, we start to enter the realm of so-called Big Data, where the sheer scale of information available allows us to start processing it in more interesting ways. As a good jumping-off point for discussions on how Big Data research and games might interact, check out Dana Ruggiero's article[†] on the topic.

- Your game metric gathering should be structured to allow for easy experimentation, so that you can easily test out new theories and gather metrics on new features and content. Depending on your platform this may be more easily done with server-side changes than changes to a game client. Consider this when determining the architecture for your product and the data upon which it relies.

- The goal isn't to prove that your game is good. The goal should be to show you which levers to pull to make your good game even better.

- Focus on metrics that allow you to test two different scenarios (A/B) and determine what effect each has on a particular metric. This leads immediately to actionable information. As a simple example, if you're planning an email reminder to your customers to try to bring them back for a new session, and your mail will offer them a free gift if they return, try sending out two versions of the mail to

[*] http://andrewchen.co/2012/04/27/how-to-be-a-growth-hacker-an-airbnbcraigslist-case-study/
[†] http://www.gamasutra.com/blogs/DanaRuggiero/20130517/192433/Speaker_for_the_Data.php

10 percent of your user base. In one version, you can offer them two free in-game items. In another version, you can offer to give them one in-game item and let them pick a friend to gift as well. See how many users choose option A over option B. Then send out the mail that gets a better response rate to the other 90 percent of your customers.

- Make your metrics and their results accessible to your team. You want transparency here so that team members in different disciplines can understand what success looks like and how their contributions to the product can affect the end user.

- Ensure that you are able to gather and analyze your metrics in a timely fashion; ideally your study, iterate, review, and results loop should be measured in hours or days, not weeks. You can't afford to wait too long before realizing you're doing something wrong. It's just too hard to reacquire users once they've tried your game and decided it sucks. So you want to be made aware of issues as soon as possible.

- Strive to keep your metrics infrastructure separate from your other software modules. You'd like to be able to reuse this framework for other games in the future, without huge extra effort. As with the rest of your systems, it's ideal that the code and databases that gather, store, and help your team understand the metrics be easily duplicated and integrated into other games or software that you end up creating.

- Ensure that your metrics are auditable and can be cross-verified against some external source like Google Analytics.

5.8 CASE STUDY: *RAVENWOOD FAIR* AND THE USE OF METRICS IN GAME DESIGN

In 1997, John Romero threatened to "Make You His Bitch" in a notorious series of advertisements for his first-person shooter, *Daikatana*. While the games business has never let him live that down, Romero emerged in a kinder, gentler form at social game development studio Lolapps in 2010 and shipped *Ravenwood Fair* shortly thereafter. *Ravenwood Fair* is a colorful, cute game in which players work to hew out a space inside a dark wood to create a fun-filled fair. Players chop down wood, build various attractions, and care for visitors who come to visit their fair. The game launched on Facebook on October 19, 2010, and is now available on four different social networks and iOS. *Ravenwood Fair* grew in population very quickly, attracting more than 25 million players worldwide within its first six months. (See Figure 5.1.)

The team at Lolapps has been remarkably generous in sharing their data and metrics with the social game design community at large. In this section, we'll examine some of their early metric data in an effort to provide a real-world example of some of what we've discussed and also provide some context for how game designers can use metric gathering to improve their games.

Let's start with some basic information about their DAU and MAU presented in the cute collection of charts in Figure 5.2. The first thing you'll notice is that most of the *Ravenwood Fair* users return to play more than once and that more than 10 percent of the game's users

FIGURE 5.1 *Ravenwood Fair* launched in late 2010 and quickly grew to over 4 million users. The *Ravenwood Fair* team graciously shared many of their metrics data to help other designers learn from their experience.

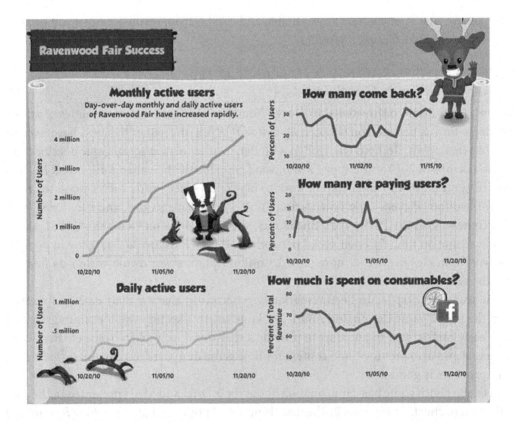

FIGURE 5.2 *Ravenwood Fair* success charts.

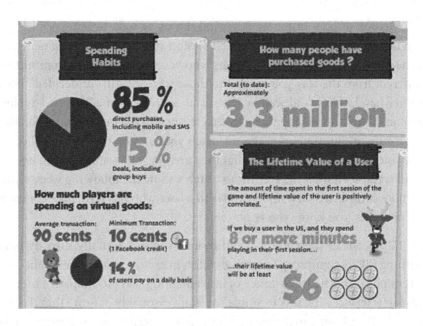

FIGURE 5.3   More information about *Ravenwood Fair*.

pay Lolapps at least some amount. The majority of this money is spent on consumable items, which means that the user can be monetized repeatedly for the same virtual item. As in most games, this sort of item is fictionalized as extra energy (which allows the user to take more turns without waiting). Ten percent is a very high conversion ratio; 3–5 percent is far more typical. In other words, *Ravenwood Fair* got off to an incredibly successful start. However, some critics of these metrics have suggested that *Ravenwood Fair* is actually only counting those users who are fully engaged in that 10 percent number—whereas the 3–5 percent number is usually thought to mean *all* users who ever try the game. So, as always with damn lies and statistics, one wants to tread carefully. We mention this debate to underscore an earlier point about how difficult it can be to determine how to read the metric data games gather. However one interprets this data, though, the game clearly enjoyed great success during its early life.

Let's evaluate the information in Figure 5.3:

- While the minimum transaction is only 1 Facebook credit, the average transaction is far higher at 90 cents. One implication of this is that users are comfortable spending anything less than $1 in a session as a sort of "impulse buy." *Ravenwood Fair* offers items for sale anywhere from $1 to $100.

- The second interesting note is that 14 percent of *Ravenwood Fair*'s users pay daily. It would be fascinating to know if this trend remains static, or if they are able to monetize a greater percentage of their users (without driving down the average purchase price) over time, by tweaking their game mechanics. This is exactly the sort of thing you'll want to use A/B testing to determine in your own game. This type of statistic speaks to the addictiveness of the game and their ability to retain users over time.

- The discussion of LTV in Figure 5.3 is interesting as well, because of the correlation drawn between playtime during the first session and total lifetime value. This implies that the way you should market to users who you've identified as "committed" could be different from the way you market to those who are still "undecided" players. On the other hand, this could well be the social equivalent of a "channel-surfing" phenomenon. Many viewers flip through ten channels in a minute looking for something they care about. But if viewers sit and watch your station through a full commercial break, you can accurately predict that they are likely to watch the full episode. And of course, those viewers who return to watch a show the following week represent an even more committed customer, similar to a user who has returned to a social game daily for weeks; you know you've got 'em.

- Since 15 percent of their users spend money without actually directly purchasing something (likely signing up for various offers in exchange for game credit), Figure 5.3 also reminds us of the importance of implementing ways to monetize users through third-party services. In this example, we can reasonably assume that if *Ravenwood Fair* had 3.3 million purchases during this timeframe, at an average of 90 cents each, and 15 percent of their purchasers didn't directly buy, they made about $445K through their deal offers. Assuming they used two full-time developers at average monthly per-head burn rates to implement the offering features, implementation of this feature more than paid for itself within the first month or two. Don't ignore alternate mechanisms for monetizing users. Implementing offer walls and other ways for users who don't directly pay you to contribute to your overall revenue is highly recommended. As we can see from Figure 5.3, it can lead to a big boost in profit margins.

We can see from Figure 5.4 that the game enjoyed a slightly surprising amount of geographical diversity. The large number of players from the Philippines likely results from the game launching with Spanish and Indonesian/Malay language versions. Their user gender demographics chart quite closely follows Facebook's average (~60 percent of players are female). But we can see that the *Ravenwood Fair* audience tends to be a bit younger than the players of many other games on Facebook.

By focusing on increasing user engagement, Lolapps and John Romero were able to create a highly successful social game. They put "fun" at the very center of their game experience by making it the player's most important stat. They sold users on the idea of regular consumable microtransactions by making energy consumables cheap and giving the users a reason to want more of it. They built an art style that is colorful and uplifting in its tone (happy raccoons, smiling mice, bears with giant heads, etc.) and appeals to the more casual gamer demographic because of its emphasis on creation, sharing, and building spaces in which fostering frivolity and social gathering is rewarded. (See Figure 5.5.) They courted an international market by releasing on several different social networks and in several different languages. Finally, they helped the rest of the world by releasing metrics like these and shared their data with other designers. If we had additional data, we could track how

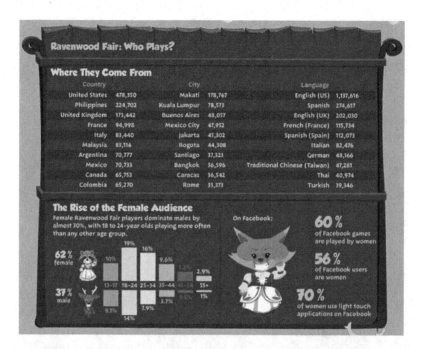

FIGURE 5.4   Geographical and gender demographics of *Ravenwood Fair* audience.

FIGURE 5.5   Screenshots from *Ravenwood Fair*.

FIGURE 5.5 (continued)   Screenshots from *Ravenwood Fair.*

changes in their design mechanics corresponded to user engagement and monetization numbers. We don't have that information for their product, but you will for yours. So gather metrics and use them wisely.

5.9 INTERVIEW WITH EVERETT LEE: "THE SCIENCE OF SOCIAL GAME DESIGN"

Everett Lee has been making games since 1996. He has worked on MMO titles, shooters, racing games, and action arcade games and has been credited as an animator, producer, and designer for companies like Microsoft as well as Wolfpack, Digital Anvil, Sony Online Entertainment, and Acclaim. OMGPOP was acquired by Zynga in 2012 for their hit title, *Draw Something*. Everett Lee left the company in the same year.

Q: Tell us a little about your history in the games business and your current role.

A: I started in this industry back in the late 1990s and have worked on PC and console titles for small developers, start-ups, and large publishers like Microsoft and Sony. My career has spanned across animation, design, and production. Most recently I joined on with OMGPOP, a New York–based social and mobile game company. I am heading up our Austin, Texas, office, where we are looking to organically grow our development team by tapping into the city's deep game developer pool and then launch some stellar titles!

Q: Many of OMGPOP's games seem to focus on very accessible game mechanics—often using just one button or a single player action. Does this reflect a commitment to a certain player demographic?

A: We are targeting a much more casual gaming audience in the social and mobile space, focusing on simple game interactions and mechanics that most anyone can pick up in a few minutes. Doing so greatly expands our addressable market, by not targeting just the traditional hard-core gamer, but rather anyone just looking for a few minutes of entertainment, from the kid at the bus stop to a housewife juggling a handful of children.

Instead of competing with TV programs, movies, and traditional games, we fill a niche I refer to as "traffic stop games." These are games that can be picked up and played in the time it takes for the light to change, and then picked up again, or not at all, at the next red light. It is not meant as a literal timer or guideline, but the metaphor of a bite-sized gaming experience that people come back to over and over again, and stop-and-go traffic fits pretty well. In the social game space we do not have an hour to teach players all the different control options and game mechanics.

Now, that is not to say that social and mobile games do not have depth to them. Many of the good ones have a layer of strategy or decision making on top of the core game loop, in which the "min/max players" try to optimize their actions for the fastest advancement or best payout. If you don't believe me, just Google a popular social game alongside the keywords "strategy guide."

Q: What sorts of monetization mechanisms do you see as being the most effective for the casual market?

A: Generally speaking, the two basic choices are to have an up-front cost for a game or to give away a game for free, initially. Merchandise with an up-front cost is a very old and well understood model, ranging from box sales at a retailer to downloadable games you can buy on Steam, iTunes, Xbox LIVE, or PSN. I give you money, you give me a game.

Games that are given away for free introduce interesting methods of monetization, or in traditional financial terms, interesting means of generating revenue.

All things being equal, you should be able to start with a higher install base, because the risk to someone trying a free game is much lower than for someone trying a game they have to buy up front; in the former case, the only thing lost is their time. Some developers try to sell users a monthly subscription to continue playing every month, which is common in the massively multiplayer games genre, both for games that are free and also for those that have up-front costs.

Some developers try to advertise in-game to the players and generate small amounts of revenue from impressions, a marketing term for when a person sees an advertisement, or click-throughs, which measures a user's acknowledging and interacting with an advertisement. Generating incremental revenue through advertising will work, primarily because of the assumedly larger install base drawn from a free game. We see this most often in banners on mobile apps or web-based games, primarily because of the guarantee of an Internet connection, but also because of the availability of third-party advertising APIs (as compared to those available for PC or console games). Sponsored apps can be a giant advertising campaign for a product wrapped around a piece of software. This is effectively generating revenue for the developer by advertising a single product for a company.

Finally, there is the microtransaction model, also called freemium or pay-to-play. This is where companies give the software away for free and then sell to the player from within the game. The basic idea is that if the game engages the player, he or she will be more likely to pay to progress, get additional content, etc. This method of monetization has been around for over a decade in East Asia but is just now really gaining traction in the Western world with the success of Zynga in Facebook games and games like *Tap Tap Revenge* on the mobile side. While other methods of monetization are still prevalent in free-to-play games, microtransaction games tend to top the top-grossing charts on the mobile side and utterly dominate in the web-based social games space.

The designer will always need to think about how he/she will drive players to spend real money in the game, because otherwise they've just made a nice charitable donation to the game community. Quite a bit is learned from past experience, trial and error, or A/B experiments run on existing products. If it sounds more like a science than art, that's because it is, at least to some degree. Social game companies have teams of people integrating analytics, poring over the data the analytics generate, and running tests to fine-tune the monetization engine.

Q: *User acquisition for social games can be expensive. What are some ways to tackle this problem? Are there plans to leverage existing OMGPOP games to help with attracting new users to your games?*

A: Companies new to the social space usually end up advertising in the social network on which the game is hosted, on Facebook for the most part in the U.S., because the company knows that users already have access to that platform. The cost of acquiring one customer has actually gone up almost tenfold in the last three to four years, to the point that some companies could end up spending more on user acquisition than the average revenue per user (ARPU) it will generate, resulting in a net loss.

Companies with a suite of social games will often advertise the new game to users of the previously released games. This practice is called cross-promoting. Most companies will introduce a pop-up in the established games to alert their users of the newly released game. More effectively, some companies will create cross-promotional quests in their established games, directing users to install the new game in return for some reward in the established game. Either way, the company tries to drive users from their existing games into their new game, in a relatively free manner. At OMGPOP, we not only cross-promote from within our Facebook games, but also from OMGPOP.com, where we have a user base of about 3 million monthly average users.

Q: *What sorts of preconceptions do designers of traditional retail games need to let go of when entering the world of freemium games?*

A: I would start by looking at the two biggest differences between the two spaces, demographics and the business model. Gamers playing retail boxed games are generally looking for longer, more engaging game experiences than gamers playing social games. This is not to say that the two groups are mutually exclusive, because the same gamer is typically looking for a different experience when playing games in each of those spaces. When I boot up my Xbox and pop a game in, I am generally looking to sit down on the couch for at least an hour of entertainment. When I log into Facebook and pop into a social game, I am often looking for a quick five- to fifteen-minute, bite-sized chunk of entertainment. Also, because the social gamer demographic is so broad, we end up creating less twitch-based games and instead focus on slower or non-timer-based gameplay, driven by single mouse clicks, to make the game accessible to that larger audience.

Because of the different business model, freemium games need to be designed with monetization in mind from the get-go. We ask questions like, "What will you sell the players?" "What will drive the players to purchase these things?" "When will you present players with the option to purchase these things?" "How much will you charge them for these things?" "What game mechanics will drive socialization so that you acquire more users without spending advertising dollars?"

This isn't to say that the core game mechanics aren't important. They still are, but they need to complement the monetization in order to drive revenue. At the end of the day, though, players are still looking to be entertained when playing a game, even if there are differences in presentation, and developers still need to try and make money.

Designers new to the space should obviously play the successful freemium games and really study them to understand why they are successful. A comparison/contrast with unsuccessful games in the same space and genre is often useful as well. Look at daily average user data. (How many people are coming back to your game every day?) Look at monthly average user data (How big is your active user base for a given month?) and daily average user divided by monthly average user data (What percentage of your active user base comes back every day? Basically, how sticky is your game?). These kinds of stats are widely available on AppData. com. Understanding what metrics are important and how to craft an entertaining gameplay experience that boosts those metrics can be thought of as crafting an entertaining gameplay experience that scores well in usability testing and reviews, and then beyond that knowing what knobs to turn to dial in better scores.

Q: *Many of OMGPOP's games are web based. Are there ways to increase the virality of games on the web?*

A: In the past, social game developers were able to post to a user's Facebook news feed quite easily. Toward the end of last year, Facebook changed their policy to reduce what was effectively free advertising, so that users who didn't play games wouldn't see all the wall posts generated by their friends' games. Games can still drive virality through other means, though, like through cross-promotions from their established games or by encouraging players to invite their friends to install the game. In the latter example, games will offer up an incentive to an existing player to pull a friend into the game, with a concrete reward or easier advancement in the game. When not on the Facebook platform, the same principle applies, though the means of execution vary slightly, often replacing a Facebook invite notification with an email and a link to the game's website.

Traditional means of virality in advertising also work, such as a promotion linked to a celebrity or someone who is high profile or a particularly entertaining YouTube video, but a marketing specialist can better speak to that.

Q: *Social games have ushered in a new audience of game players. How has this changed the face of the players you are now creating games for?*

A: Because the social game space is expanding the addressable market, instead of cannibalizing from the traditional game space, the demographics of gamers are definitely changing. A study sponsored by PopCap last year revealed that the majority of social gamers, in the U.S. and U.K. at least, are female. In a recent presentation, Wooga boasted a user base that is 70 percent female. Beyond the gender difference, the PopCap study also asserts that the average age of the social gamer is in her early forties.

No longer are the twenty-something-year-old males, seeking hours of immersion, the target demographic. Gameplay is measured in minutes instead of hours, and developers can no longer count on a 3D graphics card as standard fare in the hardware rig.

Q: *Most games for the social networks are created in Flash. Unity is also gaining some popularity. How do you see the current technology landscape of social games, and how do you see it evolving in the future?*

A: Flash became a standard for video playback with YouTube years ago, and more recently became the de facto standard for social games as well. Some browsers, such as Chrome, come with Flash pre-bundled, so users do not even need to download the Flash player plug-in. Unity may be gaining some popularity among developers, but I do not ever see it rivaling Flash in terms of market penetration; most games will still be made in Flash because that is where the lowest barriers to entry are for reaching social gamers. Unity enables developers to create good-looking 3D games; however, we need to be mindful of the core audience for social gaming. The large base of social gamers is not comprised of hard-core gamers with the best 3D graphics cards, so some programmers may argue that Unity is overkill for most 2D games. From a business standpoint, it is difficult to justify adding an extra plug-in installation step for users before they even get into your splash screen.

Looking ahead towards the future, it looks like HTML5 may be able to rival Flash, mostly because browser developers are on board and providing native support for HTML5. Native HTML5 support would mean that developers could make the game once and it would almost immediately be supported for both desktop web gaming and mobile gaming. This time savings is quite attractive to developers and creates a foundation for support there. I personally do not believe that HTML5 will take off until one of the three leading HTML5 video codecs, H264, Theora, or WebM, becomes a clear winner. In layman's terms, this is analogous to seeing if HD-DVD or Blu-ray is going to take off, before distributors throw full support behind releasing hi-def movies en masse. Once one video codec has sufficient support and the concerns about submarine patents are proven to be immaterial in court, I believe HTML5 will take off.

Q: *What do you see as the future of social gaming? Do you envision a convergence between social and mobile gaming?*

A: If we extrapolate from current market trends, we should see more mobile games integrating social components, because most mobile devices are smartphones and are almost guaranteed to have Internet access. For example, our latest game, *Puppy World*, is taking a step in that direction, with social integration through the iOS Game Center and streamlined Facebook Wall Posts for screenshots.

Approaching things from the other side of the equation, if we pick up a web standard like HTML5, we should see more desktop social games making their way over to mobile devices, because the underlying code is pretty much already there. The biggest hurdle is making sure the UI will work well on mobile devices too, which is a very tractable problem. To the back-end servers, the platform the game client is on does not really matter, except for financial transactions that must go through for each front-end platform.

Q: *What are up-and-coming social or mobile games that you think people should keep an eye on?*

A: I unfortunately cannot comment on OMGPOP's development road map, but this next year will be an interesting one. Externally, I make sure to keep an eye on any successful Zynga game or any game that a handful of Facebook friends start playing. Each successful game builds upon mechanics and lessons learned from previous games, much like in the traditional game space, but development cycles in the social and mobile space are measured in months, not years, so the pace of change is blindingly fast.

I expect the barriers to entry in both the social and mobile spaces to be raised in the next year or two by Zynga, Electronic Arts, and Disney, who will throw more money into development to raise the quality bar and increase production value to differentiate their games from the rest of the market. This move is analogous to the consolidation and ramp up of development costs in the traditional game space that EA spearheaded in the late 1990s and early 2000s, when games went from budgets of $3 million to $20 million in the space of five or six years.

At the end of the day, though, we are still in the early stages, roughly year four now, of an expected ten-year social-mobile cycle. (The basic theory is that technology roughly moves in ten-year cycles, starting with the mainframes in the 1960s, mini-computers in the 1970s, personal computers in the 1980s and 1990s, the Internet age of the 1990s and early 2000s, and now finally the mobile Internet and social networking age that was sparked by the introduction of the iPhone in June of 2007 and Facebook opening up to non-college students in September of 2006. For more information on this theory, Google "Mary Meeker Morgan Stanley mobile internet" to learn more about Mary Meeker's April 12, 2010, presentation.)

Looking back at what happened about halfway through the shift in traditional PC games from the late 1990s, when 3D graphics cards entered the scene, through the mid-2000s, one can map out the changes in the social and mobile space that will most likely come to fruition in the next couple years. Given that history tends to repeat itself in business cycles, I fully expect the pattern to play out again. I just like knowing what to expect and to be proactive in my adjustments. The next few years are bound to be exciting ones in the social and mobile space and I look forward to seeing how things unfold!

CHAPTER 6

What Is a Social Network?

6.1 HOW DO WE MAKE ANY GAME SOCIAL?

We've already defined a social game, using as broad and inclusive a yardstick as seems reasonable. We want to make sure we don't miss any useful case studies, yet still have a topic focused enough to be digestible. When in doubt, we will err on the side of inclusivity. After all, rules are made to be broken, and categorization is a fuzzy art at best. So that we are all operating from some common understanding, a refresher:

> A social game is one in which the user's interactions with other players help drive adoption of the game and help retain players and which uses an external social network of some type to facilitate these goals.

Considering how perfectly a smartphone or an online tablet can allow users to engage in the kind of social activity these games benefit from, it is natural to extend this definition to cover many mobile games as well. Indeed, the intersection of mobile and social gaming has been one of the big stories of the game industry in the last three to five years. Two distinct market segments are rapidly becoming one.

Let's delve deeper into the latter half of our definition and investigate what we mean by an external social network. What qualifies as a social network?

"Facebook" would be an obvious answer. Facebook provides a medium through which a meaningful percentage of the Earth's population can communicate, organized loosely around the idea of mutually approved connections between friends. Sociologists will have a field day dissecting the way the concept of a "friend" has changed since the advent of Facebook, and those who study human intimacy would be well served to ponder the phrase "in a relationship" as a socially acceptable euphemism for "is having sex with." Tragically, we'll have to leave these sorts of delightful navel-gazing exercises to the academics for now. Facebook may be our canonical social network, but as we'll see later, there are dozens of similar sites that cater to different markets, to users with slightly different needs. The organization of each of these sites (i.e., sites that focus on "friend" relationships, as opposed to group membership, geographical location, or hierarchical status) greatly affects their suitability for different types of social interaction. This suitability, in turn, has significant impact on the virality and stickiness of the games that run on them and on how you'll need to design the features of your product if you hope to best take advantage of what that site has to offer.

Is a forum hosted on a website a social network? As we'll see in several of our interviews, forums are a common way for gamers to interact with one another and to form social bonds outside of the game but within the context of the broader game community. Hear a description of *Pocket Legend*'s dedicated community of nurturing fans, and it's hard not to want to include forums as social networks. They allow people to virtually congregate in groups based around subjects of mutual interest and exchange information. And yet, might this not be a little bit like proclaiming a treehouse hidden in the woods to be a Boy Scout recruitment center? It may be a place for people who already know about nature to further advance their understanding of woodcraft, or to meet with others who are already in the know. But if you wanted to bring in new disciples to Baden Powell's cause, you might be better served to build a mock tree-fort in the air-conditioned byways of a local mall.

The lesson here, then, is that a social network needs to exist as a superset of a single cause or interest, to connect people of diverse tastes and preferences, and cannot be a closed or private system. Anything that only appeals to those who have already self-selected as members isn't of much use when it comes to virally spreading a message. A community can form itself around a narrow interest, but for our purposes, such communities aren't of much use, since we're interested in exposing an existing community to a new idea (your game). That means you have to find the delicate balance between the exclusivity that comes with a shared narrow interest and an attractive viral inclusivity that will entice members to join and participate. AA meetings only appeal to those who are already trying to leave the bar. We need social networks that can expose people to a new idea they might have had no interest in were it not for the social forces that drew them in.

Over the last decade, several large companies in Asia have managed to create social networks made up of several disparate elements, including MMO games, mobile games, casual web games, and chat or instant messaging clients. Western social networks learned from their successes. Tencent is perhaps the most successful of these companies from the East, boasting over 780 million users currently, with well over $1 billion in annual revenues. Early on, Tencent recognized that the sale of virtual goods would be a key to their success. Their pioneering work pointed the way for social networks like Facebook, which initially relied only on advertising. Tencent, however, proves that there is a much more successful model than the simple ads-only approach others have followed. For every two dollars Tencent makes on advertising, they make an additional $17 on microtransaction item sales.* Facebook paid careful attention to this lesson and adopted their business model. Facebook has relied heavily on Zynga's games to transition into the virtual items business, most of which are sold in the context of in-game items. Myspace and other social networks struggled to make this transition. (And they lacked the vast number of users that Facebook and Tencent claim.)

---

* http://abovethecrowd.com/2009/03/09/how-to-monetize-a-social-network-myspace-and-facebook-should-follow-tencent/

Facebook initially monetized entirely from advertising. Companies like Zynga were able to use viral channels (spamming users with feeds from *Mafia Wars* and the like) to gather huge number of users. In 2009, Facebook recognized that they weren't profiting from these types of applications as much as they'd like, so they disallowed many of the viral channels that were currently in place. Zynga and other social game developers were forced to rely more heavily on advertising, which helped Facebook's revenue (since Facebook sold them the advertisements on a per-user or per-impression basis). Next, Facebook introduced Facebook credits and eventually mandated their use, guaranteeing themselves a 30 percent take of all virtual goods sold. They even introduced their own Offerwall, a mechanism to derive values from users who do not directly pay, to make sure that they are able to take advantage of indirect monetization of users, as well. This combination of mechanics for making money off of users, and the symbiotic relationship between game developers like Zynga and their host platforms, like Facebook, is characteristic of the modern landscape of social games. (The same relationship basically exists between the smartphone platform holders and those who develop for the devices.)

Social networks organize and connect diverse groups of people. Many of them profit from the resulting advertising that accompanies collecting users' eyeballs, but more and more, social networks are finding financial benefit from the sale of virtual goods. The social networks and app stores win so long as users are on their network, buying something from someone. In this way, they are much like the owners of a mall in which a food court resides, but in which the mall owner takes a portion of the gross receipts from every food stall. It doesn't matter what an individual wants for lunch; the mall owner wins so long as shoppers are eating something.

The game designer's job is to offer a product so tantalizing that it will distract shoppers from their real goal, whatever that may be, long enough to stop at your food stall and sample one of your dishes, instead of buying one from the stall next door or continuing past without eating. Put a different way, just because users are on a social network or wasting time on a mobile phone doesn't mean they are going to play a game, and if they do, there is no guarantee they will play *your* game. Much of the rest of this book will deal with ways to ensure that they do.

6.2 WHO IS THE AVERAGE SOCIAL GAMER? WHO IS THE AVERAGE MOBILE GAMER?

Who are these metaphorical shoppers whom roam the halls of Facebook and the other social networks? Who plays games on their phone? Who is the prototypical social network player? How does that differ from the average mobile gamer?

What's the best way to attract these players? You need to understand your audience and what motivates them to better cater to the emotional triggers they may not even consciously recognize they have. Let's start with some of the statistics as revealed to us by several of the best studies that have been done on the space. It's worth mentioning that different studies vary in the data they've gathered, the validity of their statistical analysis, and their interpretation of the resulting data. So as with all statistics, you should tread with

FIGURE 6.1 *Bejeweled Blitz* for Facebook has a tremendous following, as do many PopCap games. A study released by PopCap paints a portrait of the average social gamer as forty-three and female.

caution. However, there is enough similarity among several of these studies' conclusions that a fairly accurate portrait of the social gamer is starting to emerge.

A 2010 study conducted by PopCap, creator of popular social games such as *Bejeweled* and *Insaniquarium*, looked at game players in both the United States and the United Kingdom. This study[*] defined a social gamer as someone who plays games on social network sites like Facebook at least once a week. The results of their study indicated that the average player is a forty-three-year-old female (see Figure 6.1). This is a much different demographic than that associated with traditional video games, in terms of both age and gender. Some other interesting pieces of data obtained by their study include the following:

- More than 60 percent of Facebook users are over thirty-five.

- Women are more likely to play social games with their real-world friends than men (68 percent versus 56 percent), and women are nearly twice as likely as men to play social games with relatives (46 percent versus 29 percent).

- Social gamers have a higher income, on average, than the U.S. population at large. One-third of social gamers in the United States earn less than $35,000 a year, while 17 percent earn between $35,000 and $49,000; 21 percent make between $50,000 and 75,000 and 21 percent earn more than $75,000 a year.

- Social gamers spend 39 percent of their time on social networking sites/services playing games, as compared to chatting with/messaging friends (17 percent) and playing

---

[*] http://gigaom.com/2010/02/17/average-social-gamer-is-a-43-year-old-woman/

solo games (15 percent). Nearly half (49 percent) said that when they connect to social networks, they do so specifically to play social games.

- A little over half (53 percent) of social gamers say they've earned and/or spent virtual currency in a game; 28 percent have purchased virtual currency with real-world money, and 32 percent have purchased virtual gifts.

The lack of specialized hardware requirements (no console, controllers, plastic guitars, or joysticks needed), the low cost to enter the game (they are often free to play), shorter time commitments, and the focus of many social games on cooperative play have all been offered up as reasons for this shift in demographic. Almost all of these reasons are contributing factors. Moreover, the "share with friends" nature of many social games, the general lack of gratuitous violence, the accessibility of the gaming experience, and the ability to easily play with friends and family all combine to be appealing to groups who have traditionally felt excluded from the "boys' club" of traditional gaming. Those games that do have violence at their core (the so-called *X-Wars* model) have generally been eclipsed by the more collaborative *X-Ville* models, or games like *Candy Crush*, which rely on even simpler mechanics and more universally appealing themes (Who doesn't like colorful candy?). In almost all cases, there is only one button to master in the interface for Facebook games (mouse left-click). And the ease of getting any tablet, PC, or Mac online has led to a far greater user base than any console has mustered.

Here's a little more insight directly from the PopCap study:*

- *Playing Preferences*
  - Social gamers cited "fun and excitement" as the most popular motivation for playing (53 percent). Stress relief (45 percent) and "competitive spirit" (43 percent) were next, followed by "mental workout" (32 percent) and "connect with others" (24 percent).

- *Viral Growth/Consumption*
  - Word-of-mouth is the most common way that social gamers hear about new social games (57 percent), while 38 percent said they learn about new games from ads and 27 percent cited standard web searches.
  - Social gamers have played an average of 6.1 different social games; 39 percent have played between three and five social games and 13 percent say they've played more than ten.

- *Virtual Currencies*
  - More than half (53 percent) of social gamers say they've earned and/or spent virtual currency in a social game, but only 28 percent have purchased virtual currency with real-world money and only 32 percent have purchased a virtual gift.

---

* http://popcap.mediaroom.com/index.php?s=43&item=149

- Nearly a third (32 percent) of social gamers say they're likely to purchase virtual items with real-world currency.

- Fully a quarter (25 percent) of social gamers say they've been misled by an ad or other "special offer" tied to a social game they've played.

- *Social Gaming Relationships*

  - 62 percent say they play social games with real-world friends, while 56 percent play with friends they've made online and 37 percent play with strangers.

  - U.S. social gamers are far more likely to play with strangers than their U.K. counterparts (41 percent versus 29 percent).

  - Nearly half (43 percent) of social gamers also play social games with their parents, children, and/or other relatives.

  - 62 percent of social gamers agree that social games allowed them to reconnect with "old friends, colleagues, classmates etc."; a similar percentage (63 percent) say that social games have been a source of new friendships and 70 percent say that social games make them feel more connected.

But what conclusions have other groups come to about this exciting new target market? GamesIndustry.com, a respected business intelligence and professional networking site, conducted a different survey[*] in 2010, polling more than 13,000 players, ranging from eight years old and up. Interestingly, their conclusions differ from PopCap's:

- The average age of players in the United States is 29.2 years old (though their infographic lists several different conclusions, often on the same chart).

- International players are slightly younger, particularly in France, where the average age of a social gamer is reported to be 26.8 years old.

- The GamesIndustry.com survey concurs with PopCap's findings in that more women play social games than men, claiming that 60 percent of U.S. social gamers are female.

CNN, the U.S. news outlet, also weighed in on the debate in early 2010. They focused on analyzing data from Zynga's player base, primarily from *FarmVille*. They concluded the following:

- Approximately 60 percent of Zynga's customers are female.

- The average age seems to range widely based on the specific game played. (*Mafia Wars* and *FishVille* have much lower average ages than *Zynga Poker* and *Café World*, for example.)

---

[*] http://www.industrygamers.com/news/social-game-players-average-age-below-30-says-survey/

According to CNN, Zynga understood some key design philosophies that many traditional game developers missed. As a result of looking at game design differently, or borrowing from those who did, Zynga was able to capture a new market segment, who had traditionally felt alienated by more "hard-core" gaming experiences.

Zynga's founder, Mark Pincus, was quoted as saying, "A great social game should be like a great cocktail party. If you want it to appeal to absolutely everyone you invite, it has to be broad in its content so that everyone gets it."

Ultimately, regardless of which of the exact set of statistics we believe, we encourage readers to keep Mr. Pincus's comment in mind. Every day, large segments of the population are getting online, and many of them are playing games for the first time. This is true across many different platforms, from Facebook, to competing social networks, to consoles, to increasingly powerful mobile devices. Many of these potential gamers are unlikely to be interested in the types of blockbuster games that appeal to traditional hard-core audiences. Appealing to these new gamers is a great way to tap into a market with access to disposable income and a strong desire to play socially.

None of this is to mean that you need only design games dealing with sharing, flowers, animals, and the color pink. Indeed, we feel that such cynical designs both belittle the massive gaming public and lead to tawdry experiences cynically designed not to be great games but to appeal to a misguided stereotype of "what women want." Instead, consider carefully the mechanics and lessons that can be mined from more traditional games, what themes are quick to stick, and which styles resonate across cultural, gender, and age boundaries. Seek to design and promote games that harvest from the best of each of these disparate sources. When you read the interviews herein, review the case studies presented, or think about the design discussions presented later, try to consider how to broadly apply the lessons to many different types of games, with themes broad enough to appeal widely or with mechanics that can be replicated across several different themes.

How do mobile gamer demographics differ?

As usual, opinions vary, but the good people at SponsorPay,[*] a group focused on mobile customers as a market for advertising, and the experts at Flurry[†] give us the following data as of February 2013:

- Females make up 53 percent of the mobile gaming market.

- 66 percent of mobile gamers are under forty-five years of age (50 percent of mobile gamers are between twenty-five and forty-five).

- 11 percent of mobile gamers play games while in the bathroom; 31 percent while in bed.

- 57 percent of mobile gamers play a game daily; 54 percent play more than one hour per day.

- The mobile gaming market is estimated to have taken in $8B in 2012.

[*] http://www.insidesocialgames.com/2013/02/12/sponsorpay-reveals-socialmobile-demographics/
[†] http://blog.flurry.com/default.aspx?Tag=Mobile%20Social%20Gaming

Finally, given the convergence between these different types of gamers, a present in which many people game on multiple devices, the emergence of a so-called mid-core of gamers, it may behoove us to zoom out just a bit and consider the demographics of all gamers as best we can. To help us in this goal, we can turn to a 2012 study* from the Entertainment Software Association (ESA), a North American group dedicated to advancing the interests of the gaming sector. The ESA concluded the following:

- The average gamer is thirty years old.
- Gamers are 53 percent male.
- Women eighteen and over represent 30 percent of the game-playing population.
- 42 percent of gamers identify as playing puzzle, board, trivia, or card games, making so-called casual games the largest single market segment.
- 33 percent of gamers play social games.
- U.S. gamers spent $24.75 billion on gaming in 2011.

While the varied statistics from these different sources may not completely line up in all cases or across all territories, taken in aggregate they begin to give us a pretty clear picture of who plays games. Were we to boil all of this data down into a fine extract, the most salient conclusion we can draw is this: Gamers reflect all of the wild diversity of the human population as a whole, spanning all ages and cutting across both genders relatively equally.

6.3 WHAT SOCIAL NETWORKS ARE POPULAR TODAY?

A pithy answer would be "Facebook" and then end this section of the book. And while it's true that Facebook is far and above the most successful of the Western social networks today, there are a number of others that collectively…still don't come close to matching its popularity. And yet, not even mighty Rome lasted forever. So let's take a look at some of the other social networks that exist. These are all large ecosystems, and it's a good idea to be aware of them, even those that aren't necessarily candidates for building games…for now. Some of these networks may still have value for promoting games (Twitter, for example) even though they don't function as a platform for applications per se. And in others, we may find the seeds of inspiration, be it from the clever "Circles" UI metaphor presented by Google+, to the interesting peaceful coexistence business model of hi5. Each of these social networks has its niche and its strengths, be they market or mechanics. Finally, a game that can release on multiple platforms will be the stronger for it.

In a world where users are the only real measure of success ("eyeballs" in Silicon Valley speak), we'll rank the current family of social networks by their total number of active users. It's worth noting that "actual number of users" is a highly controversial matter, since every social network wants to be able to claim vast seas of daily customers: the better to appeal to their potential advertisers. This data is pulled from sources that are considered among the most reliable in a field shadowed by speculation and estimation.

---

* http://www.theesa.com/facts/pdfs/ESA_EF_2012.pdf

6.3.1 Top Social Networking Websites of 2013

This data was obtained from The E-Biz MBA website, validated by Alexa Global Traffic Rank, and U.S. Traffic Rank from Compete and Quantcast.[*]

6.3.1.1 No. 1: Facebook

Facebook rules the roost with 750 million active monthly users, as of the time of this writing. Consider briefly the staggering size of such a market, then the wealth of viral channels Facebook makes available, their unified currency system, and the host of other features they provide developers, and it's easy to see why Facebook is considered by many the number one gaming platform in the world right now.

6.3.1.2 No. 2: Twitter

Twitter is the next most popular with 250 million active users. However, while Twitter is almost a canonical definition of a pure social network, where users follow simple updates or "tweets" from other individuals within their ecosystem, there's been little real gaming possibility, as it's not a platform for anything more than sending out text-based messages of up to 140 characters at a time. While some users have developed "games" like scavenger hunts, contests, goal-based flash mobs, and similar around Twitter, these aren't the types of games we're concerned with here. But Twitter is critical for marketing and spreading news about social games, even if just for tweeting information about the existence of a new game or changes in features that might interest your community of players. However, new features that exist as part of the "Twitter Cards" system allow developers to let users tweet "deep link" into their games; this could end up allowing tweets to help spread games virally in a much more direct manner than they've been able to thus far.[†]

6.3.1.3 No. 3: LinkedIn

LinkedIn is the professional's social network. Boasting just over 110 million users who post messages related to jobs, share articles of interest to a particular industry, or host discussions about varied professional topics, LinkedIn is a superb place for literal "socially networking" of the traditional sort—to advance one's career—but currently it doesn't offer a platform for gaming.

6.3.1.4 No. 4: PlayStation Network

Between getting a late start and falling prey to some vicious and repeated hacker attacks in early 2011, PlayStation's online network had a rocky first few years. However, the PSN (as it's commonly abbreviated) claimed over 90 million users as of March 2012 (across three platforms) and a virtual currency sold in many stores in the form of PlayStation Network Cards. The service features friend lists, instant messaging, matchmaking, leaderboards, a trophy system, virtual avatars, and virtual spaces, as well as a host of online games. In the fall of 2013, Sony plans to launch the PlayStation 4, which will add features to PSN.

---

[*] http://www.ebizmba.com/articles/social-networking-websites
[†] http://gamasutra.com/blogs/RyanHoover/20130405/189975/Twitter_Just_Became_a_Games_Platform.php

6.3.1.5 No. 5: Pinterest

Pinterest is a relative newcomer to this list. It boasts over 85 million users, who are able to easily share things they find of interest on the web. Since these can certainly be gamer-culture related, there is a thriving community who post about topics of interest to gamers, though there are no games per se.

6.3.1.6 No. 6: Myspace

Myspace is the perennial has-been of the social networking world but has taken huge strides to revamp its image in the last year or two. Unfortunately, this doesn't seem to have increased the Myspace user base any. With just over 70 million active users, Myspace tends to focus on music (band pages are popular), television shows, and other types of entertainment media (including some games). Once owned by the mighty News Corp, Myspace took off like a rocket in 2002 to become the most popular social network in the world by 2006, a title it retained until 2008. Unfortunately, hard-to-navigate pages, excessive user-customization, pages clogged with advertising, and a super-saturation of real activities allowed Facebook to overtake Myspace. Recently, Myspace has undergone a beautiful redesign.

Myspace offers a robust platform for game developers, and it boasts a number of successful titles, including *Sorority Life* by Playdom, *Millionaire City* by Digital Chocolate, the venerable *Habbo Hotel*, and a plethora of games by Zynga and other top publishers. The short of the matter is, with 70 million users, there is still a compelling argument in favor of porting your games to Myspace and monetizing them through Myspace's GWallet system. Myspace has made this task easier by partnering with Microsoft, as well as several engine and middleware providers like Unity and Pushbutton, who offer free or reduced cost tools for developers.

While it can't boast anywhere near the number of users of Facebook, Myspace is still a very serious player in the social network gaming business. They offer a host of tools to help developers monetize their products:

- *gWallet*, which serves up 2D and video ads for Myspace apps and games.
- *TrialPay*, which allows developers to easily accept payments from credit cards, PayPal, and so on. *TrialPay* also offers brand tie-ins and promotions as an embedded advertising-type solution.
- *Ad.ly* provides another source for contextually targeted advertising using the Myspace Real Time Stream.
- *PayPal* lets users pay for in-game purchases using a secure PayPal account that can be funded in a variety of ways.
- *Spare Change* makes it easier to implement microtransactions in your game.
- *Click and Buy* accepts payments from users in different countries around the world.
- *Social Gold* promises easy integration of payment processing.
- *Moneybookers* is another global payment system that uses the "digital wallet" metaphor.

6.3.1.7 No. 7: Ning

Ning is a novel platform that allows users to "create their own social networks" around different types of content. Since there is a price attached to the creation of what Ning calls a "social website," this tends to attract those with a message or a product to sell. Political campaigns, nonprofits, and the like have been known to favor Ning. At its heart, Ning is more of a platform for creating highly interactive websites than it is a true social network. Ning offers game aggregator integration ability from sites like MindJolt and Heyzap. Developers should consider Ning something more akin to a toolset and hosting service than a "traditional" social network for publishing games. Realizing your vision or porting your product to Ning will require a custom implementation, as well as some clever planning around how you position your product. Ning claims 65 million unique visitors, who visit about 90,000 total "Ning Networks," which implies that Ning may be an effective network for marketing products to end users.

6.3.1.8 No. 8: Steam

Valve Software's *Half-Life* revolutionized the PC first-person shooter in 1998, combining thoughtful gameplay with a terrific science fiction storyline. *Counterstrike* followed, arguably the most successful game "mod" of all time. (A mod is a reskinned version of a game, which alters some gameplay mechanics and visuals to create a new experience.) As Valve looked to update these products with patches and fixes, they faced the interesting problem of how to update software that millions of players were already using. The conceptual framework for Steam was born, and over the subsequent fifteen years, the service has grown into a full-fledged digital distribution platform for games, software, and media, as well as a social network in its own right. Steam allows users to communicate about the games they are playing, and even buy and gift games to their friends. Steam currently has over 54 million users, all of whom could safely be described as approaching hard-core gamer status. It has been estimated that Steam controls as much as 70 percent of the digital distribution market for non-browser-based PC games, and there are more than 1800 different games available on the platform. Recently, Steam has also made inroads to capture part of the television market by introducing the Steam Big Picture mode, designed for consumer HDTV sets.

6.3.1.9 No. 9: Tagged

Tagged claims more than 18 million monthly unique users and is definitely one to watch. With a strong focus on social games and meeting new people, and an aggressive presence outside of North America, Tagged also has managed to maintain a growth trend despite the rise of Facebook. Tagged has recruited leaders from EA and other gaming powerhouses. In addition to allowing games by other developers (like Zynga), Tagged focuses on in-house developed games, a strategy that makes them unusual among social gaming sites.

Tagged also has been subject to numerous legal problems associated with their practices of "scraping" and "spamming" and their slow-to-respond reaction to reports of online trading of child pornography on the network. In 2010, New York State's Attorney General Andrew Cuomo spoke out against Tagged for the second time in his career. Some conservative countries have even banned Tagged over similar issues. In late 2011 Tagged acquired social gaming site hi5.

6.3.1.10 No. 10: hi5

hi5 is a popular social gaming site formerly led by game industry veteran Alex St. John. The site boasts 46 million unique users per month, though this number has declined slightly in the last few quarters. hi5 features an avatar system similar to Wii or XBLA, in which users can customize a representation of themselves for use on the network. In addition, they offer simple Flash games and some of the latest social games by groups like Digital Chocolate (but none by Zynga). These games tend to lack the cutting-edge sophistication of some of the newer generation of Facebook games, but they do feature dual currency systems, and the types of social interaction that became standard in the second generation of social gaming. hi5 hosts a virtual storefront where users can purchase and download games for Windows, including titles like the *Grand Theft Auto* series and *Gears of War*. The site has a universal system of coin, and some games claim to offer "cash prizes." hi5's "Game Developer Program" offers a portal for designers and developers with a significant amount of information, APIs, and advice on how to become a "Preferred Partner."

Achieving Preferred Partner status means that hi5 will contribute marketing resources to the games they expect will be popular or to high-profile titles that are exclusive to the platform. These sorts of incentives are attractive, as is the hi5 platform called "SocioPath," which has a companion suite of tools for monetization called "SocioPay." SocioPath is primarily a UI flow differentiator, which seeks to reduce some of the early game friction associated with inviting new users. Specifically, rather than force users to register or log in to the site to play a game or join a friend who has invited them, the SocioPath UI flow automatically creates a guest account for the user behind the scenes which allows them to begin playing instantly. Then if users want to save their progress, they are prompted to log in or create an account. SocioPay takes a similar look at ways to monetize users more effectively, for example by tracking player purchasing habits and by letting games promote custom offers to different types of players.

These sorts of innovations show that hi5 is serious about being a games platform and focused on reducing barriers faced by new players interested in their games. This alone makes hi5 worth watching; they are innovating in the social games space, and they operate under a well-funded mandate to "own" social gaming.

6.3.1.11 No. 11: Xbox LIVE

Online gameplay didn't appear on consoles in any major way until the Xbox, and then not until the platform had been available for almost two years. But it wasn't until the release of the Xbox 360, which featured robust online matchmaking, leaderboards, voice and text chat, and a way to investigate what games friends were playing, that any console truly had online market share. Since the release of Xbox LIVE on Xbox 360 in 2005, the software behemoth has continually improved the service, which offers both freemium and subscription models. The service currently boasts more than 40 million registered users, almost all of whom regularly play and purchase games. With the impending fall 2013 release of the oddly named Xbox One (Microsoft's third console platform), Xbox Live continues its migration towards a social platform that seeks to extend its grasp into television, spots, and other types of leisure activity.

6.3.1.12 No. 12: Orkut

Orkut, named for its Turkish creator, Orkut Büyükkökten, claims approximately 33 million users, about 17.5 million of whom are active monthly. Notably, Orkut is a significant operator in emerging markets like India and Brazil. Users from these two countries make up more than 80 percent of Orkut's total customer base. Orkut was created by Google in 2004 in an effort to gain a foothold in the then-emerging social market space. The network has had a somewhat troubled history (including reports of worms and other cyberattacks, as well as more traditional criminal activity). Games are available as part of the Orkut Apps Gallery. At present, few of these feature the sophistication of Facebook or Myspace games, and they tend to feature a collection of broken links and trivial Flash apps. However, several specialized publishers of localized games for Orkut now exist, and a number of new social gaming companies are targeting Orkut. While the arrival of Google+ initially cast some doubt on Orkut's future, Google recently confirmed that they had every intention of continuing to operate Orkut out of Google Brazil and were investigating possible synergies between the two networks.*

6.3.1.13 No. 13: MeetMe

MeetMe, formerly called myYearbook, is a comparatively smaller site, with 7.4 million users, which was created by two high school students in 2005. It features a proprietary currency called Lunch Money, which can be won by playing a variety of Flash-based games on the site; currency and items can also be traded on the site. Like several other social networking sites, MeetMe lets Facebook users log in using their Facebook ID, suggesting that they are comfortable being a specialized adjunct to Facebook (rather than situating themselves as a direct competitor). MeetMe's popular offerings include a Blind Date social hookup game, as well as "Battles," which are an advanced version of HotOrNot.com. Their games are divided up by category: Arcade, Casino, Word, Card, and so on. MeetMe is currently hosting games by a very limited number of third-party developers but seem to be open to further third-party development; however, this is a closed platform, meaning that you need to negotiate directly with the platform owners before you begin developing for the network. Overall, while small, MeetMe seems to offer a specific, demographic-focused market for applications with built-in currency features. In July of 2011 myYearbook sold to Latin social networking company QuePasa for $100 million and launched mobile and tablet versions of the site the same year.

6.3.1.14 No. 14: Meetup

Meetup is a geographically focused site that allows users of like interests to organize real-world meetings for protests, consciousness-raising efforts, environmental cleanups, exercise, parties, and a thousand other types of events. While gaming does play a role—gamer groups

---

* http://news.yahoo.com/orkut-continue-alongside-google-possible-future-osmosis-045805883.html

of every sort organize tournaments, LAN parties, and so on—there are no online games on Meetup, and it's hard to imagine what a Meetup-exclusive game would look like. Meetup has 7.5 million active users and seems to be primarily focused on users in North America.

6.3.1.15 No. 15: Badoo

Badoo is a Russian-based social networking and profile rating site which is now run from London. Badoo is notorious for poor privacy standards and for use of an invasive Facebook app accused of tricking users into revealing their personal information.[*] While Badoo claims over 150 million users, other authorities suggest that the site may actually have closer to 7 million active users. Badoo offers a version of *Chat Roulette*, called *Twister*, in which random webcam users are paired up for flirting. The site has a strong presence in Africa, Latin America, Spain, Italy, and France. Social gaming does not seem to be a strong component of Badoo; instead, Badoo's revenue is primarily derived from advertising and member user profile "upgrades," which grant participants access to additional features and make it easier for users to meet each other.

6.3.1.16 No. 16: Bebo

Bebo is a social networking site launched in 2005, acquired by AOL in 2008, and sold off for pennies on the dollar two years later. Bebo hit 10 million regular users at its peak, most of whom focus on blogging. Users are allowed to customize their pages to some degree and can include a wide variety of third-party applications (including games) on their page. Bebo also focuses on social gaming and is a member of the OpenSocial community, a community that offers APIs (application programming interfaces) that make it easier for third parties to develop applications like games. While their total number of users is small, Bebo's generally solid security reputation, focus on games, and investment in developer tools and support make them a quality target for social game developers. Bebo users exhibit a strong preference for online role-playing, especially using characters derived from popular fictional properties, such as *Twilight, Harry Potter, James Bond*, and similar. Bebo's popularity seems to have suffered in recent years, and it no longer makes the list of top fifteen social networks; it is included here due to its focus on social gaming.

6.3.1.17 No. 17: MyLife

MyLife was formed as an amalgamation of several reunion and high school alumni matchup sites and focuses on helping users reconnect with old friends. As with many of these sites, reports on total number of users vary greatly, but reliable tracking statistics suggest MyLife has around 5.4 million regular users. Because MyLife focuses on helping users find people, social games are not currently a component of the network. MyLife has suffered from poor user complaint resolution and a number of lawsuits in California and Washington State.

6.3.1.18 No. 18: Friendster

Friendster was an early entry into the social networking space and remained a popular complement to Facebook until recently. As of mid-2011, the site turned its focus almost

---

[*] http://www.trustpilot.com/review/www.badoo.com

exclusively to online social gaming and now claims 115 million registered users, though reports suggest closer to one million unique monthly users in 2011. Tremendously popular in Asia, particularly the Philippines, Friendster describes itself as a "social entertainment site" and openly states a goal of supplementing, rather than competing with, Facebook. In a gesture of surrender, Friendster encouraged users to download any content they had posted on the site and stated that blogs, profile information, and the rest would be deleted by the end of June 2011. Friendster has since reinvented itself as a pure gaming and music hub and currently features a web portal as well as a mobile version with limited game access. Friendster allows users to log in with their Facebook account and seems to be adding new games to the site at a prodigious rate. The site maintains an open policy to developers and offers a wide array of tools for third-party "widget" (application) providers or game makers. Over 90 percent of the site's users are reported to be from Asia.

6.3.1.19 No. 19: Sonico
Sonico is a social networking site with a gaming focus geared toward Latin American users. Sonico features a collection of free Flash games for users, including a *Simpsons*-themed game. While few of these games show the sophistication of the current generation of Facebook games, there are a large number of choices available. Interestingly, very few seem to feature monetization of any kind. Instead, Sonico's revenue seems to come primarily from advertising. Sonico boasts over 4 million registered users and is particularly popular in Brazil.

6.3.1.20 No. 20: Google+
Google+ (Google Plus), launched in June of 2011, has rapidly risen to more than 500 million registered users. However, Google+ is dissimilar to most other social networks, due to its deep integration with the Chrome browser, Gmail, Android devices, and other Google properties; it acts as a unifying layer atop Google's web dominance more than as a traditional destination site. Google+ features forty or so games.

6.4 GAMES ARE GLOBAL
One thing that most readers will have immediately noticed in the preceding list is how many of the social networks are more prominent in other parts of the world than they are in North America. In many parts of the world, people who never owned a personal computer or a dedicated gaming console now have smartphones, with high-speed access to the Internet. (There are over 850 million mobile phones in India alone. This is far more than all the gaming consoles ever sold by Microsoft, Nintendo, Sony, and Atari combined.) Gaming is a global hobby, and it regularly seems to bridge cultural and socioeconomic divides.

Often, particular social networks end up becoming associated with a particular country, the way Friendster is currently associated with the Philippines, for example. (Over 90 percent of Friendster's traffic comes from Asia, with the bulk of users originating in the Philippines.) Orkut, alternatively, has captured a large percentage of the Brazilian market, which has grown considerably in affluence and purchasing power in the last few years as a result of strong economic policies and high oil prices.

Likewise, of the four dominant mobile platforms (iPhone, Android, Windows Phone, and soon-to-be-deceased Blackberry) market saturation differs greatly between countries. Globally, Android is beyond dominant: In the United States, Android overtook the iPhone in mid-2012; in China, Android now controls more than 80 percent of the market.[*]

As a result of this global market, localization is a critical part of creating a successful social or mobile game. The simplest aspect of localizing a game is translating the various text strings into assorted languages and ensuring that users are given a chance to select the language they prefer. More advanced localization can involve creating customized versions of the software that pay attention to local cultural symbols and preferences to increase user satisfaction. This process can become quite involved, with some big-budget retail products going so far as to alter characters or plotlines to be more appealing to certain cultural sensibilities.

Since players in different countries use different currencies and may have very different economic backgrounds, game developers should take care to consider how currency localization will affect their particular game. With many social networks starting to provide their own forms of currency, the logistics of payment systems and currency exchange rates may end up being abstracted, but pricing, gifting, and the like still bear country-specific consideration. The most popular user platforms are being flooded with various gaming choices; the more you can do to tailor your game to the preferences of a particular audience, the stickier your concept in that market, and the more profitable your game.

As a general rule of thumb, English-speaking countries (the United States, Canada, the United Kingdom, Ireland, and Australia) have tended to monetize at greater per-user lifetime rates. However, it is more expensive to acquire users in these territories because they are saturated with games and advertising. English is a common enough language in some other countries that it can be monetized without special efforts made toward localization (e.g., the Philippines, Romania), but these countries tend to monetize at a lower rate. However, this is offset by a lower cost to acquire users typically. Generally, localized games monetize better than those that are presented in a foreign language (like English) for fairly obvious reasons.

6.5 IT'S ALL ABOUT SCALE

If there's anything this chapter should have convinced you of this far, it's the sheer scale of these social networks and the terrific mass of potential mobile game customers globally. Taken in aggregate, there are over a billion users, well more than 10 percent of the total population of planet Earth, who interact with social networks and mobile phones on a daily basis. This shift in consumer behavior dwarfs the industrial revolution and all of the great migrations in human history for its raw number of participants. By way of comparison, fewer people ever lived and died as part of the Holy Roman Empire than will log into a social network this week.

Beyond the simple gross numbers of their users, social networks represent a relatively egalitarian cross section of humanity. These user bases cut across gender and cultural divides and include members in almost every age group and education level. Put succinctly,

---

[*] http://www.tech-thoughts.net/2012/12/smartphone-market-share-trends-by-country.html#.UU_VGhzFXNs

social and mobile networks represent a mass market in the truest sense of the phrase, with a reach that quite exceeds what traditional PC and console games could aspire to.

Astute developers may have noticed that while we talked a bit about console games and gaming in this volume, console online service networks were listed fairly low in our hierarchy of social networks. It's not that they aren't "cool" or that they aren't important; it's just that they generally aren't important *enough* in terms of user population to financially compete with the bigger sites. Indeed, Zynga has completely eschewed console development. Zynga designer Brian Reynolds said the following:

> We're after a lot of demographic. If I explain what we think is the core magic of social, I think that will explain the relative attraction, or the lens through which we view the relative attraction of different platforms. The thing that seems to make social gaming and networking magical is the fact that all my friends are potentially there and they might see the things that I'm posting or doing or expressing.
>
> [Xbox LIVE's] too small a demographic. Think about, of my friends, how many of them own an Xbox 360? Well, I'm a game developer and I even come from a triple-A space so we might even be in the double digits… Twenty or maybe even thirty percent of my friends might have an Xbox 360, but effectively 100 percent of them have Facebook and effectively 100 percent of them have a mobile phone. Of them, probably 90 percent have a smartphone.
>
> So when you think about the social potential of a platform…if we made a game on Xbox LIVE, I think—forgetting about the fact that I might have an artificially high percentage of friends that do it because of what my profession is—the number of anyone's friends that [are] going to be able to participate in the social experience is going to be a very small number, so the amount of social capital that there is isn't going to be very high. That's why right now we're on Facebook for sure, and mobile is the obvious next place for us to go because it is an inherently social platform. I mean, we've got to be on several different kinds of platforms, but especially if we can figure out a way to have people socialize cross-platform. Then, hey, we're helping with the problem. We're helping people socialize that wouldn't be able to.

Instead, like most social game developers, Zynga has chosen to focus on Facebook, then on mobile devices. Let's look at some of their user demographics in a bit greater detail.

- Facebook currently lists over 800 million users and is growing every day. It's likely a few hundred new souls have joined since I began typing this sentence.

- A considerable majority of Facebook users live outside the United States.

- There are more females than males on Facebook in total, and in every individual age bracket.

- While eighteen- to twenty-five-year-olds represent the largest single age group on Facebook, the majority of Facebook users are twenty-five or older.

These figures should help solidify our earlier comments about game design, thematic focus, and the need to consider localization for social and mobile games. For traditional game developers, the need to rethink exactly who our markets are in light of this market sea change is paramount to achieving success.

6.6 USING SOCIAL NETWORKS TO EXTEND TRADITIONAL GAMES

Over the last few years it became the norm for almost every AAA product released to make some use of social media or mobile tie-in. In the simplest cases this amounted to little more than a Facebook page allowing for some direct marketing to people who informed Facebook that they "liked" the product. Since Facebook (and other social media) tends to be very free with information about their users, marketers have jumped on the bandwagon and often find that they can get better metrics and a clearer picture of their target audience through Facebook than they can through traditional venues such as dedicated websites. The same does not tend to be true of mobile devices; they just don't feed back demographic information to software creators in the same way as social networks do.

But many games have taken a cautious step further down the rabbit hole, building social media hooks into their console, mobile, or PC products, seeking to leverage the power of external social media sites in an effort to help their decidedly nonsocial games benefit from the increased adoption and stickiness that social media appears to yield. Let's look at a few examples of products that have pursued this route and have found success as a result.

Uncharted 2: Among Thieves, the seminal third-person action game from highly respected Santa Monica studio Naughty Dog, was one of the first console products to put out Twitter updates about in-game events. In *Uncharted 2*, you play the role of Drake, an Indiana Jones–type swashbuckling explorer who collects treasures and shoots baddies in a variety of exotic locations. Following up on the success of the eponymous *Uncharted: Drake's Fortune*, the game achieves superb character-to-environment interaction and was eagerly awaited by fans and the press alike. The development team chose to integrate (what was then) a novel feature: when your character (Drake) earns a trophy, reaches a level milestone, or does any of a number of other things on the PlayStation console, the game posts an update to your Twitter account, which automatically reposts to your Facebook account. (See Figure 6.2.)

Their core notion was a superb one, but they quickly found a need to tweak the details of their Twitter integration; friends and followers of early reviewers of the game were mercilessly spammed with updates about what was happening inside Drake's world.

This feature received such immediate negative feedback that on September 29, 2009, two weeks before the game was released, the developers disabled the feature to make changes that would reduce the amount of spam. When they released the game, to great fanfare, a much more restrained version of the feature allowed users to select what would be posted and how often. The result was a game that had nothing to do with a social network, and in fact was predominately impressive for its single-player campaign, yet still managed to leverage the power of social networks. The game went on to win numerous accolades, including at least one Game of the Year award. Subsequent games from Naughty Dog have continued to improve the integration of social features into the PlayStation platform.

FIGURE 6.2 *Uncharted 2* made superb use of social networking features to let users brag about their in-game exploits. Many AAA retail products now have social network tie-ins, which help spread awareness of the game.

However, the lesson about being very careful about how much information to post to a user's feed was one to which many other developers paid close attention. Using social media to help spread the word about a game by letting users automatically tell their friends about their exploits can be quite powerful, but without being carefully tuned, this practice can end up being seen as "spammy" and draw fire from customers. (And their friends!)

Another title that pioneered a different approach, which would soon become standard, was Peter Moleneaux's *Fable 2*. An open-world, epic fantasy adventure RPG set in the land of Albion, *Fable 2* broke new ground by offering *Fable Pub Games*, a downloadable title for Microsoft's Xbox LIVE Arcade. These *Pub Games* allowed players to earn gold by competing in three gambling-themed mini-games. What was innovative (in 2008) about this move was that the gold earned in the *Pub Games* transferred over into the retail product, *Fable 2*. This technique, using a small and inexpensive or free product to tease users and stimulate excitement in advance of a full retail release, and additionally give users orthogonal tie-ins to their favorite games, would soon become a standard technique. Such games are now commonly exploited for major console and PC products. One of the key notions *Fable Pub Games* proved is that the social or secondary tie-in product need not feature gameplay similar to the core product that is being promoted. The brand association, and the ability to transfer data between the two mediums, is sufficient to stimulate interest among users and to keep users invested in the game world.

Within a few years, Blizzard proved out a similar example of orthogonal gameplay, creating another situation where a tie-in product extended the stickiness of a core game. In 2010, the MMORPG giant released *World of Warcraft Armory*, which provides Auction House access for players, directly from their mobile phones. *World of Warcraft* already boasted more than 10 million users, each paying more than $15 per month to adventure in the incredibly realized world of Azeroth. This add-on application allows users to communicate with their in-game friends, tapping into the power of *World of Warcraft*'s highly evolved and custom designed social network. The *Armory* allows users to retain some element of access to game world, while they live their real lives outside of Azeroth. Blizzard

FIGURE 6.3 The *World of Warcraft Armory* lets users study their characters and trade in the "Auction House" for a chance to earn more gold. Creating multiple "entry points" into the game world can help a game become more widely successful and provide incremental revenue.

proved again that players want to continue to connect with their favorite games even when they aren't actually "playing," in the sense imagined by the game designers. Further, the Auction House application shows that users are willing to pay an *additional* subscription ($3 USD per month at the time of this writing) for these sorts of external tie-in applications. Thus, developers should remember that mobile applications can be used to further monetize what might already be a successful product. (See Figures 6.3 and 6.4.)

Not to be outdone, developer BioWare and publisher Electronic Arts took these concepts to the next level, creating a site called the BioWare Social Network to accompany their massive AAA role-playing game *Dragon Age: Origins*, which was released in 2009. This is a site designed to engage fans of all BioWare products, giving them a place to discuss the games and share user-generated content. The content includes huge numbers of screenshot albums for *Dragon Age*, a collection of unmoderated blogs (which seem to have devolved mostly into spambots trying to sell one another Viagra or Coach purses), and, more impressively, several thousand fan-created modules for *Dragon Age: Origins*. These range from the lurid ("Sappho's Daughters") to the unexpected ("Little Red Riding Hood Redux") to the nearly professional-level ("Kal-Sharok: The Crumbling City"). The site is interesting due to the rabid fanbase, if not for the significant numbers they draw.

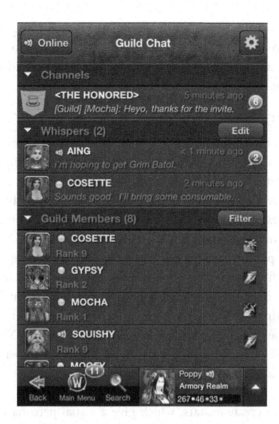

FIGURE 6.4   *World of Warcraft Mobile Guild Chat* application lets players stay in touch with their in-game friends even when they aren't at their computer. Using external applications to help users always be as connected to your game as they want to be helps increase social stickiness.

BioWare followed up *Dragon Age* by releasing *Dragon Age 2* along with *Dragon Age Legends*, a Facebook and Google+ companion product to the franchise, which offers users a chance to play in a more social setting. (The retail game offered only a single-player campaign, deep conversation, and tactical combat-heavy experience with thousands of lines of spoken dialogue and hours of in-game cut scenes.) *Dragon Age Legends*, instead, allows users to play a strategy RPG where successes unlock unique items within *Dragon Age 2*. Interestingly, *Dragon Age 2* seems almost to completely ignore the BioWare Social Network concept, which implies that BioWare has more or less abandoned their effort at social network creation.

Beyond the somewhat dubious claim of being "The First Real Game on Facebook," *Dragon Age Legends* offers some basic character customization and an overall flavor of gameplay designed to appeal to fans of the primary product line. Players can kill monsters in a simple tactical model, collect treasures, and level up their characters. The game uses a dual currency system and attempts to offer fans the opportunity to stay in the *Dragon Age* universe, even when playing on Facebook. A mobile version of the game quickly followed. While the games have never reached the number of users that would put them in the realm of true "successes" (based on their relatively low number of users), they proved nicely that social networking and mobile tie-in products can be used to extend even the least social of game franchises, by raising brand awareness and creating additional user investment in the world of the game. Since this time, the practice has become commonplace, if not ubiquitous for AAA console products. If you've invested enough to launch a AAA game on a console, it makes a lot of sense to amortize the development and marketing efforts by extending the brand across social and mobile mediums as well.

6.7 CREATING SOCIAL NETWORKS AS A PLATFORM HOLDER

Not wanting to be left out in the cold, a few companies with platforms of their own have tried to harvest some of the fruits of the social network trees and integrate these features into their own platforms. The goal has seemed to be to find a way of creating a meta-social network that sits above all games on the particular publisher's system. Microsoft's Xbox LIVE system is the best example of this, followed by Apple's Game Center. Let's look at each to see what we can learn about the core components of an effective social network so that we can better adopt our games to take advantage of the most important key features.

Microsoft was the first of the console or mobile manufacturers to realize that to create a truly sticky experience they needed to layer social features on top of their existing console games. Learning from their fledgling efforts with the early Xbox LIVE Service, they've evolved into the clean integration of an online system on the Xbox 360. This success gave Microsoft the following to leapfrog well ahead of Sony's competing PlayStation platform. Some features that successfully created a "sticky" social network include the following:

- Allowing users to create avatars, which give a visual persona to their online presence. While this move was at first derided as being silly, or an attempt to "rip off" Nintendo's Wii, there was far more at work here than was first apparent. The avatars allowed for additional extra-game monetization by selling avatar gear, which quickly became associated with strong brands on the platform.

- Xbox LIVE also allows users a way to see which games their friends were playing, and it gives the overall platform a sense of being part of a community, which adds to stickiness.

- The addition of extra-game trophies (called "achievements") that contribute to an overall gamer score (a classic meta-game) encourages players to explore games their friends might be playing and to compete to see who can play the most games.

- The inclusion of Leaderboard APIs, which allows many of their lower-cost Xbox LIVE Arcade games a venue for comparing player scores. The end effect is that the leaderboards turn single-player games into social experiences.

- The inclusion of other information, such as when players last logged in, as well as some advanced video chat features that help bring "friends" and the idea of an Xbox ecosystem to the forefront of players' minds.

- A downloadable Facebook application on the service unfortunately failed to do more than provide a window into a different social network, rather than integrating the two networks in any real sense. As a result, the inclusion of this application on the platform feels like an afterthought, rather than a potent way of merging two social networks. Unless something about the relationship between Microsoft and Facebook changes, users and developers shouldn't expect to ever see much tighter integration of Facebook into Xbox LIVE.

In short, with the Xbox 360 LIVE service, Microsoft managed first to extract a monthly fee from users who sought to play their games online. Moreover, it turned the console business, which up until recently had been self-defining as a solo experience, into a full-blown social experience and one that evolved into a social network unto itself.

Sony followed, in fits and starts, and the PlayStation Network now serves up a pretty decent approximation of the feature set offered by the Xbox, but with far clumsier integration of the actual social bits.

For their next generation of consoles, however, both Sony and Microsoft seem to be promising still better social feature integration. Hence their inclusion here. While at the moment the free-to-play and mobile market are running roughshod over console sales, it appears that there is still a lot of fight left in the major console manufacturers, and it is possible that their new offerings will reinvigorate the sector and take advantage of many of the advantages social networks provide that we've been discussing here.

6.8 IS APPLE'S GAME CENTER A SOCIAL NETWORK?

Recognizing that the hundreds of thousands of largely stand-alone games on their incredibly successful iOS platform needed similar social hooks, Apple released the Game Center, beginning with version iOS 4.2. Game Center allows users to connect with friends, send friend requests, and host online multiplayer games. It allows games to offer achievements and makes it easier for games to offer leaderboards. The Game Center's core concept is straightforward, but it seems only nominally to offer the level of stickiness that the other social networks we've discussed manage. Moreover, it does little to promote adoption of its games by nongamers, though Apple's efforts to provide a boost to this goal by including it in the default main menu for all capable devices makes it clear that they hope it will ultimately help lure iPhone and iPad users into being gamers on their platform. Indeed, the rise of a far greater gamer class is almost essential to the planned obsolescence that their hardware-sales business model relies upon; just as games pushed PC computing hardware to ever greater technological heights, so too with mobile devices. Games give people a much better reason to need more powerful machines than do email and web browsing.

As more games begin to take advantage of the social features made possible by the platform, it is likely that Game Center will become a much more lively social space, with greater utility for developers. If Apple wanted to truly promote some level of virality among games on their platform, they would be well served to study other, more established social networks, from Facebook to Xbox LIVE, and begin to emulate some of the features on those platforms.

As a result of some of these shortcomings in the Apple iOS platform, other companies moved in to fill the gaps. The short-lived OpenFeint was one, ngmoco's Mobage is another, and GREE is a third. Most of these exist as a platform-within-a-platform, by providing developers with a collection of APIs that simplify common development tasks (Banking and

Currency Exchange, Analytics Dashboard, Social Features, and Distribution). These companies often also provide co-marketing support, driving users to popular games for products they think will help showcase the platform or return well. In exchange for these services, they take a cut of development revenues for titles that appear on the platform. The net result of this is an interesting example of a software service that seeks to exist inside the ecosystem created by the platform holder; fundamentally, this is quite similar to the functions served by traditional publishers of retail games, just writ across a slew of socially enabled devices.

6.9 CONCLUSIONS

Now we've got a good understanding of what a social network is, and how wide a collection of devices can participate in one. We've looked at an overview of the major social networks in play right now, both those that support gaming and those that exist for other reasons. We've looked at how traditional games can use social networks to extend their appeal, and we've evaluated how some hardware platform holders have sought to enhance their platforms by adding social network features.

Perhaps most importantly, we've looked at studies that tell us clearly that the types of people who now play social games defy simple categorization. They are of mixed gender, across a wide spectrum of ages. They are from almost every country. They speak a variety of languages, and they have a vast hunger for accessible content that engages them.

Next we'll begin to dig into how to use these social networks to attract, retain, and monetize all these diverse users.

6.10 INTERVIEW WITH JANUS ANDERSON: "GAMING AND THE SOCIAL GRAPH"

Janus Anderson has been creating social games since 1997. After several years with Zynga, he is currently a studio director for Disney Mobile based out of Prague and a studio in

Austin, Texas. He has built games for Sierra Online, Vivendi, Westwood, Electronic Arts, Wolfpack, NCSoft, Ubisoft, Zynga, and Challenge Games as a programmer, designer, and creative director. This interview was conducted in summer 2011.

Q: *Tell us a little bit about your background.*
A: My name is Janus Anderson. I'm the creative director and executive producer for one of the two Zynga games in development here in Austin.
Q: *You've got a deep history with social game design. What can you tell us about your time in the games business?*
A: My background is in MMO development. I've spent about fifteen years working on MMOs. My first professional job was working with Sierra Online, working on one of the first MMOs with graphics (*The Realm*), back in the pre–*Ultima Online, Meridian 59* days. We were pioneering in that space, and I went on to chase MMOs for a while. I think I only really ultimately successfully shipped one other one, which was *Earth and Beyond* in 2003. The MMO space is rife with projects getting canceled and rugs getting pulled out from under development teams. After that I worked with Wolfpack Studios prototyping something in the Marvel Universe, then started my own company for a while. I went back to Wolfpack and worked on *Heroes of Might and Magic Online*, which didn't go anywhere. Got snapped up by NCSoft, where I did two or three years in external business development, and as a creative director. I basically saw hundreds of game pitches and concepts in all different stages of completion, which was very educational. I got paid for years to look at game pitches and evaluate them, and look at projects in various stages of completion and evaluate them. It was definitely an experience.

Then I joined Andrew Busey at Challenge Games in 2007. At that time, the goal was to build asynchronous short-form entertainment for the web. Games you could log into, play for fifteen minutes. Think massively multiplayer lite— games where you could play online but wouldn't really be playing against another person. Which is interesting, because that's exactly what Facebook games are. We built a couple of successful games, at least successful on the web scale. One was called *Warstorm*, which was a collectible card game. That was my baby.

The entire time we were making web games, I was fascinated with Facebook. Coming from MMOs, I thought, "Wow, MMOs and a social graph...there's got to be something here."

Right when I started, Andrew gave me a budget of about $2500 and contacts for an external outsourced Indian development company. We built a game called *Nobility*. I spent about three months banging my head against that wall. And *Nobility* was really interesting, conceptually. It didn't work out in the long run because it was too hard-core in a lot of ways. But it was my most beautiful, purely social game experiment in some ways. This was around the time that another game where you could buy and sell your friends had just gone big. And big at that time was like a million MAU.

In *Nobility* you are a king or queen with a court. When you recruit a friend, they become a pawn in your court. And they can have a tree underneath them of people who they've recruited. And you earn Influence every day based on the number of people in the pyramid under you. And people under you also have their own pyramids, and they're earning Influence. And you could use Influence to steal parts of the pyramid from other people. So it was straight up PVP, where I could try to take other people's courts away from them, by bidding Influence points. So the whole pyramid was constantly moving around as people bought pieces and parts from one another. And there were other pieces you could buy, like catapults and gifts to give to people in your court to make them happy, and make them harder to steal away. It was mostly text, with very simple graphics, but it taught me a lot about this.

After that we did another game, which was a riff on *Kingdom of Loathing* for Facebook. And back then there was no Flash; everything was PHP driven, simple stuff. We made the mistake there of building the game in FBML, which was a disaster. The game was fun, but the performance was terrible. Once again this was me and two engineers, and maybe a part-time artist. Spent about a month on that game, and it didn't really go anywhere. And there was this struggle about making games for Facebook. "Why are you making games for Facebook? We aren't making any money there. This is silly!"

But I was looking at the raw number of people who were playing these and thinking, "You've got to be kidding!" Maybe these people were monetizeable, and maybe not right now. But if you're getting that much attention, then there's gotta be something there. There's got to be a way to monetize somewhere there. All of the web games we had made were free to play, microtransaction based. We were already kind of experts in that area. Obviously, we didn't get the viral part or using social graphs, 'cause we didn't have access to any of that.

So we built another game, and this was after we started seeing a few Zynga games on the market. I'd had a design on the back burner for a while for a game I really wanted to do, called *Ponzi*. And it was basically an office game where you built up an office and did dastardly things to other people in a kind of tongue-in-cheek way. And originally it started off as kind of a *Mafia Wars* clone, which was getting a lot of traction then. But I decided to make it real-time, with an awesome set of artists. We went the whole Flash way, and we shipped *Ponzi* in three months. A real challenge from beginning to end, with a pretty small team. I think there might have been a dozen of us. And we knocked it out of the park, at least compared to anything we'd done before.

Ponzi very quickly broke a million MAU, which was a huge number back then. Skyrocket. So then we were doing Facebook games. We ported *Warstorm* to Facebook, and that also did extremely well for us. It got the attention of Zynga, because everyone at Zynga was playing *Warstorm* and *Ponzi*!

Q: Starting with old-school MMOs, you had a bunch of sophisticated users. Some of your early Facebook games were a little hard-core. What did you learn about users from that experience?

A: Well, I don't think *Kingdom of Loathing* was too hard-core. That was a technology failure. But *Nobility* was definitely hard-core because you could steal assets from other players, so it was basically PvP. Coming in right out of the gate, you didn't know anything about this game, and all of a sudden you become a pawn and get traded back and forth, undermined by people more powerful than you. It was incredibly hard to balance. Shielding new players from the core nature of the game was hard…

Q: So were there lessons there about accessibility and how to design games for the mass market?

A: Yes. I've made a lot of strides. It's been difficult because *Warstorm* was not a mass-market game in a lot of ways. And when it was picked up by Zynga, it didn't do anywhere near the numbers we were hoping, because it wasn't terribly accessible. Basically, it was a *Magic: The Gathering* type of game—though a lot more accessible than *Magic* because you got to play asynchronously. You could kinda play without understanding the rules of the game. But just because it was a card game, where you're looking at the cards and clicking on them on the screen, 95 percent of your market looked at it and thought, "That's nerdville." From a presentation standpoint.

The problem is that people who make games a lot of times are gamers, and we build games for gamers. And gamers like lots of numbers, and they like stats, and interesting complexities and strategies and details. And they want to take something that they've seen before and change it… A common design mistake that I've seen before with a lot of designers is they'll take something and want to add a bunch of stuff to it. "I really like that game, but it needs to have this, and have this other thing!" And what happens is you increase the complexity and increase the barrier to entry. The first-time user's experience is harder for people to get their heads around. If you think about it in terms of the original *Madden* football game, it was easy for people to pick it up and play. But if you take a modern *Madden* that is rolling out of EA, I wouldn't even know where to start with that game. Because there are so many different modes and different things that you can do. And it's just because they wanted to appeal to that one audience, and each edition had to add some more stuff to it. And they never took anything away from it. And it became a complicated mess. I'm very much a reductionist designer. There's a quote I like: "Perfection is not achieved when there's nothing left to add. Perfection is when there is nothing left to take away." So when I design games, I always start with the simplest set of things that really shine together, then I very carefully add elements to the mix, one at a time, and make sure that everything you add really adds to the system as a whole, and works well with the other elements. So it's a very methodical process.

Q: When we look at some social games, they seem to be multiplayer games in which I never actually play with another player. And not just because they are asynchronous. When you think about the way you design games for social networks, do you think first of a single-player game, or first as a multiplayer game?

A: My belief is that people just haven't cracked that nut yet. It's very convenient to play asynchronously. That's a good, solid core for games. But I think a lot of the social elements, even the best-of-class social elements, aren't really social the way an MMO would be. There is a presence of another person in your game, but that presence kinda gets washed out in a lot of ways, because it's not incredibly meaningful. If I'm playing an MMO and someone gives me some item I've been looking for that I need to craft some ultimate thing that I've been working on for a long time, and I had to track him down… That's social interaction that matters. Much more so than if I open the ZMC in a Zynga game and hit "accept" forty-two times when all these people have given me gifts. I may briefly see that my friends stopped by and did something, but that's it.

Q: There's a big difference between someone riding up and killing me with a broadsword and just noticing that someone has logged in and sent me a gift. Do you think keeping people at arm's length is ideal?

A: Definitely. In a lot of ways, that's MMO rule #1. You build MMOs in such a way that people can't adversely affect each another unless it's in a controlled fashion. If you think of *World of Warcraft* as the pinnacle of this, you can't even talk to the bad guys. All you can do is kill them, and you can't take it personally 'cause you know it's their job to kill you. And you have to be in a special zone on a special server to even have that kind of interaction. So on every level they bake in ways to stop people from interacting negatively with each other.

And actually, just the presence of other people can be terribly intimidating to new players who are trying to get on their feet.

My buddy, Dallas Snell, likes to talk about this concept of "playing alone together." I know there are some papers that have been written on this topic. The difference between a social game and a nonsocial game is, if you have any indication that other people are around you and playing along with you, you don't necessarily have to have direct interactions with them for those interactions that you have with the game to become a lot more meaningful. Just knowing that other people could see what you have done changes things. In a lot of MMOs I'm much more of a solo player than I am a part of a big guild, or a raid kind of player. But it doesn't matter. Even if I never interact with anyone, it's still social. A fantastic RPG like *Oblivion* might hold my attention for a week or two, but I'll play *World of Warcraft* for a year, even if I'm not talking to anyone! It's the same behavior as if you're working on a paper and you go to a coffee shop, just to be around other people. That social interaction doesn't have to involve you talking to people. It makes what you're doing more important to the brain.

Q: *You're probably learned a ton about how to monetize users—everything from the sub-scription model to the retail model to freemium microtransaction stuff. What are your thoughts on how that space has evolved and how Facebook has changed the world for us?*

A: I feel really sorry for the people who are still chasing subscription models, I'll tell you that. I saw the forefront of this at NCSoft. All the MMOs in America at the time were obviously subscription-based. But after a bunch of trips to Korea where I saw the massive success over there with free-to-play MMOs, where they would just do microtransactions... Microtransactions were super-superior in a thousand ways, as far as revenue potential. And there was a lot of discussion about "Would that make it to the West? How long will it take for the West to act like that?" And I thought, "This is gonna happen tomorrow!" And sure enough, in game terms, Facebook kind of opened that and has shown, clearly, that it's the way to go.

Number one, you never want to provide a barrier to entry for people to come in and play the game. Any barrier to entry, any cost up front, any idea that you're gonna have to take my credit card is a tremendous barrier to most people. It makes them not want to even check out what you're doing. And you obviously want to get as many people as you can looking at your product.

Second thing is, I've been in the games industry forever, and I remember the shareware model. You'd get to play three levels of a game and at some point, you'd need to pay your $10 or $15 and you'd get the full game. The problem is, you really never know when the user is going to convert. They might decide five seconds in that they like your game and want to pay money. Or they might decide it wasn't three levels that did it; ten was the magic point at which they were ready to reach into their wallet. If you design a system around freemium and do it well, then players can have a satisfying experience playing free, but there's always this carrot dangling in front of them. If you just pay a little more money—not much—just to convert them, then their experience is going to be just a little better. And people who fall in love with your game are constantly being reminded that if they could just spend a little more, then they'd enjoy the experience more. And that's the best way to snag them and turn them into payers.

Lastly, the most important part of the freemium model is that it never caps what your players can spend. If you design the game right, people can spend money hand over fist. You're going to have whales out there who will knock your socks off with the amount of money that they are willing to spend on your game. Way beyond what they would have spent on a subscription, and way beyond your highest expectations. I'm sure it's a bell curve with your whales at the top, but those whales can definitely pour a lot of money into your coffers.

Q: *Why do you think that in the mobile space we're seeing freemium, but not yet in the console space?*

A: That's a good question. I've not thought about the console space in a while. I love consoles, but I find myself so attached to the PC space. I think it probably has to do with players' habits of locating content on consoles. And even though they are all networked now, I don't think they're as social as Facebook games or MMOs. Playing a Wii party game with your friends is definitely more social than anything else out there, but when I play console games, I don't think about them being web enabled. I don't think about going to check message boards, or a forum, or chat with other people, or read a FAQ to see what's cool about the game. I'm sure it'll evolve that way. It has to.

Q: *In the mobile space, then, it seems like people are quickly catching up. Tell me about how social games can work in the mobile space.*

A: Let's just say that Zynga has a big interest in the mobile space. I think they see that as the next big horizon. Social games are still fledgling on mobile, probably because they don't have a baked-in social graph. There's no clear virality; you have to invent those viral systems. The reason Zynga had success is that they entered the social game space when viral channels were wide open. They were able to acquire tons and tons of customers for free using the baked-in social features of that platform. I don't think that there are traditional ways of networking with your friends on mobile yet. Zynga has the underlying social architecture, so they can create and maintain big social graphs underneath the hood. So I think they'll have a leg up in that space too.

Q: *What about other social networks?*

A: Those are all fine, but it's an economy of scale. What you get on Facebook is this: if you can find a profitable business model where you can make money off a customer, provided that your cost of acquisition is at least a little less than the amount of revenue that you're going to get off that player, then you can turn that knob from zero to 750 million players overnight. It's not quite that simple, but this is one of the reasons that we shifted from web games to Facebook. We just found the scalability and traffic that we could get was just blindingly better than any other platform at the time. Including the web. Clearly everyone is on the web, but there's just no easy way to go and get them. So I think the problem with the other guys is they just don't have enough members, enough faces, for you to get the kind of numbers that you want. If you're making a dime off of each player, it's much better to reach 100 million players than it is to reach 5 million players.

Q: *Do you have any thoughts on Google+ as a potential competitor to Facebook?*

A: It's probably too early to tell. They'll probably acquire a bunch of customers, but I saw a lot of my friends do exactly what I did, which was go check it out, then go back to Facebook. Partially, Facebook keeps people because it has tons of content. That's where the games are, that's where the applications are, that's where their friends are. People need a clear reason to migrate to a new social network. Admittedly, I was a Friendster user, then a MySpace user, now a Facebook user. I migrated twice to new social networks, and I found it a pain in the ass. But it would take something clearly superior, and although I like the Google Circles feature, it's not enough to make me want to move. Now if Google had a much better interface…

They could definitely become a player, though, because they can push a request indicator to any Google service people use, and people get the message that their friends are doing stuff. That could eventually change the tide for them, but I think it's going to take a while.

Q: *Do you have any advice for game designers coming from a traditional space who want to enter the social games sector?*

A: Lots of advice. Where to begin? I've seen a lot of friends come and dance around in the space. It's full of trials and tribulations for sure. First, I think you really need to understand what makes the social graph and the viral channels special. And that's something that Zynga has a lot of practice with and has built a whole culture around. They spend an inordinate amount of their time optimizing and maximizing the free customers that you can get on Facebook. It's definitely nothing like in the heyday when you could acquire those customers for free, because Facebook has ratcheted down those viral channels. Still, I think the fundamental difference between products Zynga launches and products competitors launch is that Zynga builds their products around core viral activities, so that the player creates virals in such a way that it feels natural to the game. And in a lot of ways it's even rewarding for the player to do it.

Q: *An example would be nominating someone to serve as your Chief of Staff in* Empires & Allies?

A: Exactly. That's fun; it's interesting! People feel pleased that their friend asked them to be chief of staff. That core viral loop is both social and viral and doesn't feel tacked on. A lot of competitors have very slick experiences, but they aren't really thinking about the virals. They've tacked on some bubblegum viral stuff after the fact. And you can tell.

Definitely if you are getting into the space, play your competitors' games and write down "What makes this game social?" "What makes this game viral?" and try to integrate that stuff deeply into your design. Don't just tack it on.

Q: *What are up-and-coming social or mobile games that you think people should keep an eye on?*

A: Most of the things I think are indie and interesting are outside of the Facebook market right now. I sense a wave of innovation coming into Facebook soon. There's definitely some stuff inside of Zynga that I'm definitely very interested in. Obviously, I'm biased towards my own project. I think we're gonna be making a big splash here shortly. It'll be quite a bit different than anything else out there.

I think Facebook is a double-edged blade. Games on Facebook feel like they're back in the 90s. There's massive room for innovation there. People could take games in lots of directions, but everybody seems to be scared to. And they're all rehashing the fifth iteration of *FarmVille*, or the thirteenth iteration of *Mafia Wars* or cloning and not really innovating, because that's kind of the safe path.

I think those days are going to slowly end. I think there's only so many plow, plant, and harvest games you can create before nobody wants to play those anymore. And we've definitely seen the death of the *X-Wars* model over the years, because once you've played one of those things you sure don't want to play ten more.

So I definitely see some new innovation; people are trying to take this stuff and look at it in new and exciting ways. We're nothing like console games, where things feel so stagnant. It's the fourteenth version of *Madden*, and EA likes to ship hit after hit, which are carbon copies of the previous ones with one more thing tacked on. Social games in general—the sky is the limit.

And we're just starting to see some of those innovative titles. Like *Army Attack*, and little turn-based strategy games that are kind of breaking out of the traditional mold.

Q: *Any other thoughts to offer people on the future of social game design?*

A: One of the things that really attracted me to this space, and one of the things that is close to my heart—the Holy Grail here—is to merge MMOs and the social graph in a very complete way. Right now, there's nothing like a real MMO on Facebook. I've seen a few MMOs that you can play in browser plug-ins, but that doesn't count. It's kind of like taking the best of what we think of as modern super-polished Facebook games and merging it with games that give players a real presence, create a real economy, make things inside the economy really valuable instead of just bubblegum gifting. "Hey man, I crafted this super cool thing, and you really want it because it's gonna make your life awesome!" There's a deeper level of social interaction than what we've got right now.

Q: *So does Blizzard showing up on the Facebook platform give you nightmares?*

A: I'm not really worried about any competitors showing up in the space. They've got a few years of things to learn. The cost of acquisition is really high, making money off of free players is a really hard problem, so setting up a game that doesn't lose money initially is difficult. On top of that, viral channels are still useful, but you can't expect to have greater-than-one viral coefficients, like back in the day, where "I get millions of customers for free!" Well, you can forget that now, because there are too many ways in which Facebook has clamped down. And on top of that there's the "Facebook tax" where they take 30 percent off the top.

Tread carefully. Pay careful attention to what your competitors are doing. Finding a business model that someone else did that really worked is a great place to start. Look at Ravenwood Fair. It was really just a clone of FrontierVille, with some nice art. But those guys knocked it out of the park by paying close attention to the way things were constructed. It's not a bad thing to clone other games if you think there's not a lot of competition, or if you think you can bring something new to the table.

CHAPTER 7

How to Acquire, Keep, and Regain Users

7.1 HOW TO BUILD IT SO THEY'LL COME

Let's look at the core problems with the current business model for social and most mobile games:

1. How do I gain new users?

2. How do I retain these users?

3. How do I make my money?

We'll talk about the concept of the "funnel," which describes the lifecycle of a social game user. We'll talk about acquiring new players: both how to and how to determine how much to spend. We'll talk about virality and how you can turn fans into advocates. We'll look at how Zynga, King.com, Kabam, and other top players convert their disparate tribes into a coherent nation by unifying them under one "family" of games. We'll look at some of the giants in the space, and we'll explore how smaller shops might stand a chance either with them or against them. We'll consider how to hold on to users once you've got them, and how to stay aware of when and why your users quit playing. We'll talk about the ways that leaderboards and other social gameplay features can help user retention numbers, and other best practices for bringing lapsed players back into the fold.

We'll start with the core theory behind the consumer purchase business model and how it differs for social and free-to-play mobile games.

7.2 THE PURCHASE FUNNEL

The concept of the purchase funnel has been around since the late nineteenth century. St. Elmo Lewis, one of the fathers of American advertising, pioneered the concept as part of his theoretical work on consumer behavior. The model describes the steps a customer must go through before spending money on any kind of product or offer. Because we are all products of a highly commercialized age, an age in which an understanding of the mechanics of creating consumer demand is a basic part of our social education, the core concept of the funnel may seem somewhat obvious now. But its implications for customer acquisition in the social space are both profound and useful.

The funnel expresses four primary phases for a consumer:

- AWARENESS of the product or service

- INTEREST in the potential purchase

- DESIRE to take advantage of an offer

- ACTION which fulfills that desire

The funnel takes its shape and metaphor from the decreasing percentage of the population who proceeds on to each new step. Regardless of the slickness of your ad campaign to motivate a user in the first three stages and no matter how compelling the game content, screenshots, trial version, or whatever other components you use to entice the user to give you money, you will have fewer people who purchase than who are aware. You lose customers as they move toward the bottom of the theoretical funnel. The more effective you can get at provoking each of these consumer responses, the fewer customers you lose each step down the funnel and the bigger the pool of actuated users you'll have.

So why should we care about this dusty consumer-marketing theory?

Because with the freemium model of games, which has come to dominate the mobile and social market, where you only monetize users when they feel inclined to pay you, your revenue is destined to be based on a small percentage of your total customers. Most Facebook games monetize between 3 and 5 percent of their users. This means that if you want to make piles of money, it is critical that your game have a large number of customers. You must always work to increase the number of potential customers who enter the funnel and the conversion rate of those who make it through to actuation (and actual spending). In the social and digital games space, there is relatively little friction between a customers' first awareness of a product and their ability to purchase it. Gone are the days in which snowed-in farmers from a *My Antonia*–style village would read about a new product in a Sears and Roebuck catalog, hitch up horses to the wagon to drive into town, place an order, and wait for the general store to receive the goods from afar. Instead, your banner ad generates instant awareness; the catchiness of your consumer promise motivates immediate interest (or it fails to do so); the interested customers click through to express their desire; and within seconds, you're accepting their virtual currency or wondering why you've lost them. Ideally, your game is compelling enough that your viewers immediately "desire" the next part of the funnel, and a tight loop is built. They view, they desire, and they're monetized...and when they're not playing, they're telling their friends.

More specifically, in the social and mobile space, there are three key problems upon which you should constantly focus:

1. How do I acquire new players? (i.e., How do I drive awareness, generate interest, create desire?)

2. How do I monetize the players I have? (i.e., How do I turn desire into action? How do I get them to spend?)

3. How do I retain my players? (i.e., How do I keep them in the system to be monetized repeatedly?)

Social games, by their nature, add another layer of complexity to the funnel metaphor; fulfilling your user's desire once simply isn't enough. You need your users to come back for more, as often as possible, and preferably with friends. You need them to spread the message and to spread it enthusiastically. While this concept isn't unique to social media—our hypothetical farmer from a hundred years ago might have told his neighbors about the great new product he just received—the speed and scale at which certain connected influencers can spread your message makes your product's social stickiness as important as its underlying quality. The impact of your users' opinions affects the virality of your game, and in this medium, your virality is almost always the foundation of your marketing. Social media makes it ever more possible for Malcom Gladwell's mavens and connectors to reach truly terrific numbers of other potential customers, and that's what distinguishes an *Angry Birds* from the legion of great games out there...that you've never heard of.

Research group Kontagent has refined the classic funnel model to something they call the ARM model. ARM stands for Acquisition, Retention and Monetization. This revision on the model adds two important characteristics. The first of these is the user virality, which can help to infect new users (adding these users to the top of the funnel). The second factor incorporates the immediate revenue generation of a well-monetized social game. When handled correctly, this revenue can be used immediately and be reinvested into quality advertising that generates new users.

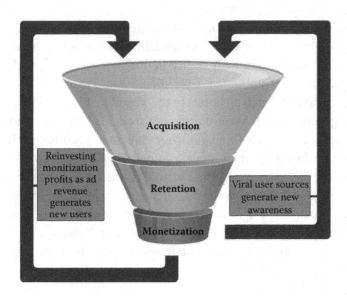

The key takeaway from this revised model is that once you've built and tuned a successful funnel, you can increase the scale of your success by reinvesting money into additional player acquisitions. These acquisitions, then, can use their own social networks to further expand the realm of influence enjoyed by your game. Again, there's nothing particularly unique about this model where social games are concerned, but thinking through this model should help focus your attention on your ability to gather metrics, to responsively tune your model, and then hopefully to "go big." Indeed, for most free-to-play publishers in business these days, a game's development costs aren't the biggest concern. Instead, most successful players in the space are hyper-focused on metrics that help them determine when a game is sticky enough and has a high enough conversion rate to justify turning on the hose of user acquisitions; then the marketing dollars go to work to pour new users into the mouth of the funnel.

With this core model in mind, let's look at player acquisition in a bit more depth. In doing so, we'll try to answer the question, how do you drive awareness, generate interest, and create desire in the minds of potential paying customers?

7.3 ACQUISITION: HOW TO GET PLAYERS

Depending on your platform and your budgets, you have a number of different ways to generate that initial critical level of awareness from your potential customers. Once you've got a fan base you can rely on word of mouth or the power of social networks to help spread your message, but initially you must spend *something* to get the message out. The night before day one you have zero customers. Somehow you need to turn that into a hundred million. The first question to ask yourself is, what's the best way for the world to learn about my game?

On Xbox LIVE publishers can purchase showcase slots that drive customers to the marketplace, where customers can then explore and hopefully purchase their game. Web games can use Google AdWords for targeted ads that appear alongside users' Google searches. Retail products can purchase advertising in magazines or on television. Any type of product can send out a press release through the Business Wire in the hopes that media outlets pick up the message and spread the word for them. The world is full of fan conferences where you can host PR stunts. (As I'm writing this, I'm watching a score of zombies shamble down the streets of San Diego's Gaslamp district, part of a promotion for a game debuting at San Diego's annual Comic-Con festival.) But ultimately, even the most innovative of publicity stunts, press releases, or ad campaigns amount to *buying* advertising, and this costs money.

For games on mobile and social platforms, the amount of money required to attract users continues to rise. Despite the innate virality of social platforms, both the number of offerings and the users are changing in ways that have reduced the effective infection rates one used to expect from games designed for that platform. The fundamental issue is that despite ever rising numbers of users, the sheer tidal volume of games released makes it extremely unlikely that a user will just stumble upon your game.

On Facebook, in the early days of the network (just a few years ago), one user might install and play a game, and almost assuredly several of her friends would join and also try the game out for themselves. How could they not, with the constant barrage of game advertising that would appear on their news feed? But Facebook's designers have shut down many of the "spammy" viral channels that promoted this kind of effect (and annoyed so many non-gamer users in the process). Facebook makes a great deal of its money on advertising and recognized that they were losing revenue by promoting "free" viral user acquisition. And the sheer number of applications available on Facebook now makes it much harder to break through the noise, in those few occasions where a breakthrough is still possible. Instead, in 2011, rates of user attraction were reported to be around 0.05 per user. They have only dropped since. Thus, it is very difficult to grow a user base on Facebook or any mobile platform through purely viral means.

Most successful applications on Facebook (which we'll count as those that have passed and stayed past the 100,000 daily average user mark) have been forced to spend heavily on advertising to attract new users. And since of those 100,000 or so average daily users, only 3–5 percent of them can be counted on to pay, and some drop by the wayside each day, we can easily see why there is a need for near continual advertising spend to "feed the funnel." The 2010 Social Gaming Summit estimated that roughly $3 million in advertising spend would be required to take a game to 1 million daily active users. The amount required has only increased since. For an excellent discussion of the reasons advertising becomes progressively less effective, I recommend Andrew Chen's fine blog.*

On mobile devices the problem is exacerbated by the reduced power of virality. Mobile games now must either spend heavily to acquire users or have a sufficient in with Apple or Google that they are featured on one of the many Top 10 or Top 50 lists in the App Stores. In case further proof of the intersection of social and mobile gaming were needed mobile game developers and publishers can now purchase targeted ads on Facebook that allow users to (nearly) instantly download games to their mobile phone. In fact, these

---

* http://andrewchen.co/2012/04/05/the-law-of-shitty-clickthroughs/#

have proven so successful that they have been used to drive over 25 million installs of applications, helping Facebook's bottom line.[*]

7.4 ACQUIRING NEW USERS ON FACEBOOK

Here are some of the ways that money can be spent within the context of fishing for users on Facebook, along with some information on the effectiveness of each method:

- Banner install ads are one of the most common ways to generate awareness of a product on this social network. These banner ads exist inside of other Facebook applications (and potentially even in competitor's games). If users are sufficiently interested, they can click the ad and be taken to a page that will allow them to install your game. The network that serves up the ads charges the advertiser for any new users who are driven to install the game by clicking through the banner. (Note: the charge is for the number who install the application and not for the total number of overall impressions.) Banner ads have the advantage of a fixed and known price per install, so costs cannot run away from you (without, at least, generating new users). The ads also tend to be nicely targeted, in that the users who see and interact with them are already part of that subset of the population who install other Facebook applications. But, banner install ads don't offer much deep targeting of particular users. (In other words, just because a user is on a cooking recipe application doesn't necessarily mean they'll want to install my zombie killer game.) Facebook (and other networks) continue to improve the heuristics they use to target users, though, and the targeted ads continue to be more precise.

- Incentivized installation ads are ads that exist inside an application (usually a game) that reward users with in-game currency (usually Facebook credits, as of the time of this writing) for installing another game. These types of "offer walls" give back to the original application for each install and are a good way to monetize users who won't pay directly. This type of user acquisition also has a fixed cost per install (CPI), and can be a very inexpensive way of attracting new users. However, the install traffic your game attracts from these types of ads is inherently poor, because users are not (initially) interested in your game at all; they install your product as a way of getting currency they can spend in a different game. Moreover, since they opt to install other applications rather than spend their own money, the possibility of direct monetization is likely to be low. This is a bit like trying to sell life insurance to people who answer ads for free stuff on Craigslist.

- Direct Facebook install ads cost per impression and are purchased directly from Facebook (Figure 7.1). These live on the right side column of every Facebook page, and Facebook charges advertisers per impression (in thousand impression increments) as well as for click-throughs. These types of ads tend to reach a terrific number of users in a short period of time and also tend to have high user engagement rates

FIGURE 7.1 Facebook offers direct advertising, charged per impression. Facebook direct advertising is considered to be significantly more effective than offer wall advertising, but also can be significantly more expensive.

once users do click through to investigate further. However, because advertisers are charged by impressions or click-throughs rather than installs, this can end up being an expensive way to acquire users.

When it comes to attracting and retaining users, one Facebook install ad is about as effective as three banner ads, which is about as effective as 30 incentivized ad installs from an offer wall.

7.5 ACQUIRING NEW USERS ON MOBILE PLATFORMS

Due to the diversity of hardware capabilities, operating systems, networks, and other platform vagaries, user acquisition on mobile is less straightforward than on Facebook. There seem to be few standards, and practices differ between different developers and publishers. Those who are the most successful with user acquisition have a serious leg up in the monetization game. Here are some of the most common mechanisms:

- Advertise
- Popup ads inside other games
- Review Sites
- iTunes and Google Features
- Team up with a publisher or platform

We'll continue to discuss these major avenues for user acquisition as we proceed.

7.6 ADVERTISING EFFICIENTLY

In Chapter 5 we briefly mentioned a few important values you should use to measure the efficiency of your chosen advertising mechanisms. Let's refresh:

CTR (click through rate)—The number of people who click on an ad, divided by the number of people who see it. For example, if 100,000 people see an advertisement, and 400 of them click on it, the ad has a CTR of 0.4 percent. By understanding the relative CTR of different ads, developers and publishers can increase the efficiency of their marketing. Since the cost for an ad is usually fixed based on the number of views, not the number of clicks, it's important to carefully study the CTR of a potential ad before "going wide" with it and to make sure the ad you choose has the best CTR possible. Typical Facebook advertisements are reported as having CTRs of between 0.04 percent and 0.14 percent.

CVR (conversion rate)—How many of those who try your product actually go the next step and play or buy it? For example, if 400 people click on an ad for your game and get as far as the install screen, but only 20 end up installing the game, then your CVR is 5 percent. While it may seem counter-intuitive that anyone would click on an ad for an installer and not follow through with the install, experience tells us this is often, if not usually, the case. (Why would they have clicked on the ad if they weren't interested?) In fact, only around 50 percent of the people who click on an ad end up following through with the install. It is worth noting that some developers and publishers have started measuring only those users who make it through the tutorial as having converted. Others refer to CVR only as those users who actually convert to paying customers (usually a far smaller set.) The lack of standard reporting of this metric makes it critically important to seek clarity when discussing specifics.

CPI (cost per install)—A measure of the total marketing cost divided by the number of total installs. For example, if you bought 10 million impressions at $1 each, and 2 million people installed the game, then your total advertising cost would be $10 million, and your CPI would be $5.

7.7 THE RISING COST OF CPI

A successful advertising campaign on any social or mobile network is one that achieves a high conversion rate with a low cost per install. Unfortunately, as time passes after the initial start of your ad campaign, conversion rates tend to drop and your CPI tends to increase. The reason for this is that the users who were natively inclined to investigate your product have already done so, and customers not so inclined get bored with repeatedly seeing your message. Those folks are aware of your product, but they have just already decided they aren't, in fact, customers. (Remember any television ad campaign that overstayed its welcome and how quickly it went from being clever to tired?) Without constantly updating your messaging or changing the advertising in new and creative ways, the CPI can increase by two times or more in relatively short order. This phenomenon has not been lost on social game developers:

> Once you've acquired the majority of the early adopters, CPIs in a particular market can increase by three to five times from your Day 1 CPI. Fortunately, this change doesn't happen overnight. Refreshing creative [advertisements], creating a compelling message, and refining your target audience are the best ways to combat application saturation. (John Marsland, Acquisition Manager, Zynga)

Let's make sure we understand the implications of the rising cost of user acquisition as it relates to the different advertising mechanisms available. Since the cost to acquire a user goes up as the number of users increases, and since users do eventually leave the system, an unceasing effort to keep a constant influx of users coming into the funnel eventually reaches a price that will make your game unprofitable. A good rule of thumb is that the cost to bring on users currently increases about 10 percent for every additional 100,000 new players. The implication here is that eventually, all social games will reach a "carrying capacity" beyond which acquiring new users is simply too expensive to be profitable. This nearly axiomatic rule drives most social game development companies to constantly keep an eye on the "next great thing" they'll have to build. This trend-line also underscores the importance of driving your initial CPI down as far as possible. It only gets more expensive from there.

As Marsland tells us, the only way to combat this, even slightly, is to vary the messaging. In order to effectively test new messaging to see which new ideas might yield the best CTR numbers, most social games have dedicated, full-time marketing analysts. These marketing analysts make careful use of A/B or multi-variant testing to see which ads are the most effective before rolling them out on a large scale.

It should be clear from this discussion that one of the biggest risks to a new social or mobile game (after it has been designed) is that the marketing campaign will fail to capture users efficiently enough to "feed the funnel" long enough that the game can make a significant return on the initial development investment, as well as the initial round of marketing costs.

7.8 VIRALITY

"But what about virality? Isn't that the whole reason we're making a social game?"

Well, yes. Social games do get a nice lift from virality and other organic methods of transmissions, as we saw in the earlier ARM funnel image. The specifics tend to be heavily influenced by the mechanics and users of the social network on which the game is played, and those elements, more than most, evolve and change over time. For example, Facebook now exercises much tighter control over game spam than in previous years. While this is great for users who got tired of hearing about the lonely sheep that wandered into their friend's news feed, it isn't as great for social game designers, who now must pay to get eyes on their ads, eyes they used to be able to attract for free. Other social networks like Xbox LIVE, Steam, and Game Center don't really do much to help with virality either; at best, users are able to compare achievements or see what their friends have recently played. Beyond that, it is up to users' individual power to attract their friends if their choices have a chance of going "viral."

As we discussed earlier, virality on games, and Facebook games in particular, is now trending to around 0.5 as of 2012, meaning that for every two new users, you're likely to get one additional user, based on players opting-in to common in-game prompts to send out messages to friends. This value is called the Viral Coefficient.

You can measure the virality of a product by looking at its Viral Coefficient. This is a measure of both popularity and growth. The number should give you insight into how many additional new users each new user will attract. The common formula used to calculate this factor is:

$$X \text{ (number of friends each person invites)} \times$$
$$Y \text{ (the percentage of those friends who accept the invitation).}$$

Generally speaking if the result is 1, the application is experiencing linear growth. If the result is greater than 1, the popularity of the application is rising. If the result is less than 1, the application is falling in popularity. This can be a useful measure of user engagement and the overall quality of the design of a game. Understanding this value can inform the amount of money you want to spend on advertising and act as a general health index for a game.

The good news is that every one of these additional new users gained through virality or other organic means is effectively free. This is one reason it is so important to build game mechanics that encourage users to invite their friends to play. Even if you end up having to incentivize users with in-game goods or virtual currency, so long as the value of the incentive is cheaper than the game's then-current CPI, the in-game attraction is cheaper than having to purchase advertising to attract a new user.

And since each of the new users attracted in this fashion will, in turn, attract more users themselves (hopefully), virality remains a strong force for social games, even in ecosystems where the network itself tends to tamp down on viral channels and even in the more mature Facebook environment in which we operate today. No one can silence word of mouth, and if your game is good enough, if it gets better when players have the opportunity to play with their friends, then those players will call/email/text their buddies and convince them to play. And in a well-monetized game, that translates into free money for you.

7.9 REDIRECTING USERS FOR INCREASED VIRALITY

There's another way that development companies have found to siphon off some of the power of the viral effect: They ensure that when users are exposed to their games, they are also indirectly exposed to other games by the same maker. This way, when users run out of turns in a particular day or just get tired of playing one particular game, they are gently rerouted to another product by the same developer—one that conveniently pays into the

FIGURE 7.2 Zynga makes excellent use of a game bar that helps transition users who try one of their games into others. Game bars that expose users to other products in the same family can help increase the stickiness of a brand for its users.

same coffers. This also allows users who aren't interested in a particular game they've been invited to join to easily transition over to another game that might be more to their liking, helping make sure a game company doesn't lose the viral effect of newly attracted users. At the same time, it increases the brand recognition of a particular game developer, making it that much easier to attract new users to yet-to-be created products, and all without spending extra dollars on advertising. This mechanic has proven effective across social and mobile platforms. Indeed, one of the primary values of many successful game companies is the terrific number of users they have in their funnel—users they can channel to other products easily. (See Figure 7.2.)

7.10 HOW TO RETAIN USERS

Once you've brought users into your funnel, how do you make sure they don't leave, at least until they've gone for many, many trips around the monetization merry-go-round?

Keeping users playing your game and coming back to see your new products is what we mean when we talk about "stickiness." Metrics like daily average users and monthly average users help measure success in this arena; ideally, any free-to-play game's users will come back many times throughout a single day, if not remain "on" all the time. After all, if they're there and playing, they are enjoying the game and there's at least a chance of them paying. The top-rated mobile and Facebook games can provide great lessons here (as can some of the top played games on other platforms). Indeed, there's almost no way to become a great social game creator without carefully studying the most addictive games in the business. *FarmVille, Clash of Clans, Call of Duty, World of Warcraft, League of Legends, Bejeweled, Candy Crush,* and others often spoken of in hushed, reverent tones due to their sheer user numbers all tend to have game mechanics that lead to a great deal of stickiness, that keep users coming back every day and make sure those users talk about the game to their friends. Learn them all if you are serious about playing in the social or mobile games sector.

To be properly sticky, games need to be designed in such a way that users want to return very regularly. When thinking about the game design of almost any game, you should ask yourself, what makes this a game that people will forsake every other pleasure in life to come back to, at least for a few minutes every day? This may sound daunting, but it is truly the task that awaits you. A designer friend of mine used to say, "If your game isn't more fun than getting a blowjob then it's not good enough." (And his most recent game won Game of the Year from G4TV in 2012.) While his sentiment may be crass, it's also fairly accurate—assume your users can engage in any pleasurable distraction known to humankind. What will make them turn their attention away from that to play your game?

Here are a few motivations that can engage players effectively, if used properly:

- Reward every significant user action, such that all time devoted to the game pays dividends.

- Dole out energy or turns in limited, time-released doses. This keeps players coming back every day or several times throughout the day. Ensure that there is a cap on the maximum amount of energy or turns that a user can accumulate so that they lose the benefit if they stay away too long. If the game is fun, if the rewards for returning add value and that value is lost if they stay away, users will return regularly for their daily "fix."

- Leaderboards and high score mechanics continue to be a tried and true player engagement feature. We'll study these more carefully in a moment, since they can be applied to almost any game on almost any social network. Players are encouraged to compete with their friends and can even be motivated to play against themselves in order to beat their own high score. Even the oldest arcade games understood this, making sure that "high scorers" were prominently displayed even when the game wasn't in use. Almost any game can incorporate some element of the leaderboard effect and for a very low cost. (See our example of *Project Gotham Racing 2* below.)

- Make the in-game currency valuable enough to players that they care about it, that it offers them a value beyond simply a "score counter." Then give them a little each time they come back to play. Bribery works, so long as you bribe your users with something they desire.

- Give players a reason to care about what's going on in the game world when they are away. MMOs and other "living world" type games are great at this. Make sure your players feel that when they aren't playing your game their friends *are* and are having fun adventures without them. These can be real friends, in a true social gaming sense, or engaging characters and storylines that progress outside of the timeline set by the user. Even single player games can imply that things happen in the game as time passes, even when a particular player isn't playing. Messaging users about these types of events can keep them engaged, even when they aren't online.

- Punish users (gently) if they are away too long. This mechanic can backfire easily, because it can make users feel like they've lost their opportunity to go back to a game they like. But if used properly, users will want to come back every day to avoid whatever minor penalty a game will bestow upon them. *FarmVille,* for example, is notorious for making users' crops rot. And as long as the penalties don't "stack" too heartily, if recouping the ground they've lost is fun rather than frustrating, even a little in-game penalty can be motivation to return to your game.

- Carefully study compulsion and reward loops in other games. From *Call of Duty*'s multiplayer XP model to the noises a slot machine makes in a casino, there is a particular psychological strategy to giving users tiny, regular rewards in response to their actions. Many games go so far as to reward users for almost every click. (Notice the stars and coins that explode all over the screen in *Empires and Allies* or *CityVille* every time you click on almost anything.) For your game, there will be a "sweet spot" in the reward strategy that gives users the feeling of success that they crave, while making them work for it, just hard enough, such that it doesn't lose its appeal.

These kinds of motivations that lead directly to user engagement are critical to achieving positive retention metrics, numbers that measure daily visits and average time spent per visit. By keeping your users coming back and making sure that when they do return they're engaged and having fun, you also increase virality by making them want to tell their friends about the game. This creates the positive feedback loop that leads to very successful products. The big point is, keep your user engagement high so they are always coming back.

7.11 TRACKING RETENTION

The unexamined life may or may not be worth living, but the unexamined mobile or social game almost assuredly is not worth playing. As we've emphasized throughout this book, without properly studying metrics, there's just no way to improve the quality and stickiness of your game. So how should you track user retention?

First, you should track users along several different scales. We recommend daily, weekly, and monthly tracking for active user values, tracked within particular cohorts. This will make it easier to track the effects of changing demographics, as well as the effects of changes the development team makes to the game. Finally, by comparing against other major events in the industry (like the release of a competitor's game), a team will be able to work from a clear picture of the role their offering plays in the greater marketplace. Keeping track of customers based on what version they started on or their start date can be helpful, as well.

There's also value in tracking information about the number of different visits any given user makes in a day. This will help in tuning the types of game design mechanics we discussed above, since having such numbers makes it much easier to do A/B testing on micromechanics designed to bring users back for multiple sessions within a particular day.

Tracking time per visit can be beneficial, as well; this information clarifies what types of engagement users have with your game, what they are really doing in the game. This lets you understand the delta between how users actually play and what your design team intended. A collection of 30-second visits implies that users are just checking in. Lengthier stays mean a greater level of engagement with the gameplay itself. Both of these might be okay, but only if either interaction creates value for the user and a monetization opportunity for you.

Understanding the average lifetime per user will help you understand your retention rate at a macro-level. If most users are churning out after a few days, there's probably a reason. Are they running out of engaging gameplay? Have their friends moved on to something new? Is there some difficulty spike that is frustrating them into finding new ways to spend their time? Have they been staring at the same content for too long? If you know when users leave your system, never to return, you can potentially fix those issues and keep them in your funnel longer.

7.12 USING LEADERBOARDS AND MESSAGING TO ADD STICKINESS

Let's dig a bit deeper now and look at two particularly useful tools for increasing user engagement, the leaderboard and the message reminder.

As we've discussed, the very term "social game" can be seen as a clever sleight of hand, since some of the most successful social games have only the most rudimentary of multiplayer-components. Instead, many games are able to build single-player experiences that effectively use design systems and services to set the player's actions within the context of a social network. Using leaderboards that allow users to compare their performances against friends and other players is one of the oldest and most successful mechanisms for accomplishing this goal. From the first arcade games, leaderboards ("Scoreboards") have been used to turn a single player game into a social experience that creates a sense of community. As any gamer over thirty remembers (and almost everyone will have a story about), old school Scoreboards inspired players to plug quarter after quarter into stand-up arcade machines, because players enjoyed playing the game, but moreover players hoped to beat the machine's "high score," a score that could have been achieved by them, their friends, or perhaps by someone who was anonymous but for their initials. Later arcade games (like *Gauntlet Legends, Golden Tee Golf,* and a variety of the "bar game" machines) began to use networks that let users compare their scores to players in other arcades or bars around the world, further locating the single-player game within a real community of players.

So how do we use leaderboards now to help create that sense of community and reinforce the social network effect? The following are some techniques that the top developers use:

- *Use multi-faceted scores.* Give users a score based on multiple variables rather than just one. For example, don't just give points for every enemy killed; instead, offer points for enemies killed, give bonuses for stringing kills together in a short period of time, subtract points for taking damage, and so on. This gives you a far wider range of possible scores, helping to increase the granularity that differentiates between two users of similar skill, and makes the "perfect score" far more difficult to achieve. Techniques like these prevent your leaderboards from going stale and provide many different types of players the opportunity to make a leaderboard appearance.

- *Context is everything.* Players care more about how they match up to their friends than they do to strangers. Almost all existing social networks make it easy for you to track and filter results by relationship to the user. Secondarily, players care more about players (even strangers) who score close to them on the leaderboards than those who are stratospherically far above or abysmally far below them. Players tend to care about their competition more than those who play far outside their league. This is another important reason to have well granulated scoring mechanisms. What players perceive as their "league" may be different from a general stack ranking of player point scores.

- *Display scores in interesting ways.* Flat, two-dimensional leaderboards are at best dull and at worst lazy and old school. Present information about your players and their friends in innovative ways that become part of the entertainment experience rather than merely an external measurement. *Project Gotham Racing 2* for the Xbox was an early pioneer of this technique (Figure 7.3). By giving a unique name to their scoring system—"Kudos" were earned for driving with style as well as speed—they managed to make the scoring model feel integrated rather than tacked on as an afterthought. Second, and more important, the game displays a constant newsfeed-style crawler along the bottom of the main menu to show the player when a friend bests their score on a particular track or in a certain event. The game added the ability to race against the "ghost" of a friend by showing a greyed out version of their car racing alongside yours, following the line they raced in their best session. This further added value to the leaderboard system by allowing users to effectively race against one another in an asymmetric fashion.

- *Give users different events in which they might compete.* A single leaderboard is too simplistic and reduces player engagement because only a particular kind of player who exhibits very particular types of skills can excel. It's hard to get excited about being ranked 12,334,667[th] out of 39,775,448 players, even if it does mean you're in the top one-third of all players. In addition to filtering players into smaller, more meaningful groups by social network, region, or similar, consider offering different types of events. One player may want to be recognized for the most creatively designed farm, while another might hope to be known as the player who harvested

FIGURE 7.3 *Project Gotham Racing 2* for Xbox featured a leaderboard system that constantly reminded players of their friends' accomplishments in the game and allowed users to race against "ghosts" of their friend's top scores. These types of innovations in leaderboard presentation can help create a sense of community among players, which tends to increase player retention.

the most rutabaga in the month of March. By breaking your game scoring up into a number of different tracked events, you can give players more focused goals and smaller groups to compete against. The more people who play your game and feel like winners, the stronger your player engagement, the more friends they bring in, and the more opportunities you have to monetize.

- *The gold stars matter only if they teach you.* Generally speaking, no one cares about the top score unless it happens to be them, if they are close to beating it, or it's a friend whom they happen to be close to beating. However, you can drive user interest in the superstars of your game by allowing users to learn something from them. The brilliant and fiendishly difficult 2009 release *Demon's Souls*, available only on PlayStation 3, featured a temple in the game world where the top fifty players were awarded statues of their characters (Figure 7.4). Other players could investigate these statues to see what types of equipment those players used when achieving their great feats, thereby giving these more novice players ideas on how they might best the game's challenges. This feature was part of a larger suite of innovative asynchronous multiplayer design mechanics, many of which remain unharvested by mainstream social games. Later, games like *League of Legends* added highly publicized tournaments and a spectator mode, which encouraged players to watch the champions (whose rock-star status is only slightly belied by their pallor) compete in significant matches.

FIGURE 7.4   In addition to numerous other multiplayer innovations, *Demon's Souls* let players see statues of the top-scoring heroes and investigate their equipment. Players tend to care about top scores only if they can learn something from the players who achieved them.

- *Tie replays into leaderboards.* Some games have taken this concept to an excitingly deep level, allowing players to record and share entire matches with the rest of their social network. Games like *StarCraft 2* and many of the later games in the *Halo* series (Figure 7.5) offer robust replay features. These types of features allow players to study world-class competitive players (many of whom are in fact "professional gamers" with agents, sponsorships, etc.) and how their matches were resolved, much as newspapers publish notations allowing chess fanatics to mentally recreate each move of a championship match. While these types of features can be technically complex, perhaps too technically complex for integration into most social game engines today, they still provide a ripe area of investigation for future social network games.

FIGURE 7.5   *Halo 3* introduced a replay system that lets players watch multiplayer matches. Replay systems can help drive user engagement with leaderboards by letting players study the "top stars," hopefully to improve their own techniques.

7.13 USING MESSAGES TO REMIND USERS TO RETURN

Sometimes even the most dedicated gamer gets distracted by the pressures of real life or by some of the non-gaming pleasures to which we alluded earlier. A little nudge to remind these players of what they are missing can be helpful, especially if those messages say more than just "you've been away, so come back" and instead let the player know of innovations they might genuinely regret missing. There are any number of ways these types of messages can be constructed. Emailing users is the traditional way of saying, "We've missed you; please come back." Posting to a user's Facebook wall, sending a text message to their phone, or messaging them inside another game (provided you have the legal right and the user's permission to do so) can all have a similar effect. Many smartphones now offer the opportunity for applications to send notifications to the OS, just like mail or voicemail notifications. Of course, you'll need to allow users to opt into and out of this kind of communication. But used effectively, notices of upcoming community events, special offers, and similar can be quite effective.

As we've discussed, acquiring new users can be very expensive, so it's worth your time and money to invest in creative ways to return lapsed users to the fold. And it's much easier to reacquire a user than to acquire a new one, since you already know how to communicate with that lapsed player. Email reminders can be a cheap way to stay in contact and are particularly useful whenever there is a new feature added to the game. Of course, message reminders need to allow users who have truly left and no longer care about a game to unsubscribe, or you risk the stickiness of your overall brand beyond any annoyance they may have with the particular game. But don't overlook the value of a simple reminder, especially if it's accompanied by an offer of more interesting game experiences or, even better, something free. Take a look at ways that games on Android, like ngmoco's highly successful *Blood Brothers,* which is published on their Mobage platform, are able to push news of community events to make users excited to see what they are missing.

Also, pay attention to ways in which you can invoke the power of a game's social connections within the message you send. "Please come back; we miss you!" is less powerful than "Play today and we'll give you a free gift worth $1!" What's more powerful still is, "Mike is exploring the continent on his own. Play now and we'll give him 2 extra galleons and you 4 extra galleons and a shiny new sword!" By offering users a valuable gift, telling them about a new feature, or ideally doing both and giving them a way of helping themselves and their friends by returning to your game, you can regain a convert (far more cheaply than you can acquire a new user).

7.14 ONLY THE LAST INCH MATTERS

We've talked through ways to attract and retain users and ways to regain users once they've stopped playing. We've evaluated various metrics that help social and mobile game developers better understand the behaviors of their users. We've looked at virality, why it's so powerful, why it's significantly more difficult to achieve on Facebook these days, and some of the ways that you might be able to take advantage of organic growth mechanisms on mobile devices. We've dissected some of the more effective ways leaderboards can be designed in order to increase the stickiness of a game, using a broad spectrum of examples from great games of the past that we hope inspires game developers to think of new ways to build compelling scoring mechanics.

Next let's look at the heart of the monetization problem. What models for monetizing users currently exist? Which monetization strategies are most effective for the different types of games? What mechanics can be built into games to make these models more effective?

After all, gaining users and even keeping them doesn't help your bottom line unless those users are also paying. While there is satisfaction in creating something that players can enjoy free of charge, most companies create games for a less noble, but perhaps more practical motive. Next we'll dive into how to generate a profit, but not until we've made a brief stop in Vancouver to visit with an up-and-coming social and mobile game development studio.

7.15 INTERVIEW WITH EXPLODING BARREL: "GIVE THEM WHAT THEY WANT"

Heather Price joined the games industry as an advertising manager in 2001, after a career in the packaged goods industry. She has served as a director of marketing at Electronic Arts and a director of product strategy at Microsoft Game Studios. She currently leads Exploding Barrel Games as the studio's general manager. Heather has a BS in Engineering from Rutgers University. In 2013, Exploding Barrel was purchased by Kabam, a leader in the mobile and social space.

Scott Blackwood has been making games since 1994 and has expertise in multiple genres across all platforms. During his tenure at Electronic Arts he worked on sixteen AAA titles, created two original IPs, and was responsible for development budgets in excess of $20 million. Prior to founding Exploding Barrel Games, Scott most recently built a 140-person team from the ground up at EA BlackBox to create the award-winning franchise *Skate*.

Jeff Howell has been building software tools and games since 2002. He has worked as a programmer at Relic Entertainment and technical director at Electronic Arts. He is currently the CTO for Exploding Barrel Games. He holds a BS in Computer Science from the University of Calgary.

Q: Tell me a little bit about who you are and what you're doing.

HP: Exploding Barrel Games was founded by Scott Blackwood, our president, in October 2009. He was most recently the executive producer on the *Skate* franchise, which he built from the ground up to a 140-person team. He spent fifteen years at Electronic Arts and shipped sixteen AAA titles. After deciding to leave EA, he got very excited about the emerging social and mobile market and the potential to bring AAA experiences to that space. He saw the promise in Facebook as a platform, as well as the mobile space, and this concept of free-to-play socially connected games.

In the early days he brought on several partners, like Wilson Tang, the Chief Visual Officer, who had been at EA for six years on the *Need for Speed* franchise. Before that he spent many years at Industrial Light and Magic, working with the likes of Spielberg on a couple of *Star Wars* films, as well as *A.I.* and *The Hulk.* Wilson was excited about this space because he believed that there is an opportunity with presentation fidelity that wasn't being mined. Wilson is also an amazing concept artist, so he's perfect for quick iteration.

Jeff Howell joined us even earlier. He was on the forefront of socially connected and online spaces before many other people were. He was paying a lot of attention to Xbox LIVE, which is still a viable, socially powerful network. He was also doing things with console games like letting users capture video and push that video out to YouTube with one click of a controller button. He has been at the forefront of online for years. He saw an opportunity here to win by building great tools for rapid iteration and data-driven design, arming designers with great tools and so they can iterate quickly.

Q: You guys are building Jimmy Buffett's Margaritaville *for traditional social platforms, as well as mobile, is that right?*

HP: Correct. For Facebook and iOS. We love the iPad as a gaming platform. We love the iPhone as a gaming platform. If this game were just for Facebook I think we would have been less excited about it. Whether you are playing on Facebook or on an iPad, it is the same experience. As far as we know that has not been done yet. For the iPhone, we've made a *Margaritaville* experience that is a compliment to the other two games. You can't really have the scale of world in that size footprint, so we're focusing on experiences that make sense for how people play games on their iPhone. For the iPhone, the focus is on our minigames, which we have a lot of. On iPad and Facebook, the focus is on exploration and adventure.

Q: I'm not aware of many other licensed social games that have been done to this level of quality. What's it like bringing the Margaritaville *license to life in this way?*

HP: One thing that the leadership team is super-passionate about is digging into a culture. If you were to ask me if I wanted to dig into a Pepsi game, that would scare me. The *Margaritaville* brand isn't just some songs and a restaurant. There are books.

There are Parrotheads, who are people who hang on every word Jimmy Buffett says. Beyond that group of people, there is this concept of a great "staycation." Who in a winter month does not want to escape to a world of gin-clear water and go fishing on a snowy January day? Having that core fanbase and fiction that we can mine and respect and having the opportunity to bring some of those book characters to life in this world was exciting. Using brands can help discovery and user acquisition on these platforms when they come with a core fan base, but the brand has to lend itself to something that will make a great game.

Q: The game is free-to-play initially. How do you monetize users?

HP: We looked at what was working in the social space, casual MMOs, and free-to-play MMOs in both the West and in Asia. We use the energy mechanic, because that just works. There are obviously vanity items and also the concept of accelerators, which we think is powerful. We have both temporary and lasting accelerators. If you don't want to grind and really want to catch that specific kind of fish, we'll let you go to the Bait Store and buy that great lure you want. There are also some new ideas that we are going to try out and see what people attach to. It is important to us to look to the data to see how people are behaving and give them more of what they want.

Q: You guys are using great-looking avatar characters for players, and you're doing some neat stuff with player-to-player avatar interaction. Can you tell me more about that?

HP: A lot of social games aren't social. You can play asynchronously with your friends and help each other in the gameplay, but you usually can't see them in your world. That's something we think can be improved.

SB: It gives the perception of synchronous play. Facebook isn't ideally geared toward synchronous play, but this way I can feel like I'm sharing a moment with friends.

Q: Is all this perceived synchronous play cooperative?

SB: It's just about your friends having a presence. I can see you walking around in my world. I can walk up to you and you can say something from a list of different random things; you might talk about the weather or ask about the hurricane last night. You might tell me something that I need to know for the game or you can be working on my boat. You could be the captain of my boat or working in my bar. So there are a lot of different ways you can play with that.

Q: So you're integrating friends' avatars into the game as NPCs?

SB: Yeah. The NPCs are mostly there to provide some color and as a reflection of how well you are doing in the game. As your bar gets better, more people will enjoy being in your oasis, being on your beach. They'll be out there mingling or dancing a la *Beach Blanket Bingo*. Some of them will be your friends, who also fulfill a purpose.

In the game you can have a five-piece band. If you don't have a steel-drummer yet, we drop the steel drums out of the music. I want a drummer in my band or else my bar isn't operating as well as it could be; my vibe isn't as good as it could be.

Q: You mentioned steel-drumming and some minigames earlier. Can I expect a drumming minigame here?

SB: Yes, It is a turn-based memory game. You start it by playing against Bobby G, who is a character from Jimmy Buffett's fiction. There was a story where they had to go into the jungle to find this guy because he was hiding out from the authorities. We played that up a bit. He'll play a couple notes and I'll have to play them on my drum. The sequence gets longer and longer and it makes a song. Just like *Guitar Hero*, if I play a bad note it'll play a false note and sound off.

Q: How do minigames affect monetization?

HP: They cost energy to play. Minigames are so important to the experience, so it can feel as big and rich and fun as it is. While there is an energy mechanic in the minigames on iPad and Facebook, we are also making them the core of the iPhone version, so people can just have fun playing with them.

SB: On *Top Bar* we originally didn't have an energy mechanic. We found that people would come in and play a minigame like *Beer Pong* for an average of forty minutes! So we were giving away too much for free. Then we turned it into a one free-play per day, and you had to pay for more, and people screamed bloody murder. We learned, don't give away too much at first! Go the other way. Be stingy, and then give more over time.

It's amazing because it's free to play, but people don't think of it that way. They just think of it as something they put a lot of time into. 98 percent of them never pay a dime. They'll even write in and tell us, "I spent so much money on this game!" and we'll look it up and know that they never spent any real money on the game.

You've got to be really careful when you take away even the tiniest things. In *Top Bar* we had a *Patron Toss* minigame, where you threw other patrons into various items, including a giant swinging donut, and you got a prize worth $.10. And we realized there was a cheat; there was a way to get perfect every time. I couldn't do it, but other people could. So then we had to limit it so that you could only win real currency the first time; then you'd just get a prize coin. Again, unbelievable how mad a few people got! So that was good learning from *Top Bar*.

HP: Scott brings up a great point on the mindset of people playing these free-to-play games. They feel like their time is every bit as important as money, emotionally. They have been trained that if they spend twenty hours playing the game a week, whether they gave a dime or not, that's of real value. It's important to them. They invested time, dammit! You've gotta be very careful with that.

SB: Some of them value time even more than money. If you've spent two months with something for a half hour a day, you've become heavily invested. If the developer does something bad... This happened to me in a game I was playing that I was very addicted to. There is an example of a game I was playing for several months, where they went and changed some features that made all the load times longer. I never went back because I had sixteen different areas I had to visit to maintain every day. I couldn't wait for a thirty second load for each one, and they lost me. I'd put probably $400 into that game but they changed it to where there was just too much friction, and I was gone. You've got to be really careful with any kind of changes you make.

HP: You asked earlier about minigames. Another thing that we believe in is leaderboards. We think social benchmarking, knowing where you stand among your friends on all these minigames, is a very powerful thing. If I know that you have caught a bigger fish than me and I'm one person away from the top of that leaderboard, I'm going to spend a little more time fishing. And that's a very powerful motivator. It's good-natured competition.

SB: It's comparative, not competitive. It is how people play social games, rather than the hardcore "I wanna shoot my friends in the face" mentality of a lot of eighteen-year-olds playing Xbox; people want to compete, but it is generally less malicious. I'm sure if games had a feature where I could come in and wipe out your farm with a nuke, then a lot of people would say, "That's it. I'm never playing this game again." People don't want that. They want to look good and be able to show off their progress to their friends rather than compete directly.

Q: Tell us about the technology you guys have built to create social games.

JH: Probably the biggest thing is that we've built ourselves new technology that scales a lot better than a lot of the old technology. A lot of the older social media developers are stuck on an old LAMP system, which basically means they are using PHP and SQL to drive their stack. The problem with these technologies is that they aren't really built out of the box to scale up really fast. There's a lot of work you need to do to handle the scaling problems. There have been a lot of new technologies in the past year that have made this a lot more possible, and that's what we're built on. This is our backend I'm talking about here.

SB: This is why we decided to build our own backend. We were using a third party before to do all our hosting. We've just found that for a bunch of reasons, we were better off to spend the money and build our own.

JH: There are two big reasons: scalability and cost. And these are pretty big factors. The cost is important, especially with free-to-play games, because every additional dollar I'm spending to host the game is counting against my revenue. It needs to be as cheap to run as possible.

Secondly, we're a small company, so we can't afford huge capital costs to buy huge servers and data centers. We have to build things for the cloud. Scalability is huge. If you look, you'll see some social games that go down for a day or more undergoing maintenance, because they weren't ready for their demand and because they hadn't planned for scalability at the social level. These games can go zero to hero in just a few days, so you need to be ready for that kind of scale. If you haven't planned for that, you can have a lot of problems.

So first, we're built on the cloud, for the cloud. We use a solution that abstracts the cloud for us and handles a lot of the scaling. It will figure out what the load is over time and start up new servers as needed. This is nice because if you're paying for servers, you don't want to be paying for 400 servers for the entire day.

Instead, when it's lunchtime on the East Coast, scale up to x number of servers, then scale back down later in the day, and so on.

We built all our stuff on Amazon, but we can easily swap our stuff between Amazon and Rackspace.

SB: And that's important, because sometimes those services go down. We've been asked numerous times what happened when Amazon went down recently for a day or so. How did it affect us? It didn't.

JH: And people get this horrible misconception that the cloud is reliable and perfect, and that everything that you put there just works. It's just not. Sometimes things crash and you can lose a server. You must build your stuff to be able to handle multiple machines going down. That's really important.

JH: The cost is about 1/3 of what we've seen out of other systems, and an even smaller fraction of what some of the older games cost in hosting and support costs. We looked at the costs here compared to what we'd done in the past and realized that if our game did well on those systems, we'd be paying a quarter million dollars a month. Now we'd pay about $60,000. That is a lot of money to save.

Q: *Are there proprietary tools you guys have built for building and tuning content?*

JH: We started with Unity, because we weren't happy with Flash. We're not 2D people. We work in 3D, and we knew at some point... If you look at social games, they've kind of gone through the last twenty years of gaming history in the last three years. At some point, they're going to go 3D because people are going to get bored with clicking and interacting with just 2D stuff. We think Unity is on the forefront.

HP: And 3D isn't just 3D camera stuff. That includes physics which we can use in design.

JH: Unity is a AAA game tool. You can build anything from *FarmVille* to *Call of Duty* in it if you want to. It was really flexible for us. We found that it was missing a few things for us, though, and that's where our system, Fuse, comes in. That provides a sort of data-driven visual scripting language like you would see in Unreal's Kismet tool. That way we can put all of the power in the hands of the designers instead of the programmers. This is important because we've made some really serious changes to design throughout our development. You'd never be able to do that quickly if it were all code-driven behavior. We've got a whole cinematic system that we've built and all of these things tie back into our Sparks Analytics client that we've built.

JH: One thing that people can really screw up, though, is with games this big, you've got to be really careful about download sizes and install speeds. That needs to be way less than ten seconds, because you can't have users sitting around on a load screen; they'll all quit. So we've had to optimize heavily.

JH: We've built our own analytics system from the ground up. We had to do that. There are third-party systems, like Kontagent and others, you can use to figure our analytics. The way browsers work... you can't instrument every action in the game without making a lot of weird calls to those services. It makes it really difficult to get a beautiful picture of what is really happening with all your users. When you get into analytics, you find there are a lot of different ways to answer most questions, and some are a lot easier than others. We built our own analytics package because social games are so data driven and you really have to be able to understand where people are spending money and who is spending money.

SB: And with the big analytics packages, you have to pay per each event you want to track, and that can get really expensive.

JH: You can spend $10,000 to $15,000 a month on analytics. That sucks because then you feel limited in what you can track. With our system, it pretty much costs us nothing.

SB: We've got customer service portals, localization systems, and it's all parceled out so that if a publisher or partner wants to own a particular piece of something, or implement their own virtual currency system or something, they can.

JH: Our build systems let us press one button and get a build live within ten minutes. We've pushed out ten or fifteen live builds in a day, which makes testing very easy. We can bundle by platform, so we have iOS bundling where we can press one button and it'll bundle up an iPad version and send an email to everyone with an entitlement for that version to tell them to install the newest version.

Our localization system lets you keep a string table for all of your different language versions of the game, and it actually uses Google Translate to do the first pass translation for all of them.

We have a bunch of community tools, too. We can look up any user in the game, see all their play sessions, and see all of their transactions. Give them something if they're mad and that kind of thing. We've built a diagnostic logging system, too, which shows us in real time everyone who is logged in and lets us track all of their behaviors. There is a crash reporter that sends off a report and a call stack if there's a crash.

SB: But of course, you guys write bug-free code so that never happens.

JH: Exactly! [Laughs]

Q: Can you tell us a little about the technology in the game, especially the modifications you've made to help people get into the game quickly?

SB: There's a good lesson here about why you need to pay attention to data and pick one thing at a time and try to make it better. If you're trying to fix ten things at once with a thousand different levers, it's just not possible to infer anything relevant from the results. There are too many different variables in that equation to solve—ever.

When we launched our first Facebook game, we had a big problem—70–80 percent of people who showed up didn't want to install Unity, and they would leave forever. That's a big problem… in fact, there's no bigger problem. So we really dug into that once we had our back-end up and we knew we were getting the right kind of data and could ask the right kinds of questions. We worked carefully to turn one knob at a time to drive that number down and reduce friction. We were able to make it a very friendly, easy way to get in, and not have a big bad install screen hit you in the face and bury a file somewhere that is hard to find.

HP: When you're looking at the data, don't let the pendulum swing too far with your solution. When you look at the data and determine you have an issue, don't think, "Oh my god!" and try to go completely the other way to try to fix it. You'll fail. What I'll tell everybody is to make shifts in increments. Make sure you're asking the right questions and don't let the pendulum swing too far.

SB: It's just like tuning gameplay. If you have a bunch of levers and you change forty-nine of them and get a really awesome result, you will have no idea how you got there. You lucked out.

The nice thing about social games is you get your data back immediately. The more people you have playing, the faster you get good data. It doesn't take long to find out what is going on and test out a fix. You don't have to wait days, because you get immediate feedback. For us, it's like a stock ticker. Anything we want to track, what anyone who plays our game is doing, we can see in real time. We can know the second someone buys a specific item.

Q: How do I know what questions to ask of my analytics?

HP: It'll have different answers based on what stage of the game they are in. There's a set of questions you'll ask at the beginning. First is user acquisition. "How do we get our CPI down as low as we possibly can?" And this kind of comes down to old-timey advertising and optimizing. So there we ask, "Are we presenting the right message in the right way?"

Then once we've acquired that user, it becomes, "Where is the friction?" "What are the chokepoints?" "How much time does it take players to get from point A to point B?" If we're losing everything in the tutorial, maybe it's too wordy. Maybe it's too confusing. Then, if we're losing people after three weeks of play, "Why?" Where are they in progression? Did they just get bored with it? Or is there something in the game that's actually chasing people out?

"Why are people buying?" "Where are people spending their money?"

SB: "How often are they coming back?" If they're not coming back enough, maybe your return mechanics aren't tight enough and you need to build some more compelling loops to bring them back every day.

HP: So the critical thing is to ask questions that think of every two minutes as a vertical slice. Think carefully about what you really can change. What can you fix? Data is useless if it is not actionable, so don't ask questions if you can't do anything about the answer. Focus on actionable, strategic questions that break down play into concise increments of time. Focus there, and make sure you get that right.

HP: As game makers, to be able to give the people what they want should be something you focus on. We believe the customers know best.

Q: What advice do you guys have for game designers who are coming from the traditional space and are diving into making social games?

HP: Don't think it's easy. Don't think that you're going to get it immediately. Be willing to try a few things. Going to one GDC Online and taking some notes isn't enough. It's harder than it looks.

SB: You've got to play a lot. Study it. Respect the space. More people get that now than when we started, which was almost two years ago. There's a lot here that's different from building AAA console games, but we think there's a lot that we can bring from the console world—something that's additive. It's still pretty embryonic, what's being done with social games. There's a lot of room to run. As more folks from AAA console space get involved, they'll bring what they have, and things will get really interesting.

CHAPTER 8

Monetization Strategies

8.1 SHOW US THE MONEY

We've touched on some of the different ways games have found to make money from their users, but in this chapter we'll take a much closer look at the different monetization options available for games, social, mobile, and others. Naturally, different types of games lend themselves to different types of players and play profiles; thus, we'll need to talk about which monetization strategies are best suited to particular types of games. In recent years, the free-to-play microtransaction model has become ascendant, so we'll spend particular time on it. We'll review the most common virtual items sold in today's dominant mobile and Facebook games and peek into the design mechanics that make this model so successful. Finally we'll look at an interesting case study of a game that combines a hybrid of old and new monetization models in order to appeal to a varied audience.

8.2 CLASSIC PREMIUM DOWNLOAD MODEL

You've built a great game, you've tested it carefully, and you're ready to sell it.

Under this model, the user learns all about your game through clever pre-release marketing and PR, or they hear about it from their friends, then go to a hosted site to download it. Possibly you've linked this site to your game's Facebook page, where you advertise special deals on certain days, encourage players to invite their friends, and generally drive customer awareness by taking advantage of modern social media marketing. Perhaps you've partnered with an online retailer who has a virtual storefront, or maybe you're directly managing the download process. Either way, what we're describing is a classic premium download model. This is uncommon on Facebook (though there's no law that says it has to be that way). But Facebook aside, let's look at some of the places where this model thrives.

8.2.1 Mobile Application Stores

The mobile app stores began with a traditional near-retail model of sales. The user would buy a product with a credit card or PayPal, the vendor would take a portion (30 percent in Apple's iTunes case), and once payment cleared, the virtual good would be downloaded to the purchaser's device. A complicated legal agreement would cover what rights to the product the user would actually be purchasing. No one ever reads it, and the transaction is fairly straightforward. This is still the way the iTunes App Store works for games players might purchase for their iPad, iPhone, and so on. This is also the basic model for Android on the Google Play Store, the Amazon Appstore, and almost all of the lesser known app stores. Microsoft's Windows Phone and tablet has a similar OS-specific online storefront, and so on.

Currently, the major problem with these types of marketplaces is getting enough user mindshare to break through the white noise created by all the competition. There are literally hundreds of thousands of apps available on the iTunes store, with the number increasing every day, and many of these applications are games. Finding a particular game on the target device (your mobile phone, iPad, Windows Surface, etc.) is extremely difficult if the customer doesn't enter the marketplace with a particular name in mind. The desktop version of the store makes it slightly easier to browse the marketplace, but with such a terrific array of software available, developers are forced to claw their way toward the top of the "featured" or "Top Apps" charts if they hope to garner much attention. It's the overly crowded storefront problem all over again, just a few orders of magnitude greater.

There are a number of ways to manipulate this system to your advantage. There are tales of publishers buying enough copies of their own game to get it into the "Top Sellers" lists. Other games make deals with third-party companies who give users in-game currency in exchange for downloading a game. There's a shadowy world of quiet relationships and legal graft that has been known to help get games onto various "featured" lists, as well. Taken in aggregate, this all boils down to a strong likelihood that you will need to spend money, perhaps on several complex and indirect forms of advertising, to acquire your initial set of users. Generally speaking, building the game represents only a fraction of the cost required to get the game deployed to a significant number of customers. Raising awareness is everything in the social and mobile space now.

However, designing your game to take best possible advantage of social and organic growth elements can help keep this spend under control. If your game is socially infectious by its very nature like, say, *Words With Friends,* you may be able to drive user awareness through word of mouth. Or better still, if your game has built-in mechanisms for inviting friends to play and rewards current players for doing so, you can potentially increase your user numbers without having to "purchase" them through expensive and unreliable marketing and eventually work your way into the coveted "Top Paid Games" lists.

While an examination of iTunes is necessary, if a bit depressing, it is important to remember that iTunes isn't the only application store out there. Devoted mobile companies like ngmoco have opened up Android phone app stores—theirs is called Mobage—that seek to impose a bit of order on the fairly chaotic open platform devices. AppBrain serves a similar function, allowing users to search for Android applications by using a variety of different, and perhaps tighter, criteria. Many of the games for this platform have started adopting variants on the freemium business models we've discussed for social games, out of an effort to beat the piracy that runs rampant on the Android platform.* Even on iOS,

---

* http://www.guardian.co.uk/technology/blog/2011/mar/17/android-market-pirated-games-concerns

where piracy is a considerably smaller problem, free-to-play has emerged as a near dominant business model.

8.2.2 Steam

A similar "digital-retail" model exists and thrives for games played on the PC and Mac.
Valve Software's Steam is both a storefront and a miniature social network. Designed by
the company that created the seminal PC hits *Half-Life, Half-Life 2,* and *Team Fortress,*
Steam offers a wide array of marketplace and social features. Initially, Steam was created
to allow Valve to address technical and logistic problems associated with patching their
mega-hit *Counterstrike,* but it quickly evolved into a standard digital storefront for PC
gaming. Users can download game demos, review screenshots, see video trailers, purchase
full games, buy add-on content for games, join groups of like-minded gamers, send messages to other Steam players, and so on.

Steam also features a collection of social elements. Gamers can browse games by popularity, chat with like-minded gamers, and see what their friends are playing, all of which
serves as a type of recommendation engine, providing Steam with some level of virality.
Gamers are also able to purchase and gift games to their friends on Steam, as well as form
social groups and "clubs" accessible through the platform.

Steam processes payments tendered from customers and in return takes a portion of the
proceeds. (Valve is notoriously tight-lipped about the specifics of the income they take in
from this platform, but by all estimates, it is a great deal of money.) Users are restricted to
purchasing and playing games in their own country of residence, and prices vary by country. Game purchases are supported in USD, the Euro, Pounds Sterling, and the Webmoney
online currency. Steam (Figure 8.1) handles the patching updates for its games and facilitates

FIGURE 8.1 Valve's Steam platform for PC and Mac is both a digital storefront and a miniature
social-network. Approximately 30 million users are active on Steam, playing over 1200 different games.

user access to their purchases on multiple client machines. (For instance, a player can make one purchase, then play the game both at home and at the office.) The overall quality of the games offered on Steam is very high, with many mainstream retail releases also opting to appear on the platform. Among the hundreds of developers who support the platform are the largest and most well-known in the industry, such as Activision, Electronic Arts, Bethesda, and 2K. Moreover, Steam has demanded a high level of quality from their offerings, which makes their marketplace far less of a free-for-all. With only about 1300 games available at the time of this writing, Steam has a much more manageable noise-to-signal ratio than, for instance, iTunes. The platform makes it easy to find games, which makes it easier to sell your game on Steam.

For the most part, Steam offers a classic premium download model for PC and Mac gamers that provides fast, secure, appealing, and convenient service. While some products offered on Steam may dabble in internal monetization strategies, for the most part Steam functions as an effective marketplace for a traditional retail sales model, just without the brick-and-mortar location (and the overhead costs that go along with it).

8.2.3 Alternatives to Steam

There are a number of competitors to Steam for distributing PC games. Some of these alternatives are proprietary or cater only to games made by a particular company. Others specialize in deeply discounted software, indie games, or vintage software. None of these services come anywhere near Steam in terms of popularity, but all provide viable market-places. Moreover there are naturally some types of games for which Steam is either pro-hibitively expensive or unavailable, so these alternative services can offer access to markets that might otherwise go untouched.

Electronic Arts has recently launched Origin, their online game retailer, which seems to serve the function of an online marketplace without offering any of the social features provided by Steam. North American users can order games for their console or handheld devices, which are then shipped out via FedEx or USPS. Gamers can also directly download PC products—there are currently none offered for the Mac—both from EA and other publishers. Origin has a sufficient back catalog of offerings to make this an interesting tool to investigate, if only to see how a major publisher is approaching direct digital sales on the PC.

Direct2Drive serves as another online marketplace, where users can pick up digital copies of games for both the PC and the Mac. The Direct2Drive catalog is robust, but the download manager lacks the sophistication of Steam, and they have yet to incorporate any concept of a community. Direct2Drive is a store, not a social network, but it is a good place for PC and Mac games to get exposure to additional customers

Good Old Games has taken an old-school nerd's love of classic games and turned it into a business model. GoG offers games no longer available from retail or publisher frontline catalogs and allows users to directly download them for the PC. Games like *Fallout* (the 2D version) and classics ranging from *Alone in the Dark* to *Zork* fill out the shelves of this virtual storefront. Prices are surprisingly steep for titles that almost assuredly aren't getting play anywhere else, and community features are skinny at best, offering a few hundred forums, mostly dealing with game specific discussion. However, Good Old Games is keeping great games of the past alive and selling, and for that they deserve accolades. They also regularly offer sales that are quite a good value. Good Old Games is still accepting new titles into their storehouse, and an enterprising social game developer could likely find a way to relaunch a classic IP with a new social or mobile focus or tie-in product, and sell it through GoG.

Impulse, by Stardock, is an online store and community that once catered primarily to independent games for the international PC market. It has recently been acquired by GameStop and now serves as an online storefront for the retail behemoth, under the new name GameStop App. With a vast catalog, professional fulfillment, and the power of a vast network behind them, Impulse clearly has Steam in its sights but lacks the advanced social features or the huge member base. Still, independent game developers looking to gain exposure for their games would be well served to consider a partnership with Impulse. Given GameStop's massive resources and recent focus on promoting online games through their Kongregate, Impulse and the GameStop network is a space worth watching; it is a somewhat fragmented marketplace, but one with tentacles that reach deep into the gaming community, particularly in North America.

Gamer's Gate offers direct downloads and retains the focus on indie and lesser known games. Gamer's Gate regularly offers products at significant discounts (*Cthulhu Saves the World* for only $2.69!) but also features mainstream games like *Dead Island* or *Dragon's Age*. Users are encouraged to foster a sense of community by offering reviews and are rewarded with discounts or Blue Coins, the site's virtual currency, for helping other users with their gaming problems and for purchasing games from the site, effectively using a loyalty program to incentivize community. The site features more than 5000 games available for download.

8.3 SUBSCRIPTIONS

The subscription model, where users pay for access to a game based on the amount of time they want to spend in the game world, has its roots in the traditional mechanic of paying for server time by amount of use (such as how Compuserve and America Online used to charge for internet access, in days long past), as well as in the pay-to-partake model used by print newspapers and magazines for more than a century. The provider provides access to a service, fresh content, or both, and in return, a willing consumer agrees to pay for the time they spend using the product, typically billed in monthly or weekly increments. For the most part, the only games that offer a subscription model are those with significant back-end server components. More specifically, subscription models are largely the province of massively multiplayer online role-playing games (MMORPGs). Most MMOs historically have had a retail-side boxed component as well and then offered the first month or two of subscription "free" in the hopes that their users would get hooked. *World of Warcraft* and newer PC and console games like Sony's superhero-themed MMORPG *DC Universe Online*, are examples of this traditional subscription model, alive and well in the games sector today. It is interesting to note that Blizzard has managed to extend this subscription model to applications on mobile phones (like the *World of Warcraft* Armory App) for which they charge a smaller, additional monthly fee. While a dozen or more MMOs have launched, then subsequently reduced or dropped their subscription fees, *World of Warcraft* continues to prove on a monthly basis that if a product is compelling enough, users will pay retail, then continue to pay premium subscription fees for months or even years. However, the subscription model has all but died out for most games in recent years under the withering downward pressure put on prices by the rise of so many high-quality free-to-play games.

There are a few problems with a strict subscription model:

- The first is that relying on subscriptions forces you into providing a level of customer service that can be very costly. Blizzard, for instance, employs hundreds of *World of Warcraft* customer service representatives who work around the clock helping the lost find their way, resolving technical issues, and adjudicating petty disputes inside the game world of Azeroth. When you ask your customers to pay you an additional amount every month, customer retention becomes every bit as important as customer acquisition. Thus, the attractively regular, consistent flow of cash that comes from a well-managed subscription model is only sustainable alongside a regular, consistent expenditure on customer service.

- Subscription models can limit the total amount of money you can get from a user in a given timeframe. If a game is solely subscription based, there's a finite cap on the amount of money a user will pay (say, $15 per month). But even using a blended model, in which the user pays a subscription fee and can also opt in to other ways of being monetized, there are risks. If you employ a subscription model, you're asking your players to pay you some amount up front. This makes it that much less likely they'll pounce on your juicy in-game monetization offers. Some users would happily give you far more than what you request in a subscription price, but others would quickly grow resentful if they pay for access and then are refused access to the better parts of your game unless they reach again for their pocketbook. Thus, depending on your game, you might be better served charging nothing up front, so that players can save their money for in-game purchases, which might serve to be more addictive for them and thus more profitable for you.

- Payment systems are complicated for subscription models. You're forced either to partner with a third-party provider who will handle billing, dispute resolution and refunds, etc. or to provide these services yourself, which may or may not be a smart strategy for keeping your margins high. Billing systems are complex enough that they command books unto themselves. And as Sony can attest, security is paramount when you're storing user credit cards and other personal information. A failure or breach could end up costing you millions.

8.4 FREEMIUM

Free-to-play or *freemium* models, which allow users to play the game without cost and instead encourage them to pay for items or services in an *a la carte* in-game fashion, are the standard for the Flash-based games found on most social networks and have rapidly become the standard for most mobile products with much depth. This collection of models (the specific variations get byzantine and are the subject of much of the rest of this book) is also becoming ever-more common on the PC, and even on consoles (i.e., Xbox LIVE and PlayStation Network). Let's look at some of the major ways you can make money from users when the core game play is offered for free.

8.4.1 Sell Time

Looked at from a certain perspective, time is the most commonly sold luxury in most free-to-play games. Because Western users tend to frown on the idea that people can just buy their way to victory ("pay-to-win"), many game designers have elected to make things a lot faster and easier for players who are willing to part with coin, without actually preventing free players from experiencing the same content. Thus, many freemium games use a mechanic similar to one of the following examples:

- A user may only get 12 energy an hour. Energy will be used by performing different in-game tasks. However, a user can buy more energy and avoid the one hour wait by paying $1.

- A certain required resource may only spawn or "drop" once per day, which effectively gates a user's progress. However, users have the option of purchasing more of that resource in a microtransaction, thus allowing them to continue the gameplay without experiencing the drop delay.

- Some repetitive "leveling up" tasks (i.e., build 100 houses in this area, kill twenty of this monster, etc.) that typically require scarce resources or quickly expended in-game energy can be automated or simply waved away with a small cash donation.

- Certain rewards a user might earn after a certain length of play time can be unlocked by paying with real-world currency. For example, perhaps players normally have to be a Level 20 to get a certain type of sword. An in-game monetization strategy might offer them that sword after Level 5…with a $2 donation.

- Many games allow users to speed up "grind" type mechanics, in which players increase their character's power or skill by completing a lengthy series of repetitive tasks, by selling enhancements that increase the amount of reward given for the "grind." For example, *Pocket Legends* allows users to buy potions that increase the XP (experience points) earned from each monster slain. Thus, one player may pay no money but need three hours to have their character reach a certain level. Another player might choose to spend a small amount but reach a higher level during some smaller percentage of time. This type of item is called an "accelerator."

Allowing busy users to trade money for time is very popular with users and game designers alike, because it doesn't feel as if it "breaks" the game balance. Such a trade still allows players to see new content or accomplish in-game goals without putting huge amounts of time into the game.

8.4.2 Sell Virtual Goods

The sale of virtual goods is likely the most common model for monetizing users who don't pay for the core game. From avatar item sales that can make your character look "cooler" (common in dozens of RPGs), to purchasing better guns or ammunition in *Crossfire*, to the sale of user-created items in games like *Second Life*, users have proven that they are willing to spend regularly and occasionally spend very large sums on the right kinds of virtual goods. There are different schools of thought about what kinds of items to sell, how to avoid breaking game balance, and so on. In fact, these are often some of the most heated debates among game designers. For the moment, we'll simply mention this as a top way of monetizing users with microtransactions (and occasionally not-so-micro), but a later chapter will address this topic in detail.

8.4.3 Game Content Unlocks & PDLC

For decades, games have released demos for free in an effort to convince users to buy the full product. ID Software's seminal PC game *Doom* and many of the great "shareware" products of the early 1990s used the virality of BBSs and the internet to distribute these demos and even gave away install discs containing the first few levels of gameplay. This practice is still common on Steam, Xbox, PlayStation Network, and for many PC products. Fundamentally this method of giving some of the game away but asking users to pay to unlock the rest is just a variant on the practice of asking users to pay for content.

The strict division between a demo and a full game is beginning to dissolve, though. Instead of making the user's choice a binary one, you can offer many different bits of content and let users pick and choose which they want to unlock. For example, in a world with many different play spaces to explore, you can charge users a small fee to gain access to more advanced areas. Alternately you could allow users to play with one character class but charge them for the ability to play as characters of a different type. *Pinball FX* on the Xbox gives the core pinball experience away but asks players to buy different "tables" upon which they might continue their game. New songs are available for a small charge in *Rock Band*, as are certain pay-to-play side missions in games like *Dragon Age*.

Additional content of various sorts is often available for download outside of the original or core game "package." Such content often goes by the moniker of paid downloadable content (PDLC), but there is usually no good design reason that the content must be downloaded separately. This is typically an artifact of old-school technical limitations on size (which can bloat download times). Often, however, development teams will build additional content for their games after the initial product has launched, thus offering the player an additional reason to "stick with" the game. PDLC can be a great incentive for users to spend a bit more time with your game and consequently to give you a few more of their dollars. But remember that PDLC can also have a downside. Some game developers have experienced backlash from angry customers who paid extra for content they felt should have been included as part of their initial purchase. Early experiments with DLC were filled with regular missteps, from Bethesda's "horse armor" for *Oblivion,* to Capcom's PR misstep in charging for content already contained on the disc for *Street Fighter IV.* If you charge an initial entry fee into your game, be sure that your PDLC offers something additional, extra, and fun, and feels like it adds great value for your customer.

In a world where initial content is often offered for free, however, the possibilities for PDLC expand substantially, if only because of the reduced user expectations. We recommend contextualizing the locked content within the game fiction in a way that makes the game experience more immersive; also, avoid inflaming your customers' ire by blatantly reminding them that you are shaking them down for extra money. For example, a fictional gatekeeper character who demands a tribute of in-game currency before allowing the user's character to pass into the new area can help situate the act of paying for content inside the framework of the game, as opposed to feeling like an intrusive external force sticking its hand into the user's wallet.

Several games have found a great deal of success with PDLC in recent years, particularly on the console. *Rock Band* proved to the world that (at least for a year or so) groups of friends would get together every weekend and pay $3 per song to download new music and "rock out" with their friends. *Magic: The Gathering: Duels of the Planeswalkers* sold booster packs of digital Magic cards for nearly the same price they charged for tangible cards in stores.

The mobile market has also found success in this trend. Dozens of mobile publishers have offered additional paid content for their games, enticing users repeatedly to buy just a little more of what they need to expand their game experience. An advantage of building and releasing downloadable content for your game is that it keeps the game fresh in your users' minds. The news and PR stories associated with the announcement and release of new content reminds lapsed users of the game and attracts the attention of those who may have missed the game on its initial release. Perhaps more importantly, for any of the distributions with a "Top Downloads" or "Most Popular" type sorting mechanic, from the Apple iTunes store to XBLA, the new downloads from users who want the PDLC can resurrect an older title from the graveyard and bring it back to the top of the charts. Frontline game sales almost always spike when a PDLC is released.

A good rule of thumb is that for every five people playing your game, you can count on no more than one of them purchasing your DLC. (A 20 percent attach rate for downloadable content is considered quite good.) And please note, these sorts of attach rates are for traditional retail or console products, games in which the user has already made a considerable financial investment. So before investing heavily in creating DLC, it pays to have a thorough understanding of your user base. If your game has an install base of a million users, spending an additional $2–3 million in developing and testing for downloadable content that might sell for $2 per copy…well, you can do the math. However, for games with a pervasive world, a user base that remains engaged for months, and in-game mechanics that promote social-stickiness (like prestige gear that can only be found in unlocked zones), this kind of investment might make financial sense. Note that PDLC attach rates seem to be highly dependent upon the date of DLC release, and the sweet spot for rolling out additional content varies from platform to platform. So do your homework to determine the ideal time after launch to offer something new to your customers.

8.4.4 Cover Charge

One interesting hybrid approach to the free-to-play model that has begun to gain traction recently is the practice of allowing users to download the game free but then mandating that they spend a small amount of money before they are actually allowed to play. This money is then converted into in-game currency, such that the developer is basically guaranteed at least a minimum spend from each user. This is the equivalent of forcing users to pay a cover charge to enter a nightclub but then guaranteeing them two "free" drinks once they are inside. *Dust 514,* a recent FPS game by CCP, the developers behind the highly successful MMO *Eve Online,* has recently announced this model for their PlayStation 3 sku.* The model provides a way of offering the game for free but still guaranteeing that only serious users investigate the product, while at the same time bolstering at least the initial intake of revenue.

8.4.5 Sell Your Players' Eyes

Do you remember the scene in *Blade Runner* where Rutger Hauer visits the Chinese eye designer? Unfortunately the way you'll get to do this won't be nearly as cool, but on the bright side, you're much less likely to end up the victim of a psychotic Replicant. If your game has a great number of users, their time and attention has value. You can sell advertising as a way of deriving value from users who want to play your game for free. You'll need to make a deal with someone who serves up ads, then integrate their platform for ad hosting and display into your software. Luckily almost all of the platforms available for social game release now natively support these sorts of features. iAd Network is highly regarded as an advertising platform from Apple for the iOS. Android offers a variety of ad network services, from AppFlood to Mobclix.

On the web, the rules for in-application advertising vary by social network. While Facebook and the other social network creators will be more than happy to help you show ads *alongside* your app, Facebook itself will not serve up ads for display *inside* an app. However, Hi5 and other networks do offer an application for facilitation of advertising services.

The amount of revenue you eventually receive, as measured per view, will likely be quite small from advertising to customers; particularly on mobile games, this strategy isn't likely to generate tremendous revenue on its own unless you're able to command an *Angry Birds* number of users. However, it can be a way of supplementing income, or even better, of encouraging already converted users to purchase a "premium" (i.e., more expensive) version of the game.

8.4.6 Offer Walls

As discussed earlier, it costs money to attract a new user to a product. Yet a game can't survive without generating new users, so developers are usually willing to spend almost anything up to the CPI, in order to get new users installing their game. In response to this

---

* http://www.gamesindustry.biz/articles/2011-07-11-dust-514-requires-cover-charge-from-ps3-players

FIGURE 8.2 *Empires & Allies* makes use of an offer wall where users can accept special offers in exchange for virtual currency. Offer walls are a good way to monetize users who may be unwilling or unable to pay directly.

need, both social and mobile games have adopted the concept of the offer wall (Figure 8.2) in which users are rewarded with in-game currency for following offers served up by other application developers (or outside advertisers).

These may often be for completely unrelated types of products—DirectTV and Netflix ads are common, for example—or they may be for different (and sometimes even competing) games. Because these ads generally aren't targeted to the player's interests in the way that, say, Facebook ads are, these offers typically have very low value for the player. Since they are entirely an opt-in way for players to get currency for the game they like, however, they persist. Here's how an offer wall typically works:

- A developer (A) of a new game offers anyone who gets them an install $1.

- Another developer (B) integrates an offer wall into their successful game.

- Developer B offers to give their users $0.50 worth of in-game currency if they click through and install one of the products listed on the offer wall.

- When the user does, A pays B $1, B gives the user $0.50 and keeps the rest, A gets an install, *and* their application rises on the popularity charts.

In the past, TapJoy offered the most active and established offer walls, but in recent months they have moved away from the social networks in favor of focusing on mobile offerings.

Other, shadier dealers have been known to trick users into enrolling in expensive cell-phone plans or into installing types of application software that turn out to be very difficult to uninstall. Facebook and Zynga both have drawn fire (and several lawsuits in California) for allegedly being complicit in these sorts of "ScamVille" offers, but by 2011 these behaviors seemed to have been largely curbed. Still, there is a variety of controversy surrounding the specifics of using offer walls, and developers and users both should tread with caution, particularly on the Android platform, where malware is more common.

8.4.7 Popup Ads

In addition to offer wall install ads, games can serve up other types of advertising in an effort to monetize users. For example, when entering Digital Chocolate's *Zombie Lane*, users occasionally are offered an ad for a "free" in-game consumable if they agree to play a Flash advertisement (which is also a game, of sorts) that is promised to last only twenty seconds. This practice has raised some eyebrows, as it appears to act as a distraction, enticing users *away* from playing the game itself. It is a bit like standing in the front entrance of a McDonald's restaurant and offering customers a quarter off their Big Mac if they agree to take a bite of a Taco Bell taco. Nonetheless, these sorts of pop-up advertisements are ways to increase indirect monetization of users, though they may also increase user frustration.

8.4.8 Ad Placement

Beyond ad hosting and the various types of offer walls we discussed above, there are other ways to sell your non-paying users' eyeball time. Several developers have successfully integrated product placement into their games. This is common in sports and racing console titles but has recently begun appearing in social games, as well. Zynga, for example, has integrated Farmer's Insurance blimps into *FarmVille* and has partnered with convenience store chain 7-11 for a variety of promotions centered around a campaign entitled, "Buy, Earn, Play!" Of course, this type of product placement in entertainment isn't particularly new, but with the notable decline in television viewership (or, at least, commercial viewership, thanks to the advent of the DVR) and newspaper sales over the last several years, traditional advertisers for companies like Farmer's are taking a closer look at social media. Moreover, since many traditional media brands are conservative with their brand image, the friendlier, less-violent, less "adult" themes of many social games make them appealing to advertisers. Companies that would shy away from games like *Mortal Kombat* or *Call of Duty* might jump at the chance to advertise in *FarmVille* or *Angry Birds*. Indeed, some of the cross-brand promotional titles, like *Angry Birds Star Wars,* could be seen as extensions of this notion, just for brands that both bring users to the table. (See Figure 8.3.)

8.4.9 Advertainment

For years now, the occasional ad campaign has taken the benefits of in-game advertising so much to heart that it creates a stand-alone "game," whose primary job is to function as advertising. In this model, the game is usually offered for free, or at least very cheaply, in exchange for the brand awareness its creators hope the game will create. One of the earliest of these was Dominos Pizza's strange 1989 Commodore 64 and DOS game called *Avoid*

FIGURE 8.3 Product placement inside games can be a lucrative addition to freemium models. Zynga has courted traditional companies like Farmer's Insurance by offering them in-game access to a fresh market.

the Noid, in which the user played as a pizza boy who had to escape the pizza-wrecking attacks of Domino's claymation mascot, the Noid. This product was successful enough to spawn a sequel for the Nintendo Entertainment System called *Yo! Noid.* Later, companies like Doritos and Burger King funded games that were given away free to willing users. (These advertainment games can take on a life outside of the original marketing endeavor. For instance, Burger King's Xbox line of games, *Sneak King* and *Big Bumpin',* are reported to have sold more than 3 million copies.)

Of course, as a game designer, selling out your game to hawk fast food may not be particularly appealing, but developing software of this type can be an excellent way to hone your game engine and tech or to experiment with different user models. Moreover, the exercise of creating games that target a specific market for a particular purpose has great value in growing a team, and since product placement in a game can help offset development costs, it may be helpful to consider the possibility for advertisements in your game, even if the game is not completely an advertainment piece.

8.4.10 Motivate LTNV

As we've hinted at above, there are other ways to derive indirect value from your users, even if they don't pay you a penny or click on a single ad. When users invite their friends, they increase their lifetime total network value (LTNV). Even if particular players never give you a dime, there's always the chance that their friends will spend money in your game or view ads. This is the heart of why the social element of games matters and is at the heart of terms like "virality" and "organic growth." Thus, you should always seek to build game mechanics that reward (or mandate) that users invite friends into your game. Games like *Empires and Allies* ask users to "appoint" friends to key positions in their "management staff"; in *Desktop Defender,* users are rewarded for inviting friends (and rewarded further when their friends actually start playing). Allow your users to send out "help" requests when they must defeat difficult enemies or encourage users to give "gifts" to their friends that those friends can use once they're in-game. Ultimately motivating players to invite their friends through your game mechanic increases the viral nature of the game, which leads to user acquisition, which in turn is the quickest way to generate more revenue. Behaviors that maximize this motivation lead to a higher LTNV and thus a more profitable game. In general, to increase LTNV social games should do everything they can to build in mechanics that incentivize users to invite their friends to play.

8.5 PLAY THE NUMBERS

The previous section is not an exhaustive list of the varied ways you can make money from non-paying users. Certainly innovative developers are coming up with fresh ideas every day. However, the right monetization strategy may not require payment in the beginning to yield you financial success in the end. However, we've reviewed a number of models that require a near-staggering number of users before any financially satisfying results are produced. Never forget that while individual metrics differ from game to game and platform to platform, the sad fact is that only 3–5 percent of users ever pay at all in most free-to-play microtransaction games, and the individual per-user impression value for ads is tiny. If your game is able to monetize at higher rates, congratulations! You're doing something right. If upon initial launch it isn't, then you've got a long road of studying KPIs and tuning ahead.

But there is yet another way you can play the numbers, and that is to pay close attention to your individual users. Not all users are created equal; in fact, they are as varied in profitability as they are in their age, ethnicity, and gender. One phenomenon that companies like Giant Interactive, King.com, and Zynga have capitalized on is the knowledge that only a small percentage of their total users account for a disproportionate amount of the total revenue they collect. Somewhere under 0.5 percent of a social game's average user base is likely to give you far more money than is average. (As mentioned, the term favored by designers for this type of user is the "whale," which isn't intended to be as impolite as it sounds.) By using metrics properly, you can ferret out which of your customers fall into this category. These are the players you most want to cultivate and reward. Just as Vegas offers complementary rooms for their big spenders and strip bars keep a VIP section for their best customers, so too should you determine a valuable reward system for those players who have shown themselves to be most willing to reward you.

Zynga noticed this phenomenon and, according to many sources[*], formed a private club for their top spenders called the Zynga Platinum Purchase Program. This program allows users to buy credits in higher than normal amounts and offers discounts on Zynga's virtual currencies. Zynga has remained tight-lipped about this service, perhaps because it has already received some negative publicity equating Zynga to a "dealer" servicing their "addicts." Despite this sort of sensational melodrama, however, the core business principle is sound. By gathering metrics or using some of the programs built into certain platforms (like hi5's SocioPay), smart social or mobile game developers can tailor their offerings to a particular customer subset. Not interested in paying anything? We'll serve you up

[*] http://www.insidesocialgames.com/2010/09/10/zyngas-platinum-purchase-program/

more ads, and the Farmer's Blimp will visit your farm once per day (or hour, or minute). Comfortable with spending $3 per day? Let's make sure to give you game challenges that encourage sustained, daily spending at that level. Comfortable dropping $60 on some new in-game gear? Perhaps we should match you with other users who have formed a guild outfitted in only the finest that money can buy. By studying your users' pay patterns, you can custom tailor the game experience to them. This requires smart analysis of the various metrics, as well as creative, flexible game design, but sustained efforts in this area can radically boost your revenue.

8.6 COMBINATIONS

"But Tim, why can't we just do it all?" you may ask. The answer is, maybe you can! Many of the above models work well in concert, allowing developers to appeal to a variety of users and monetize them in various ways. As social games evolve in sophistication, the number that rely on only a single one of these methods will continue to shrink. For example, Activision's *Call of Duty* franchise (which could be said to have evolved into a "social game" due solely to the strength of its multiplayer community) has begun incorporating both a traditional premium sales model, the PDLC model, and a subscription model for users who want advanced functionality in their multiplayer experience.

Let's look at another title that has managed to incorporate several different monetization strategies into a fun, compelling little package that takes the strength of a hardcore game design and offers it to a wide market on mobile devices.

8.7 CASE STUDY: *HUNTERS EPISODE ONE* AND DIFFERENT MONETIZATION METHODS

Hunters Episode One (Figure 8.4), by U.K. Developer Rodeo Games, is a fiendishly addictive turn-based tactical game in the tradition of *Xcom, Fallout, Jagged Alliance,* and *Squad Leader.* Released for the iOS in early 2011 and later for the Android, Hunters features a robust character advancement backend, complete with perks, loot collection, and plenty of high-tech weaponry and gear. Rodeo released a sequel for the iOS later. A high-performance 3D engine and beautiful background artwork bring to life the gritty sci-fi fare of ruined space stations, arctic military bases, and the villains that inhabit them (Figure 8.5). In *Hunters,* you assemble a squad of mercenaries, outfit them with guns and armor, then go into drop-sites to hunt down enemy leaders, retrieve alien artifacts, and defend reactors. The pacing is tense, and the gameplay is deep enough for you to consider firing arcs and movement points, while accessible enough not to devolve into tactical minutiae.

Aware of the difficulties of monetizing the game on the crowded mobile marketplace, the team at Rodeo Games implemented several different monetization models.

First, they offered the game for premium download at a price point that set expectations for high quality ($4.99). Second, by appending "Episode One" to the title, they immediately indicate to the user that this will be an episodic game and thus will undoubtedly feature additional PDLC in the future. (In fact, this ended up being a stand-alone sequel.)

Third, they built an in-game currency system based on credits (Figure 8.6). Players get credits for successfully completing missions and for looting the corpses of fallen foes.

FIGURE 8.4   *Hunters Episode One* is a game where high-tech bounty hunters are engaged in turn-based combat. *Hunters* was released in 2011 on the iPhone and iPad.

FIGURE 8.5   *Hunters* features a high-quality 3D engine, great artwork, and a "just one more turn" design mechanic well suited to mobile devices.

Players also get credits for accomplishing secondary mission goals (i.e., "No teammates were killed") and for selling salvaged weapons and armor. The credits are used to buy newer, better equipment and to hire higher level, better-skilled mercenaries. In addition to earning credits, players who are eager to advance at a quicker-than-average pace, or who find themselves a few thousand credits short of buying that new flamethrower, can purchase credits through an in-game app store.

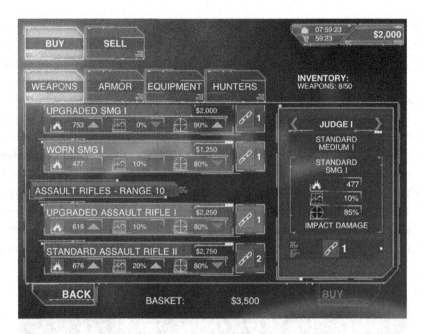

FIGURE 8.6 Deep RPG-style equipment, inventory, weapons, and talents available for in-game purchase give *Hunters* a good deal of replayability and support the in-game currency.

FIGURE 8.7 Players can earn credits by completing missions and looting the corpses of dead enemies, but can also buy currency through in-game purchases.

Credits are sold in a variety of denominations, from $0.99 for 20,000 credits, to a discounted offer of 1,000,000 credits for $16.99. These credit purchases occur in-game, so the user is subject only to a minimal break from the game fiction (Figure 8.7). By designing this feature to be optional, *Hunters* caters to players who are comfortable spending money to save time but stops short of alienating users less reluctant to part with their real-world dollars. And by offering credit packages at a variety of price points, they appeal to users with many different levels of disposable income. Since they establish a price point of 20,000 credits for $1, then give discounts for purchasing more credits, they convey to the user a sense of getting a bargain by spending more money. Understanding this type of behavioral psychology is important to motivating beneficial purchase habits in your customers.

For those users who have more time than money, *Hunters* has implemented an offer wall that allows players to "Tap Here to Win Prizes!" These are presented on the mission selection screen, which helps integrate the wall into the game fiction in a way that feels minimally intrusive. Each of these offers serves up an advertisement for an online "deal," rewarding participating users with a few thousand credits (about $0.25 worth) for installing the application. With this system, *Hunters'* user base can happily tap up enough credits to outfit their mercenaries with better rocket launchers and power armor (Figure 8.8).

While it is not technically a social game and currently features no multiplayer element, *Hunters* delivers a number of quality examples of successful monetization (Figure 8.9). By this writing, the game has been translated to several mobile and tablet platforms and sold

FIGURE 8.8 *Hunters* beautifully integrates the concept of an offer wall into the game menu, monetizing users who may not be interested in purchasing in-game currency.

FIGURE 8.9 *Hunters* sells itself as a premium download game on iTunes App Store, but it also monetizes users through an offer wall and with in-game currency purchases.

terrifically in more than a dozen countries. And though it is sold using a premium download model, the Rodeo team combines the promise of episodic content, in-game microtransactions, a custom currency promoted at cleverly designed price points, and an offer wall feature, all nicely integrated into the game fiction and menu. This multifaceted combination of monetization models illustrates the many ways a game can monetize a user.

8.8 WHY YOU SHOULD AVOID GIVING PLAYERS REAL MONEY

Gambling might seem like the most obvious way to make money from social and mobile gamers. For the house, some margin of win is guaranteed. And the human monkeys have shown that they love to pull the lever and watch the wheels spin in the hopes of winning *something*, even when they understand just how unlikely that win might be. Gambling is popular, its revenues are predictable, and even the simplest of games seem to attract startling numbers of players. Recently Zynga has even chosen to wade into the online gambling market.

Unfortunately, as tempting as it might be to build a virtual casino on Facebook, we can't advise it. There are several games that have made money by enticing users to pay into their system in the hopes of getting real money back out of the game. Hundreds of online gambling sites have done so in the past. (Just try to find an unregistered domain with the word "Poker" in it, for instance.)

Second Life and *Small World* both allow users to create and sell virtual goods to other users and convert the in-game currency back into more commonly traded currencies. These are not gambling games, though. *Second Life* gives users the ability to model and craft three-dimensional goods, and even keep the copyright for their designs, then sell replicas of these creations to other users who can use the creations to outfit their virtual houses. While it uses its own form of currency, called Linden dollars (L$), these dollars can be exchanged for US dollars and other currencies. *Second Life*'s GDP has been reported as being as high as $64 million. *Blizzard* has even dabbled with the idea, suggesting that they might allow users to sell user-created content (Starcraft maps) for real money, and of course, there is *Diablo*'s real money auction house. So why isn't this a good idea?

There are a variety of legal complications, in almost every territory from which your users might be able to access your game, as soon as they start being able to make real money. The first concern is that it becomes very easy for your users to become litigious. The minute they feel that you are not giving them money that is rightfully theirs, you could find yourself in a complex, multiparty lawsuit. Rather than simply pestering you for a refund of their purchase price, you might instead find yourself accused of fraud or worse.

- Most countries have laws that state that when you create a marketplace for selling goods, you retain a level of responsibility for those goods. Just as the owner of a shopping mall isn't allowed to turn a blind eye to the water pipe shop that is actually dealing drugs, game developers who allow the sale of virtual goods for real money have a legal obligation to police what is sold. If a user creates a painting of child pornography and sells it or "borrows" the logo of a popular clothing brand, and your game doesn't actively prohibit or discipline this type of activity properly, you can be held legally responsible.

- Gambling laws change with the mood of the times and the boundary of the country in which the player resides. For example, *Poker Stars* was a huge online gambling game operating for almost a decade and offering prizes worth as much as $11 million. In April 2011, the U.S. Attorney's Office for New York seized and shut down the servers that ran the site for allegedly being in violation of federal bank fraud and money laundering laws.

- Facebook and other social networking sites prohibit games considered to promote gambling (and even advertisements for those games). While *Second Life* certainly isn't considered a gambling game, the line gets blurry quite quickly when users are able to translate in-game currency into real-life money.

Each of these might be a surmountable problem on its own. But unless this is your full time focus *and* you have the resources to fight the numerous legal battles almost certain to ensue, we recommend staying away from this particularly problematic area of gaming. Don't let your users take money back out of the game.

Nearly every country from which your users might access your game has some sort of law regulating online gambling. And it isn't just the government who can make use of these laws. Once your game ventures out of the realm of fantasy and into the real-world genre of gambling, the problems multiply along with the possible revenue.

Our lawyers have asked us to reiterate here that we're not attorneys, and that nothing in this section or this book should be construed as legal advice. However, if you are going to go against our advice as game makers and let users take money out of the game, we strongly encourage you to seek counsel from an attorney with experience in the realm of online commerce. If you're serious about entering the realm of online gambling, you should begin to cultivate a cave of hungry lawyers raised on rare meat and get ready for fights with the authorities, customers, and your competitors.

8.9 TRANSITIONING MODELS

If your initial business model isn't working, can you change your model? Of course! Pivot! In fact, the industry has seen quite a bit of this in recent years, as game companies have moved from subscription models to free-to-play models or supplemented their traditional retail presence with free-to-play offerings. We've even seen classic game development houses tack subscription fees onto retail games for "premium" online services.

One of the best publicized of these adaptations was the shift made by Turbine with their *Dungeons & Dragons Online* (DDO) and *Lord of the Rings Online: Shadows of Angmar* (LOTRO) games. Turbine took both games from retail-plus-subscription models to free-to-play models in the last few years, to great fanfare and even greater success. Turbine ultimately elected to stop charging for subscription and began releasing the games for free, with a new, internal microtransaction model that allowed users to gain access to additional features, new areas of content, and the like by making in-game purchases.

Their first MMO to move to a free-to-play model was *Dungeons & Dragons Online*, an action based RPG game thematically based on the venerable pen and paper game. The game was released for Windows PCs in late 2006 and published by Atari.

FIGURE 8.10 *Dungeons & Dragons Online* by Turbine offers players a chance to play an action-focused PC MMO version of the classic pen and paper role-playing game. DDO moved from a subscription model to a free-to-play model in 2009.

In late 2009, DDO became free to play (Figure 8.10). Users were offered three different choices of sales model. The "VIP" players who continued to subscribe to the game (or who had purchased a lifetime subscription) were given 500 Turbine points per month, could access all races, classes, and game spaces, could play up to ten different characters, were granted immediate login at peak times, and received the highest level of customer service. "Premium" and "Free" players each received reduced versions of these various offerings, unless they elected to purchase and spend Turbine points.

With *Lord of the Rings Online,* Turbine built a compelling 3D adaptation of J.R.R. Tolkien's epic fantasy work and styled it as a subscription-based MMO, sold as a boxed product through classic retail channels. The game underwent a fairly complex and turbulent development process and was released to acclaim from both gamers and the press in April 2007. Turbine released several major updates to the game, the most notable of which was the *LOTRO: Mines of Moria.* This full-bodied expansion was sold at retail stores and as PDLC and received critical acclaim for its story-driven gameplay and attention to the details of the original source material.

Based on the tremendous success Turbine had in switching models with DDO, they elected to make LOTRO free to play in September 2010, moving away from their previous subscription cost of $9.99 per month (with an up-front $50 retail purchase of the box component). They adopted a tiered model similar to what they used with DDO. Within a month, the *Lord of the Rings* player base more than doubled, and in January of 2011 Turbine announced that their revenues with free to play were triple that of their retail and subscription products (Figure 8.11).[*]

This move was widely noted by the games industry, and soon after several other online games companies announced that they too would explore pure freemium models in the coming years. Turbine took two successful games based on popular franchises and proved

---

[*] http://www.gamasutra.com/view/news/32322/Turbine_Lord_of_the_Rings_Online_Revenues_Tripled_As_FreeToPlay_Game.php

FIGURE 8.11 *Lord of the Rings Online* gave players a chance to play in a richly detailed version of J.R.R. Tolkien's classic fantasy world. LOTRO more than tripled their monthly revenue after moving from a subscription model to a free-to-play model based around microtransactions.

that they could be even more successful when they allowed users to choose how much to spend.

8.10 WHICH MODELS FIT BEST FOR WHICH TYPE OF GAME?

While there is no perfect prescription for success, some game genres do tend to lend themselves to certain types of business models. In this section, we'll spend some time discussing the types of monetization strategies you should consider wedding to certain types of games to maximize your chance for delighted users and satisfactory returns.

8.10.1 Role-Playing Games

RPGs are well suited toward microtransactions, selling features, and expansion packs. Typically RPGs give the player a vast game world (or at least a world that appears to be so), in which they create a single character or a party of characters, then spend the majority of their time exploring the world. Along the way, most RPGs take the player's character along an epic and transformative journey, from a lowly novice who spends his time slaying rats or bunnies to a heroic and lordly grandmaster who flies, teleports, battles huge demons, etc. This kind of game progression and a reward structure based on empowering characters (often given a unique name by the player) personalizes the game experience, and thus incentivizes the player to spend on any improvements made directly to that character. The player character effectively acts as an avatar for the user in the game world, and the degree to which players identify with their characters can be very deep indeed. Players especially seem to favor items that distinguish their characters from one another, creating a sense of individuality within the game world. Thus, anything that is rare or unique gives the player bragging rights and a way to feel special inside the game world. Frequently these items can even be merely cosmetic, particularly if the game has some online or social components that let users see one another's avatars.

Selling convenience features also tends to work well in RPGs. Because the players often spend a tremendous amount of time in the game, anything that speeds up the less desirable play experiences or reduces the time they must spend on tasks that distract them from leveling up their characters tend to be popular. For example, you could sell users the ability to carry more items (such as by offering them a magic bag) so that they don't have to return to a central location and sell back their "loot" as often. Or perhaps users want to change key features about their character (like race or gender) months or years after the characters are established. This is an easy and wholly optional service for which some players will eagerly pay and other players will never even consider (but not suffer for its existence).

Alternately subscription models have traditionally been popular for online MMORPGs, but these are waning as of late. (Okay, they are all but dead, with a very few exceptions.) There are several problems with the subscription model, but the most notable of these is that users can only be monetized to the amount of the subscription if subscriptions are the only monetization mechanism in the game. Beyond the artificial spending limit created by a subscription model, the wealth of high-quality, free-to-play options that now exist in this genre suggests that the game you release should be of incredibly high quality or somehow markedly unique to attract users with so many other (cheaper) options.

Role-playing games tend to be good candidates for PDLC, as well. Since these kinds of games often focus on exploring the game world, it is a reasonable leap to offer users access to new areas, filled with new monsters to kill and new treasures to take. In fact, this has been the most common monetization scheme (after the initial retail release) for most MMORPGs for the last ten years. New game spaces tend to take large amounts of data to represent, so large "expansion packs" are commonly sold as PDLC. As streaming technologies improve and as bandwidth increases, it seems likely that more games will begin to "background download" new content as it is released, then conduct the transaction required to access it entirely in the game world using in-game currency. (Indeed, some games already do this.) This alteration to the way the content is installed and sold can drastically improve user conversion rates by reducing friction.

8.10.2 Turn-Based Building Games

Building games are among the most popular types of games on the current social networks. These games tend to focus on letting the user build up farms, cities, military bases, and the like. Almost without exception, these games focus on lightweight design elements and the sharing of materials required to build new structures or units. Games like *FarmVille*, *CityVille, Empires and Allies, Ravenwood Fair, Kingdoms of Camelot,* and *FrontierVille* have at least elements of this gameplay. Originally this type of game was pioneered by *Sim City, Little Computer People,* and the *Sims* franchise. While these games have found some success in traditional retail models, as well as by selling expansion packs, they are now most commonly known for utilizing the microtransaction model, by which extra energy is sold to users. This is a specific subset of microtransactions in which the user can pay to keep playing, rather than be forced to wait for their energy to return, or pay to bypass a time-consuming task. We'll treat this model in far greater detail and address the specific nuances of the design of this kind of microtransaction in a later chapter, but suffice to say that if you're inclined to build a game of this sort, you've got some excellent models to study and some tough competition to beat.

8.10.3 Simulation Games

Simulations are usually best suited toward single-purchase models or the selling of expansion packs that offer the user new content inside the game world. For example, *Pinball FX* on the Xbox LIVE Arcade platform sells users new pinball tables to keep the experience fresh. Sports games have generally focused on a straight retail model, though those with RPG characteristics (like Electronic Arts' *College Football*) have dabbled with feature sales (allowing users to quickly "train" their athletes for a small fee).

However, like the rest of the games business, many games of this type are starting to explore freemium microtransaction models. A number of Facebook sports simulation games (like *Top Eleven Football Manager* by Nordeus and *FIFA Online* by Electronic Arts) use a traditional in-game microtransaction model. However, since many simulation games focus on action (car racing, real-time sports, etc.), the traditional social-game microtransaction model doesn't tend to work as well without some design tweaks, in particular, because it can be disruptive to ask the user to stop racing or running after the ball long enough to decide to buy something. Unless there is a compelling mechanic that allows users to improve their performance between games or before the next match (like a season or training mechanic), it's hard to get them interested in anything other than moving on to the next event. Thus, most simulation games that rely on microtransactions adopt an RPG-like focus on character stat advancement.

Several racing or driving simulation games, like *Need for Speed: World* by Electronic Arts, feature freemium models. This online version of the street-racing franchise allows users to use microtransactions to unlock new cars to race using their in-game currency, SpeedBoost.

8.10.4 Virtual Worlds

Virtual worlds typically focus on user creation and socialization as their primary activities. This focus makes them well suited toward free-to-play models in which users are sold virtual objects they can use to outfit their personal spaces or to create new, personalized creations. Selling users the ability to send one another gifts has proven popular in some virtual world games. Since many virtual world games also feature user avatar characters, these games are good candidates for selling cosmetic items that let users augment those characters. However, since these sorts of games rarely focus on character improvement or "leveling up," much of the performance-enhancing gear popular in RPGs tends to be less so in these sorts of games. Games like *Habbo Hotel, Second Life,* and *Small World* all fall into this category. Thus far, few true virtual worlds have been highly popular on mobile clients (though simple chat with avatars is pretty similar) but there's no reason not to expect this market segment to grow. Indeed, at least a few developers have built mobile client interfaces for games like *Second Life.*

8.10.5 Non-Persistent Action and RTS Games

This catch-all category started out by offering that most familiar and basic of microtransactions, the pay-for-play model in which users inserted a quarter each time they wanted to continue playing, and the game gave them a few extra turns or lives. Arcades set the standard, but it's rare to see their model emulated anymore. Instead, most non-persistent action games tend to sell content pack upgrades. *Trials HD* is one such example on Xbox LIVE Arcade (Figure 8.12). *Trials* uses leaderboards very effectively for social stickiness and expands the initial offering with *Big Thrills* and *Big Pack* track offerings sold as PDLC.

Desktop Tower Defender on Facebook, a tower defense game from Kixeye, nicely blends real-time strategy and non-persistent action. The game uses a classic dual-currency model, in which a player purchases new tower types (which convey new abilities during gameplay). Purchases happen between games, so the monetization doesn't interfere with the gameplay (Figure 8.13). The result is that the gameplay remains fast paced, while still allowing the Facebook standard free-to-play plus microtransaction model to work.

Games like *Windup Knight* and *Temple Run* on the mobile side have moved terrific numbers of units and seem to have effectively managed to do well offering a variety of microtransactions that allow users to survive longer or rack up higher scores.

League of Legends by Riot Games is another example of a wildly successful RTS game (technically a "Multi-player Online Battle Arena" or MOBA) that focuses heavily on PvP (player versus player) combat, set in a colorful fantasy world where two teams compete for dominance of a particular map. Each character plays the role of a "summoner" who controls a champion avatar. The game is free to play but offers an in-game store from which users can purchase virtual goods through microtransactions (Figure 8.14). Summoners can unlock new types of champions, buy new cosmetic skins for their champions, purchase various types of boosts that help speed up the rewards earned through play, and so on. Because *League of Legends* exists independent of any dedicated platform, the developer

FIGURE 8.12 *Trials HD* captures fast paced arcade action on Xbox LIVE Arcade. *Trials* has done excellent business using a PDLC model that lets users download new tracks for a minimal price.

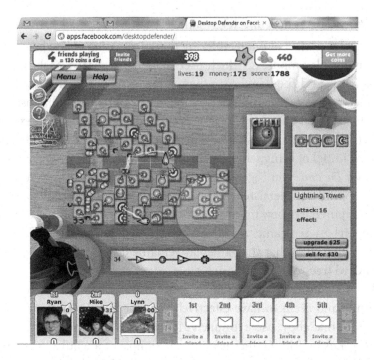

FIGURE 8.13 *Desktop Tower Defender* blends lightweight real-time strategy and fast action. For action games to effectively make use of a microtransaction model, purchases should be introduced during breaks between levels or at other natural pauses in the action.

FIGURE 8.14 A player controlling a champion fights for control of territory in *League of Legends* by Riot Games. *League of Legends* offers a fresh take on the RTS genre and has been very successful using a microtransaction model.

was forced to run its own payment systems. Players can purchase Riot Points, the game's virtual currency, by using a credit card or PayPal, or through SMS.

8.10.6 Online Trading Card Games

Collectible card games became popular in the United States in the early 1990s, when Wizards of the Coast's brilliant *Magic: The Gathering* game took high school and college campuses by storm, and made mathematician and game designer Richard Garfield a wealthy man. The game took its business model from collectible trading cards like Topps baseball cards and Garbage Pail Kids. Players could buy a starter deck for about $5, which contained enough cards to start playing, along with the basic rules of the game. Each starter deck was guaranteed to have a specific distribution of rare and very rare cards, some of which could be quite valuable. The game makers subsequently offered booster packs that featured a smaller number of cards but with a greater percentage of rare cards. Wizards of the Coast further refined this model by making subsequent issuances of new series of cards slightly more powerful than older series. Thus, players who wanted to remain competitive were all but forced to keep buying new series of cards. This model carried over nicely into dozens of online and social collectible card games, including some based on *Magic: The Gathering* (Figure 8.15). In these types of games, players can pay to download new booster

FIGURE 8.15 *Magic: The Gathering* and other collectible card games take the old business model of selling "booster packs" that have a chance of featuring rare cards and adopts it to the world of social gaming. Microtransaction card pack purchases give users a chance to improve their abilities against other players.

packs of cards to add to their collection, in the hopes of receiving a rare card that will give them an in-game advantage or that can be traded or sold to other players. The model is effectively a microtransaction model with the slight whiff of gambling (due to the randomness of the rare cards). This has proven an effective model, and Wizards of the Coast sells digital card booster packs on their web- and console-based games for the same price as they do physical trading cards.

It should be clear from this section that there are as many different hybrid approaches to monetization as there are different games. These major categories serve only to broadly invite discussion and rumination on the types of business models that are most effective for certain genres of games. The more overarching point is this: Make sure that the way you intend to monetize your players fits the game design and play characteristics of the game you're making. A lack of attention to who your players are and what best integrates with your game design risks your overall revenue.

In the next chapter we'll discuss microtransactions in far greater detail, analyzing the types of virtual goods that can be sold and how they affect game design. First, though, let's check in with one of gaming's top creative designers to hear his thoughts on social gaming.

8.11 INTERVIEW WITH RYAN CLEVEN: "SOCIAL PLATFORMS"

Ryan Cleven has been making games since 1997. He has worked as a software developer, CG supervisor, game designer, and producer at companies like Radical, Mainframe, Electronic Arts, and Microsoft. He is currently a game director with Big Park Studios in Vancouver, BC.

Q: Tell us who you are and what you do?
A: My name is Ryan Cleven. I'm a creative director at Microsoft's Big Park studio. I've been making games professionally for about fourteen years, and unprofessionally for

another seven or so before that. I've made various racing games, from snow-mobile racing games, snowboard racing games, basketball games, sports games, to more driving games. They've been mostly console games. Around 2008 I started working on the only free-to-play console game I know of on the Xbox that aimed to make money off of microtransactions.

Q: *It seems to me that Xbox LIVE is very much a social platform. What sort of features do console platforms offer that could help make games more socially sticky?*

A: Xbox LIVE is definitely a social platform. It has users who have friends, who are connected to each other. One thing that more console games could leverage better is the connectivity information on LIVE to communicate with users who have been playing the game recently. The consoles communicate who is online at a given point, yes, but when you go to play any Facebook game, there it is, front and center, who among your friends plays this game. With most console games, I get this menu listing "New Game, Load Game, Multiplayer" and so on, rather than bringing my attention to my friends who have played the game. Why is it that when I log on to the game, it doesn't say immediately, "Tim played recently, and he's Level 10, and if you go level up, you can get past him"? There's very little leveraging of the social network to actually motivate and encourage people to play with each other or compete with each other or actually involve each other in game play. *Trials HD* remains to date one of the best uses of this in a console game.

Q: *Why is that?*

A: It is primarily because designers focus so much on a single user's isolated experience with the game, as opposed to looking at the game as part of a social fabric. Facebook and other social games—their business model depends on virality. This means that they haven't already gotten their $60 from you. They need you to be playing with your friends and be telling your friends about the game as much as possible. They need your friends to buy stuff, because you are not spending any money on the game up front. The console guys already got $60. Their business model does not depend on you bringing your friends, but it would definitely enhance the player experience. You would like to know who else is playing your game. That way at work, you could have that conversation over a water cooler about the game you both play. Or you could bring someone back into a game who might previously have abandoned it. From a longevity point of view, I think it is a huge feature that people are totally missing. Games that showcase players' relationships with their friends will create more energy around their game and, in the long run, better stickiness.

Q: *Are there other platforms out there that you see as being similar in that they have thus far missed some opportunities to use the social network more effectively?*

A: I think that the key point of any social graph is how much it actually impacts the player's lifestyle—their daily life cycle. Just like a compulsion loop inside a game, if you look at the loop of a person's daily life, how much is the social network affecting their daily lives? If you look at Twitter, it has a huge effect on people's daily lives, but no games are effectively using that for anything yet. Facebook affects people's lives tremendously and there are many games using it. There are games that isolate themselves to consoles or the iPhone that are not using their spaces effectively. Some games are totally failing to do this.

How many social networks is a person touching in a day that have real impact on their lives? Probably two or three, tops. That could increase, but it would also increase fragmentation and the value of each of those networks would go down. There is probably a constant you could figure out.

Q: Three years ago you told me, "The console war is over, and Apple has just won it. But Microsoft, Sony, and Nintendo don't know it yet." Do you think Apple or Android have created a real social network yet for their games?

A: No. But they can. It is within their grasp. But right now, what is the primary social network on the iPhone? There are a few of them, like Game Center that is built in to the iPhone, plus some third-party ones. Any current Apple proprietary social network doesn't have the impact on people's lives that other social networks do. Xbox LIVE, by comparison, is integrated into the actual dashboard experience of the console. Game Center is a tangential experience inside the phone. It doesn't surface your identity to the topline dashboard. It doesn't broadcast changes at the dash level. It doesn't have any kind of "toasts" or interrupts or anything that makes it part of your daily experience. I think that Apple has really dropped the ball there. So far.

Q: So when I think about the platform that knows the most about the people I interact with on an intimate level, it's clearly my phone. So why isn't anyone building games that make use of that information?

A: That information isn't easy to get access to, and there are probably privacy laws involved. Who you are phoning or text messaging isn't captured by anyone but Apple, and they aren't surfacing that to app developers. If they did actually have a strong social network substrate that could track all the messaging and make use of that, there would be a ton of stuff there—a rich social graph. The question is, how would virality then work on the device? Would you get a push from someone else to say, "Install this app?" That would be really interesting. The lack of invites, or recommendations, or gifting, is a glaring hole in the platform.

One of the key things about social games is that they establish relationships. People often think that games have to be multiplayer to be social, but they don't. Just the act of comparing my play to yours makes it social. It's a new type of relationship. My mother-in-law can come say, "I'm better than you in *CityVille*." Or, "Do you need a pink pony? I'll send you one." That she can speak to those game elements with me, and then act on them in some way, gives us a relationship based on the game and that is the social part of the game.

The iPhone is really falling down by not giving us new verbs to use to describe relationships on the device. They are relying on the apps to do that. If you think about it, "Tweeting," or "Posting," or "Friending," or 'Liking" are all verbs that are owned by someone else. If they had those kind of verbs on the device, then you could build a social network for gaming on top of it. As it is, you are going to have to use another social network.

Q: Let's talk about ways to integrate the concept of virality into game design.

A: Virality has a fundamental relationship to how people acquire your game. It means something totally different to a console game you pay $60 to get than it does to a game that is free to play and that you can have within a few seconds. Even digital download games—they cost $10–15 and have a 200 MB download. That is a lot different from something that costs no money and effectively has no download. Most Facebook free-to-play games that are successful are extremely quick to download. Their business model requires virality. It is not just something that is nice to have. The barrier to entry is low, so the results of that virality are easy to leverage. If you are considering virality in a game, you have to think about how people get into the game in order for that virality to be useful. Now that is not to say that you can't make use of virality in a more expensive game. It is more that if your business is sitting on top of virality, you make sure that the virality will translate into people actually playing your game.

So from a game design point of view, the problem is that virality and the business model are so inextricably linked. So for the game design, it's not really about virality so much as designing around a business model. The virality is about getting people around you to come and play the game. So why are you doing that? On the one hand, it's about bringing people in so they buy stuff, and on the other it's about providing the user with a good experience. Designers can leverage existing relationships, as it can be very difficult to use virality in a place that was devoid of initial relationships.

Q: What's an example of a game that would be almost impossible to make virality work in?

A: So this will sound weird, but… *World of Warcraft.*

Q: Why?

A: Because it requires such a massive personal investment. First there is the $60 initial investment and then a $15 monthly subscription, then a many-gigabyte client download. It then requires countless hours of your day just to be in the same strata as the person you want to play with. If you have been playing for three or four months, and you are level 80, and I just joined, sure, you can go create a character that is parallel to mine, but it's not at all the same experience. Because the relationship we are using is just the personal relationship; the virality has not augmented that in any way. The game you actually care about is not overlapping with mine at all because our level of experience with the game is so different. The tight relationship we have outside the game doesn't impact the play unless one of us concedes to start again. This isn't scalable. As you add people through virality, you have to keep starting over. Conversely, WOW is great at making new friends. People develop new out-of-game relationships through the play in WOW due to the exact reason virality is challenging for it.

So there is a relationship between the depth of personal investment in play and how well virality works. If you put in virality, make sure that the play puts players on similar and comparable strata so they can actually develop relationships based on the play with each other. Otherwise, the virality is not adding anything to the play. Virality typically requires shallow play, meaning that two players, regardless of how long they have been playing, have similar play experiences. That is unless you target a certain market that already has experience with the play style you're aiming for.

WOW is trying to solve some of the barrier to entry by providing free below a level or free for a time, which definitely helps. But the 3D world, with 3D navigation with extremely challenging controls will never be a numbers match to the gathering play of Facebook games, at least when it comes to virality for a very broad audience.

Q: *So, would chess be a game that could have an inherently low level of virality because the difference in player skill can be so great?*

A: Right. The difference in player skill would mean that real, meaningful virality would be almost impossible. Sure, you can invite a friend and have a nice time together, but the chess part isn't going to help you have a nice time together. You'll invite me, I'll come in, you'll lay the smack down, and I'll lose. You can consciously choose to adjust your play style to match mine. If you play at your level and I play at mine, I'll be at such a serious disadvantage that I'll be forced to seek people who are not you in order to learn enough that I can come back and even be a part of your chess world.

Q: *So for a game to be built around virality, it has to inherently sacrifice depth?*

A: You can put depth in different places. Depth is a lot of different things. What you want to avoid is significantly disparate experiences between players. Are they playing in very different locations in the world? Are they playing against very different opponents? Is the difficulty so different that a player wouldn't be interested to play with the other?

Avoiding these robs you of some of the common ways we create depth in games but might open up some others, like customization or breadth of choice. In a lot of social games, for example, they expand the map. This does not significantly change play difficulty, there is just more to do. When I compare myself with you, sure, I've got more depth because I'm making more decisions that have impact across a bigger economy. As a new user, I'm not really confronted with any of that. Your game just looks like a bigger plot of land, and I can recognize that and still understand where we both are. And I can enjoy my relationship with you.

A lot of the modern social games are deep games; you have to do very deep numerical analysis on them if you want to mix/match them—in fact, they make that really hard to do. Players who want to can compete there if they want to by investing more time. The depth is there, it is just harder to get at, ironically, but it does not create really different experiences or exclusive status differences between players.

Q: *Let's talk about monetization. You came from a traditional games background, and have then spent a bunch of time thinking about how to monetize free-to-play games. What are things that designers from traditional games space need to understand?*

A: The biggest misconception is around what people are willing to pay for. When you come from classic console design, you keep thinking about features. You keep thinking about "more gameplay!" With social games and virtual goods, what people actually pay for are mostly cosmetic changes and status items, and progression advancements which just let them go through the number crunching a little bit faster. These are not bad. They are actually things that have a lot of value to people as a lifestyle.

People want to look at things they like to look at and they want to hear sounds that they enjoy listening to. This is not something that is inferior to buying an expansion map pack that you can churn through and then go on to the next expansion pack. It is not about more gameplay. The free-to-play game itself is the territory to play on and the things you buy are the trappings and the dressings of that territory.

When you are designing virtual goods, you should think about the game as part of their lifestyle. It does not matter if they play thirty seconds every day or three hours every day. It's about how they imagine themselves in the game world. If they come in and have an industrial farm, where do they maximize the output from their farm, and do they like to think of themselves in those terms? "I am a very productive farmer…" Then you sell them things that will help them imagine that vision. Some of that can just be things that look like that idea of efficient industrial buildings, or it could be something that lets them eke out another 10–15 percent efficiency. That way they can tell their friends, "I am the most industrious farmer!" Another farmer, who plays and just wants to noodle with their farm to make it look like their ideal retirement farm…what they want to see is the farm getting closer and closer to some aesthetic vision of perfection. They will put money into buying pink hay bales or a beautiful pond. They don't really give a rat's ass about how efficient their farm is. It is an aesthetic play for them.

That is a little of an oversimplification, though, because the brilliant social games will weave these two things together. The actual play is part of the customization process. In *CityVille*, for example, the different businesses have different tradeoffs, but they also look quite different. You can choose to have a city full of bakeries, but that will have a different performance characteristic. That way you get both types of players to play each other's games.

Q: *There has been a reluctance in the West to sell performance-enhancing items, that these are somehow akin to cheating. In the East, games like* Crossfire *have completely ignored this rule, and it seems to work for them. Is it possible to build social games for the Western market that feature performance-enhancing microtransaction items?*

A: Yes. I think it's only a matter of time. There is a lag in the culture here. In the West we do not like it to be so flagrant, but it is happening more and more. The relative strength of the $60 retail game keeps putting this "purity of game design" concept in our heads. I think as the free-to-play model continues to bloom, a generation of gamers who don't carry in those prejudices from the old world of $60 retail games will overcome that idea.

That being said, we already do it; we just hide it. In *CityVille*, you can get decorations that give you a bonus to the surrounding businesses, but only up to a certain limit. If you purchase the better ones with real money, you can get roughly double that amount of bonus. Now because this is not directly buying results, it feels different. There is a layer of indirection to it, but you can definitely outpace everyone else's economy if you buy these. People can still outperform other people by spending. The same is true of other games that use virtual goods. They will do things that make it really hard to earn the thing that will make you competitive, but it is still, in theory, earnable. So they just put a big time investment between you and that thing. The conceit is that it is earnable, but in actuality, most people are buying it.

You have to be really careful about the performance-enhancing items, though, because irrespective of the fairness, there is a player investment problem. If a player can shortcut their way through to performance, how much quicker do they go through their lifecycle within the game? From a business and game design point of view, if a person comes in and drops $20, becomes really powerful, tears through the content, and they then eject, would you have been better off if you'd asked them for $5 five different times? So you have to be careful with performance-enhancing items because they can erode the longevity of the experience, in addition to the enjoyment of that experience. Finessing this is an art.

Q: *Talk to me about user-created virtual goods.*

A: There are a few social games out there based entirely on user-created virtual goods, but the general pattern is that they make money by commission from people trading back and forth. The really interesting one out there is *Team Fortress.* They introduced a crafting system, but then they also released a storefront where users could buy both unique and craftable items. On top of that, Valve takes submissions for user-created assets. These assets, once approved, will go up for sale. Valve takes a commission from these items, and there is no possibility of buying these items with credits earned in game. The whole storefront is entirely based on real money. This is similar to games like *Second Life* where users can put in arbitrary content and sell it. The key difference is that there is a crafting system built into the game that mixes with this item ecosystem. It creates three tiers of player investment. There are buyers, crafters, and sellers. A person could be all three, but for basically a team-based, non-progression game, there is a ton of player creation and involvement.

Q: *Lots of people have proclaimed that console gaming and the retail market are dead, and that the whole world should now go free-to-play microtransaction. What do you think about that?*

A: The audience scope of social games is so enormous and the amount of money that we are charging per hour for free-to-play experiences is too low to be sustainable right now. Eventually, new people are going to stop coming into the system, and for growth to continue, we're going to have to start charging more from these people. Is that just cranking up the price of virtual goods or is it going to be a new business model? Given that these games are lifestyle games, there is a business model that already works—that's the subscription model. It has been around forever in online gaming. There is a really great opportunity to leverage subscriptions or new ways to think about subscriptions and to leverage virtual goods at the same time. The thing we have to solve, though, is the barrier to entry. $60 to try an experience to see if you like it is unreasonable. It just means too many people are not going to try the experience you put forth. A demo is not the same thing. The amount of time it takes to discover and get a demo is so slow.

The people who can give you a great experience, for free, in a few seconds, are going to win. And as those experiences get better, it is going to start to push aside experiences that cost $60 and take a day to install.

Q: Any parting thoughts for social game developers out there?

A: The audience being so large means there are opportunities for almost all appropriately sized businesses. If you are a small business, do the thing you think is interesting. Be weird and strange and fun and cool, because chances are there are a hundred thousand other people out there who will go for that. Do not copy Zynga directly, because Zynga is copying itself and so are the next three giant companies beneath them. It takes an army of people to do what Zynga does well. Pick the appropriate level to come in. With 200,000,000+ social gamers out there, there are people who would love to play a game that felt like it was made just for them.

Don't be afraid to go and do something different and interesting.

CHAPTER 9

Virtual Goods

9.1 FAKE ESTATES

The very phrase "virtual goods" is something of a delightful contradiction. Anything virtual, by definition, doesn't physically exist, and goods, at least when appearing within the context of the marketplace, are typically an article of trade. For our purposes, though, virtual goods are real enough that they generate billions of dollars in revenue each year and are so important to players that they can drive binge play sessions, provoke real-world fights, create (and destroy) marriages, and keep users spending money twenty-four hours a day, in almost every country in the world. Virtual goods may be an amusingly twenty-first century contradiction in terms, but they're also big business and a major part of social and mobile game design.

Virtual goods can end up taking on many different forms in a game. They can be literal items that a player or character buys in order to enhance their in-game abilities, or they can be instantly consumed "items" that grant the user more turns or access to some previously unavailable feature. They can also be purely cosmetic items that stroke users' vanity by letting them customize the way their character or car or card or farm animal appears to other players. These items can be a core component of gameplay, or they can be special, even seasonal items. We'll discuss popular items of all types and talk about how such items can be used to affect, alter, or destroy a game's balance. We'll discuss how to avoid some of the game-balance pitfalls often created by offering functional items for sale and ways to make visual customization features appealing to your users as a way to distinguish themselves from the crowd. We'll also briefly touch on user-created virtual goods. We'll wrap all this up with an interview discussing mobile game design from an indie perspective.

9.2 SELLING PREMIUM GOODS

If a game is going to monetize via the sale of virtual goods, it's ideal for the game design to account for this from the moment of the game's inception. To be well executed, the game's designers need to plan in advance what types of items will be sold and understand very clearly the ways in which these items will affect the game balance. Virtual items need to augment the gameplay, not distract from it. The best types of virtual goods are those that fit nicely into the game world and act as a core component of each and every move. In a city-building game, each different building the user interacts with could be considered a virtual good. In an online driving game, the subcomponents of the user's car can be the basic building blocks of the virtual goods system. For a first-person shooter, each gun or bullet could be a purchasable item, and so on. What all of these examples share in common is that the goods for sale are a critical component of almost every user's experience within the game system, and they were designed from the onset of the game to play a major role in every second of the user's experience.

Integrating the sale of virtual goods into an existing game design is difficult to do without inadvertently "breaking" the game. At best, the system is likely to feel like a tacked-on afterthought designed to extract money from customers without improving the gameplay. The best way to avoid this type of design afterthought is to carefully identify which parts of your game design could reasonably rely upon the sale of virtual goods and which parts need to remain untangled from the influence of microtransactions (Figure 9.1). Spend time analyzing other games in the market and take advice from there; would Monopoly be as much fun if you could just throw a dollar on the board every time you wanted to buy a hotel? Determine what you're going to sell for real money, and carefully integrate that plan into your overall game design.

For game designers, there is a core division between the two key types of virtual goods, and this distinction needs to be understood from the onset of the design process. In-game items (or even non-item boosts, accelerators, or features) need to be considered in terms of the degree to which they alter gameplay for the user. Purchases that change something meaningful about the game are said to confer "functional advantages." Purchases that are purely aesthetic are often no less important to users, but they serve a different function in the game's design and moment-to-moment play. These purchases are generally considered "vanity items."

FIGURE 9.1 *Team Fortress 2* by Valve is a free-to-play FPS on Steam that monetizes by selling virtual items. Games can sell items that are functional, cosmetic, or both.

9.3 FUNCTIONAL ADVANTAGES

There are many types of goods that can grant a functional advantage in a game. In a shooter, this could be something as obvious as a more damaging gun, or a gun that fires faster than those available in the game for free. In a city-building game, a functional advantage could be a certain type of bulldozer that produces new buildings faster than is possible for those players who do not chose to spend real-world money. Role-playing games tend to favor swords and armor; for a fishing game... well, you get the idea.

When considering selling players items that give them a real advantage in gameplay, game balance should be a critical consideration. If rich players are overpowering those who don't spend money, those who don't spend much money will become disenfranchised and quit playing. Alternately if players don't feel engaged because a game is too easy or too hard, they'll quit playing. There are a few ways to overcome this, since the core problem is different depending on the type of challenge offered in the game. First, there are some general issues to consider for items of this type:

- Selling functional items in a game that pits player versus player (PvP) risks making the game feel unbalanced. If one player can simply spend a few extra dollars and create an advantage so powerful that no other players feel they can compete (without also spending), players may quickly feel alienated and move on. This sensibility is particularly strong in North America, though less so in Asia based on the popularity of games like *Crossfire* and *ZTOnline*.

- To complicate matters, the risk of alienation described above can also become a major selling point, depending on your player community. Often, when users in a PvP game have been killed or "ganked" by another player, they tend to be emotional and want to strike back; this does make your players more likely to spend money in exchange for power if your game design allows them to do so. But you need to tread with caution when allowing this sort of behavior. You don't want to leave your revenue to the whims that divide gamers between their wallet and their damaged sense of pride, and you don't want to foster the type of nasty online community that exists only for those who get their kicks from spending a few pennies to "grief" new players. Certainly this is an emotion to exploit, but also to control.

- Selling functional items in a game that pits the player against AI opponents (or "bots") or against the environment (as in PvE) risks making the player feel as if there is no skill to overcoming the challenge of the game. As long as they plug in enough dollars, they can guarantee a victory through attrition.

- Items that shift or slightly tweak the game balance, creating a new variation on the overall game experience, have the opportunity to be significant sellers in the PvE space. If players are already enjoying your gameplay, something that will allow them to enjoy some variety without leaving your gamespace has great benefit for both you and them. So long as the item isn't perceived as reducing the necessary level of overall skill required to excel at the game, users are likely to spend on items that will save them a little time, improve their chances, and otherwise vary their already positive experience.

Here are some tips for reducing the feeling that users are "buying their way to victory." These guidelines can apply to both PvP and PvE games.

- Limit the duration that a purchased item can be used by any single player. For example, if players have an item that grants them faster healing, rather than allowing them to enjoy that power indefinitely, give it to them for a limited duration. This lets you repeatedly sell the item as a consumable but also helps balance out what might otherwise be overpowering to other players. Even the most vigilant will forget to "re-up" their item or decide to try to play without it. A set duration also allows your players to see the comparable value of the item. They are regularly reminded that the small expenditure increases the enjoyment of their gaming experience, or it allows them to spend their money on other items you might offer, thus increasing the variety of their game experience.

- Make the advantage indirect, such that it isn't obvious to the player's opponents when they might be using a particular "buff." For instance, imagine that you let players buy an item that allows them greater speed in the construction of new buildings; rather than simply decrease the players' time to build each building, consider designing the item instead to reduce the amount of lumber, metal, or brick required to construct the building. This way, the increased speed at which a player can build isn't patently obvious to their opponents, but your player still enjoys the same net effect (more buildings in the same time).

- If your game features a metagame loop, like the XP model in *Call of Duty* or the summoner advancement model in *League of Legends,* for example, accelerators that allow players to advance through the metagame at a faster pace tend to be quite popular. This is in contrast to items that directly make a player more powerful in mid-game, which are often perceived as cheating or as "breaking" the game.

- Balance out the items that grant players certain advantages by allowing experienced opponents to either earn or buy a specific defense or countermove. Yes, Player 1, you can buy something that makes your initial tennis serve 25 percent faster, but Player 2 may have a backhanded return that reduces any speed bonus to no more than 10 percent. Such balancing strategies will limit a player's "sure win" purchasing options and force more tactical play. You can still allow for an advantage to the player who just purchased the new item, but experienced players will be able to recognize and adjust their gameplay accordingly, reducing their frustration and enhancing everyone's competitive gaming experience.

- Rather than selling users a "nuke 'em from orbit" type ability that eliminates all obstacles or enemies on the screen, give players a powerful attack or ability that still requires their active involvement. For example, rather than a "smartbomb" type weapon that kills everyone on the screen, sell them a "flamethrower" that does terrific damage to whatever they point it toward, if they point it in the right direction at the right time. The net effect is much the same from a game balance standpoint, but one makes users feel as if they skillfully used a new ability, while the other makes players feel as if their credit card just purchased their victory.

- Consider carefully what your core game mechanic is. In game designer speak, what's "the toy" that makes the second-by-second interaction with the game enjoyable? Ensure that whatever you are selling doesn't break that toy by changing how the player interacts with your game, or at least not for very long. Instead, find tasks that are repetitive or dull, then obviate those tasks by offering for purchase a particular, shiny, "cool" item. For example, in many RPGs, characters are required to make a long and (often) boring walk back to town to sell items every time their inventory fills up. The designers of NCSoft's MMO *Dungeon Runners* allowed players to purchase a gnome who followed them around and converted useless items to gold on the spot. The time-saving element, plus the quirky gnome's method of processing, made the purchase an easy choice for many of the game's faithful.

- Selling items that aren't necessarily measurably better, but are still in some way different, can delight users without breaking the core game experience. For example, in a game about world exploration where a player must explore the space by paddling around in a rowboat, consider instead selling them a seahorse to ride. The seahorse might be unable to get as near the shore as the rowboat, but could be less affected by choppy water (or some other balance-saving detail). Thus, the item functionally is very much the same but carries with it a visual difference, along with some slight advantage/disadvantage that helps to vary the player's experience of the game without markedly changing the core "toy."

- Sell upgrades that make a player more flexible, but not necessarily more powerful. Allowing some players to carry two weapons while others only one, so long as the two are not doubly as strong, won't inherently introduce a disadvantage. What it will do, however, is change up the gameplay enough that players will have to vary their tactic, giving players more by giving players greater flexibility

9.4 GAME BALANCE CONSIDERATIONS

For any game type, there are sure to be issues of pricing and game balance, especially when you are selling items designed to confer a functional advantage. This type of game balance simply introduces an additional variable to the designers' balancing equation. The greater the degree to which an item allows a player to deviate from the standard curve of in-game performance, the more expensive it should be. Ideally your game will be such that you can calculate what the real-world dollar value is of each statistical advantage players may receive, if they purchase the item you're considering offering. This advantage, in turn, will need to be reduced to a money-for-time equation to properly quantify the effect the item will have on the world and the offsetting balance that will need to be achieved to sustain proper gameplay.

For example, in a PvE-focused fantasy RPG-type game, if an appropriately leveled player of average skill takes on average 1000 seconds to fight her way through a particular dungeon, and she receives on average 1000 gold for doing so, then the average ratio of gold/time in that dungeon is 1:1. Let us imagine that a sword that does 10 percent more damage is sold for 10,000 gold, so the player is able to fight through the dungeon 10 percent faster. This player would now be able to run through the dungeon in 900 seconds. This item has just increased the gold/time ratio to 10:9. Imagine that you sell gold to the player at the rate of $1 for 1000 gold. This means that the real-world ratio between dollars and time is 16.6 gold per second saved. Consequently, the value of the 10,000 gold sword, which will save the user 100 seconds per dungeon run, should be about $1.60. Clear as a MUD?

Obviously the specifics of how to balance time, difficulty, and two different currencies (in-game and real-world dollars) will need to be entirely customized for each individual game design. But getting these specifics right is of critical importance, especially when selling items that can give players a functional advantage over one another or over the game itself (Figure 9.2). The alternative is an unbalanced game and alienated players. Games that are either entirely PvE or entirely PvP are considerably easier to balance than are those attempting to straddle the line between the two. In blended games, which offer both types of challenges, the designer ends up needing to account for the tastes of a few very different types of players. This problem is difficult enough without allowing for external influences on the game balance (like functional item purchases). However, because a game that

FIGURE 9.2 *League of Legends* sells new champions, new skins, and new runes for your summoner in its online store. Selling items that improve player performance can be risky, especially in PvP games, and doing so requires great care and attention to balance.

manages to appeal to both types of players can potentially have a far greater customer base, this is a challenge that is well worth undertaking.

9.5 AESTHETIC "VANITY" ITEMS

Is there anything about a handbag from Louis Vuitton that makes it fundamentally better than a similar handbag sold in Target? Perhaps (but probably not). At a gross level, they perform an identical function, and provided they are the same size and shape, there is very little practical difference between the two. So why is one many, many times more expensive than the other? Because people like status items that help distinguish them from one another based on their accoutrements.

Selling vanity items is a relatively straightforward proposition, because such items don't have any real effect on gameplay. From a shiny red hat for players' avatars to sweet, blacked-out rims for their favorite car, allowing players to customize their game experience can be a very powerful user draw. Even games without any player avatar can accomplish this personalization by offering players prestige skins for… almost anything. On the Xbox LIVE version of *Magic: The Gathering,* for example, players can buy shiny tinfoil backing for their decks of cards. And they do, in droves.

Planning what sort of items you'll allow your players to customize is integral to the design and feel of your overall software project. It should be something you consider from the start, because customization can be very difficult to retrofit, depending on what you hope to achieve. For example, a character system with the ability to add "ragdoll"-style character customization might be very costly to add later if the foundation wasn't in place when the game was first architected. However, swapping out player icons or even customizing UI elements in exchange for a dollar or two can be quite popular, and often involves little more than some advanced planning and a little extra 2D artwork.

One of the great features of vanity items is that they are, in effect, viral. If players see someone else walking around wearing an item they want to wear, the value of that item is increased, and some players will go to elaborate lengths to acquire that item. Because goods that cost real money are automatically rare (since, statistically more people play than purchase), scarcity is preserved, adding value to the virtual goods. *World of Warcraft* has consistently found success in exploiting this feature, by allowing the introduction of new gear that can be found only in a certain area that *just happens* to be part of an expansion pack. Of course, while the gear must be found in the new area, players are free to wear it in the old. When players discover that the only way they can get the new and wonderful items is to buy the pack and explore new lands, they're motivated to purchase the expansion pack.

When designing vanity items or skins, remember that your games (should) exist in a global marketplace. Consider the different sorts of items that might appeal to varied markets. National flags tend to be very popular, because they allow gamers to identify themselves by region. Symbols associated with different districts, sports teams, or belief systems can be popular, as well. Of course, you'll want to take care as to the sorts of iconography you allow. Swastikas, for example, may be popular among certain subgroups, but you probably want to avoid them in your game. For every icon that gets players excited, there's another that could upset players to the point that they abandon your game. For this reason, allowing users to create their own symbols, icons, or skins is likely to expose your team to a number of headaches. A happy medium can be found in allowing users to create their own custom liveries from a predetermined set of icons, colors, and the like. Both *Need for Speed* and *Call of Duty* have made great use of such features, allowing for limited user insignia customization while avoiding the problems of completely freeform user creation.

9.6 RARITY

People love a bargain, and when their motivation is to feel unique or express themselves, they want to feel as if the item they are buying isn't something everyone else will have. One way to accommodate both of these goals is to have limited-time sales offers and release certain goods only in a limited number. ("Only 1828 Golden Hammers remain! Buy one now for only 200 points!") By offering an item in such a way that it has perceived scarcity, you create demand and appeal to the user's desire to get a special bargain.

Most of the sales and marketing tricks surrounding the concept of rarity hearken back to traditional advertising models. "Buy one, get one free!" has always been a great enticement for consumable items. "Upsize for an additional $0.50" is a good way to sell users on a slightly larger amount of product than perhaps they actually need. (In the dual currency world, this often manifests as a bulk "discount" for purchasing virtual currencies in larger denominations.) And, of course, the same tricks used by retailers related to product positioning apply in the virtual storefront. Want to sell more of an item? Put it at the top of the list or give it a brightly colored icon.

Likewise, consider offering items that are tied to the calendar in some way. For example, Santa hats are always a top seller around Christmas time, at least in some parts of the world. Here, again, a little attention to global trends can go a long way. Are there special goods you can sell that will help users celebrate Chinese New Year in your game world? What about Guy Fawkes masks? Depending on your game engine and the flexibility of your store and backend systems, you may be able to customize offers for a particular territory, which can help you target sales to those most likely to be interested in them.

Almost anything that can be sold in real life—and quite a wide array of things that cannot—can be sold as virtual goods in a social game. Since the game world is limited only by the imagination of the designer, there is no feature, offering, or fantasy that a user cannot be enticed to indulge. Your game can sell seahorses to ride, shiny-tin foil rims for a virtual car, a literal horse of a different color, or a magic flamethrower that lets users extract petty revenge on a player who has recently wronged them. Deciding what to sell and what properties to imbue each virtual item with can be an incredible challenge, as can balancing the ways these items interact with other game systems. As we move forward, we'll look at some of the ways that designers can further nuance these decisions by offering different types of items for different types of currencies.

9.7 INTERVIEW WITH DIMITRI DELATTRE, FOUNDER OF DEADPAN DODO: "INDIE PERSPECTIVE"

Dimitri Delattre has been making games since 2002. He has worked as a localization expert, lead game designer, producer, and creative director for Electronic Arts (Vancouver, Canada), Visual Impact (Paris, France), 2D Art Factory (Paris, France), and SGN (Buenos Aires, Argentina). He is the founder and the CEO of Deadpan Dodo, a mobile game studio based in France and Argentina.

Q: Tell us a little bit about yourself and your history in gaming. What made you decide to make the switch to mobile game development?

A: I had the chance to discover gaming pretty early. My dad brought home one of those first Amstrad CPC 6128s arriving in France when I was still a young boy, and I would spend hours recopying, from magazines, lines of code in BASIC (of which I didn't understand anything!) just to see what the machine was going to do with all those characters. As I grew older, computers and consoles became at least twice as powerful every year (and back then, that was making a huge difference). The games were probably one of the best indicators of what a new machine could do. The game genres were still not as defined as today. Every game felt unique. *DOOM* was the FPS, *Mario* the platformer, *Monkey Island* the scripted puzzle, *The Incredible Machine* the physics puzzle... Anyone over 30 can relate, I'm sure!

While still playing regularly, I actually never thought that I would have a career in the gaming industry. (I went on to study business, economics and finance, which eventually became useful after a few years in the industry.) There was no school dedicated to this world, no "perfect career path" to follow. And I have to admit that it is pure luck that I found a job in the industry, by the smallest door that exists: the QA department, in the biggest company there was back then: EA. I never regretted starting so low. For me it was the perfect "nursery" to truly begin to understand the other side of the industry, the side that we developers see every day: the bugs, and the creativity!

Six years at Electronic Arts from tester to assistant producer gave me a unique opportunity to work on dozens of games across all major platforms, alongside highly competent juniors and veterans, and to realize the complexity of creating a game, to say nothing of a good game. I returned to France to continue my career as designer and creative director mostly in portable consoles (DS) in a small French studio (Visual Impact). Around that time, I remember gently making fun of my friends who made the jump to mobile gaming. Back then, the touch-screen smartphones didn't exist, and I just couldn't see what fun we could have playing on a microscopic screen and crappy keyboard.

In 2007, the iPhone came out, and I suddenly realized that the revolution was on. A revolution for the gamers that could now play with their fingers, but also for us, on the other side, because from one day to another, you could start thinking about creating games without all the complex machinery. No expensive development consoles, no super powerful PCs, no development cycles of several years, no need of a 20-person team to create a game, and easy ways to bring your game to the world.

At that point, I had the opportunity to become creative director for SGN in the Argentinian city of Buenos Aires, a studio that was aiming to target only touch-screen devices. I didn't hesitate long. With the team there, we could think of a game concept that we wanted to put to the test and have a working prototype within just a few days (hours sometimes!) At that point, it was clear to me that the mobile game industry could bring me much more control and opportunity to create freely, with minimum limitations and investment. I could go rogue. And I did as I launched Deadpan Dodo, my own company that does what I want and believe in: games that are not only manufactured to make money but also teach, in a fun way, and challenge our traditional ways of thinking.

Q: *What do you see as the biggest new opportunities for mobile game developers? Where do you see this market going in the next few years?*

A: What changed fundamentally with the mobile gaming is... well... the fact that gaming went mobile. Obvious yes. But what that really means now, is that you don't go to the gaming machine, the gaming machine is on you, with you, constantly. Anyone with a smartphone is a potential gamer, when once, this wasn't the case.

Playing is in our nature, and probably the best way to learn. So for me, while the existing gaming industry will still target the "original" gamers, the new opportunities are in the way we use gaming to achieve something else: developing oneself without efforts, just through fun. Be careful here. I am not talking about education through gaming. I mean gaming first and through it only, some kind of education, not necessarily academic.

I also see gamers taking a bigger role than before. Once, gamers were just end-consumers, and all was needed from them was to buy the products. Now they have a say in the games as their reviews are extremely important for the success of a game, and they became the prime advocates of great games. And this will push developers to pump up the quality of their games and releases. I think this is excellent news!

Q: What have you learned from the games you've released on mobile so far?

A: Haha, tricky question! The mobile gaming industry is still a really young branch of the gaming tree. Many games were successes back in 2008 and would go completely unnoticed today; the audience has drastically changed and keeps changing. The old and clear monetization system that we knew so well became, if not obsolete, anecdotic at best.

But in condensed form, here are my findings: First, releasing an unfinished game just because we developers can now update them along the way is a very big mistake. The competition has never been as high as now, and this is just a beginning, and no half-finished game has a chance to sell well. Polishing is not an extra anymore, it is a must-do. Second, even though not every gamer will buy, developers should still aim at improving their retention rates not only for the buyers but also for the rest of the players. They will be advocates of a great game, can be used as "feeding grounds" for paying players, and might still become monetizable in the future. This is a very hard job to do well. Third, in the current market, your game should be free with IAP, but not a cheap demo. Give pleasure to your customer, and bring him into a mindset where he actually wants to spend. And finally, and unfortunately, money-marketing still plays a big role in getting your game played by the masses.

Q: Do you see mobile gaming and social games as converging or diverging in the coming years?

A: Playing is fun. Playing with (or against) random players is usually better. Playing with friends is always the best, though. It is not applicable to all game types, but in most cases, it is true. And the social component of a game can determine its success. *Draw Something* is an excellent example of a game that could only work by being social. Now does that mean that every mobile game will have Facebook integration and will be playable from the device or a computer? I don't believe so, as I don't believe that a device's player is necessarily the same as a Facebook's player. But most developers already noticed that retention is one of the key pieces of a success, and that the social components of a game impact largely the retention of players, so social elements are here to stay.

Q: In such a crowded marketplace, what are ways you'd recommend other game developers try to get their games discovered?

A: Do quality. Do beautiful. Do different. Do what you love. Be creative... There is no cheap, magical recipe to reach the top of the charts. But if you believe in your product, and non-related (to you) people start believing in it too, you surely are on the right track.

It is probably one of the hardest things to do for a developer: drop your lines of code and your mouse, and look at your game with fresh eyes. But it is a very important step to ensure that your game is valid and has a real chance in the gaming jungle. Personally I try to complete a game and then start right away on another development. And when the time is right, I look again at the former "complete" game and start dressing a list of the dozens of little things that should be better.

Finally, once you are satisfied with your final product, the real work starts. Developing and creating is all fun, but when it comes to tell the world, it's a completely new business and it has to be handled as seriously as the development phase. That means dedicating a large part of your time to talk about your game, to explain why it is better, smarter, funnier, somethinger more than the others. There are hundreds of people out there that will want to see your game, review your game, talk about your game if they like it. Those people will help you start the rain, and then only your players can transform those few drops into a real tornado. So keep in mind that your end consumer is a player, satisfy him and good things should come.

Q: After you launch a game, how much energy are you spending on studying, improving, and maintaining that game, as opposed to developing your next idea?

A: At Deadpan Dodo, we have this motto: "If we don't have an average of at least 4 stars reviews, we are doing something really, really wrong." Games leave our doors only when we are sure they are complete and polished, and new versions are top priorities if we hear of any, even minor, issues. So I would say that at least a fifth of our time is spent on making sure our games are of the top quality, rightly priced and tuned, and keep receiving new content. Another fifth of our time and energy is also spent on studying the results, the analytics, and looking at what the competition does, why it is interesting, and how we can learn from their products.

Q: What is the game development community in Buenos Aires like?

A: There are two levels really: larger studios (30+ people) are in a never-ending competition, sometimes quite ridiculous. The smaller studios, on the opposite, work often closely together to provide tips, feedbacks, data on sales, retention, etc., to each other. I personally meet at least once a week with other developers, either indie or small business owners. There is for sure in Argentina a great load of excellent developers and talent, and some of the best artists I've met in my career, with an extremely good ratio of cost/quality.

Q: How could those coming from the traditional games industry in North America or Europe do a better job serving the emerging markets in mobile and social gaming in the rest of the world?

A: This is a difficult question. And I believe that currently, those markets are not quite ripe anyway, as the monetization seems to obey completely different rules than in North America. To reach those markets, there is the obvious need to localize languages (which is too often overlooked) as a key piece of this puzzle. Deeper than that, there are cultural differences in those new markets, and different expectations from those audiences, which need to be fixed from the ground up. One size doesn't fit all anymore. This is certainly something to watch closely in the next few years.

Q: If there were 1000 times as many smartphones in the world as there are today, and each of them were 1000 times more powerful than what's in your pocket right now, what are the game design opportunities that would open up as a result?

A: That is an excellent question, and I often wonder about this. I am still undecided, but I have a tendency to believe that it's not necessarily the power of the devices that create gaming opportunities, but rather the new features. The motion of the Wii, the stylus-touchscreen of the DS, the finger-touchscreen of the smartphones, the gyro or the Kinect brought more to the table in terms of design opportunities than any new graphic processor since the Amiga. Basically, in the coming years, I will be watching more closely the Google glasses and skin sensors rather than the new processors. Right now, there are already some amazing 3D capabilities on touch screens. Yet, the higher selling games are 2D or 2D isometric. Now, give me a feature where my device doesn't need to be touched anymore but I can just fly my hand in 3D over the screen and then I am sure we will see new gameplay types.

Q: Any final advice for those seeking to break into the mobile game development space?

A: Don't wait for a job to make your career. Use all the time you have to get your hands dirty, to analyze what works and what doesn't, to understand the higher mechanics of some of the best games, to understand all the roles of the gaming industry and how they all benefit to the product. As surprising as it may sound, there is a lot to learn from *Pac-Man* or *Tetris*. And there is even more to learn from doing your own version of *Pac-Man* or *Tetris*. There are more and more free tools to code with a very low bare minimum of development knowledge, from App Inventor to the open source Moai. For the designers out there, this is the way to go: play with those tools and learn from them, understand what makes a game good, what mechanics can bring an ok-game to a AAA-game, understand the cycle of a production, from all the points of view (dev, artist, design, content, QA, management, etc.), stay curious, and live your passion!

CHAPTER 10

Currency

10.1 GREENSPAN FOR THE WIN

All games need an economy, even those that don't overtly have anything to do with money. In sports games, the economy might be measured in points scored or in player stats. In a fighting game, the game economy is measured in damage, speed, and health. This is how game designers balance a game so that it is fair and (more importantly) fun. Of course, in many games the in-game economy is an obvious and explicit part of the reward structure. Earning copper, silver, and gold from each monster slain is an integral part of *World of Warcraft* (and most other fantasy RPGs). Most social games give players some form of currency as a direct reward for almost every action they take; in many social games this reward mechanic is tied to the core compulsion loop, and coins and stars spring out of every mouse-click like hyperactive candy from a piñata.

For games that feature microtransactions, it often makes some sense to complicate the in-game economy a bit, by introducing a secondary form of currency that is tied to real-world money. This dual currency system is so common these days that it could almost be considered a standard design trope. Dual currency models typically divide into "soft" currencies, which are awarded in-game and have no real-world value, and "hard" currencies, which are derived from real-world money. There are both game-design and logistic reasons for adopting a dual currency model, both of which we'll explore in this chapter.

There is, of course, no law that says a game has to adopt a dual currency model. Having a single in-game currency (that could even be pegged to a real-world currency like the US dollar) is perfectly appropriate for the right kind of game (though it would likely pose a number of game-design challenges). Conversely there's no hard and fast rule against having more than two currency systems in place in your game at any one time. Indeed, with many social networks and platforms providing their own virtual currency systems, such a design plan might be ideal.

10.2 SINGLE CURRENCY MODELS

Imagine that you wanted to create a game around the real-world adventures of a lemonade stand owner, like the venerable *Lemonade Stand* game from the days of the Apple II. You could set the price of lemons, maybe even tie it to a real-world daily lookup function that averaged the price of citrus in the user's region. Likewise, you could tie the price of sugar and labor to rates in the area, then let users set their per-cup price and watch a (admittedly fairly dull) lemonade stand unfold. While a social game in which everyone is busy selling lemonade to their friends might start to read like a Phillip K. Dick sketch before long, one could certainly build such a game. Then, as your microtransaction model, you could let users whose stands weren't doing too well give you US dollars, at a 1:1 ratio, for every dollar they wanted to gain in game. This is what a single currency system would look like, integrated into one of gaming's earliest consumer pricing simulators.

What are the problems with this model? (Aside from the *Lemonade Stand* game being boring in comparison to some of the more complex game mechanics now standard in the modern age.) For starters, asking people to perform game actions using real-world dollars forces them regularly to think about the relationship between the game and real life. If I need to buy a bag of lemons in order to progress, and it costs me $3, I am immediately forced to think about the other things I could be doing with that $3. I had to work for those $3, and I may not want to spend them on virtual lemons. By way of comparison, if a bag of lemons costs me 23 Sourbucks, I'm much less inclined to be yanked from the fantasy by thoughts of rent, tuition, or whatever other real-world expenses compete for my dollars. At least on a surface level I'm not spending my dollars; I'm spending Sourbucks.

Another problem with a single currency system is that it becomes very difficult to reward the user without giving away real-world currency, which may involve state and federal legal issues and in general isn't the best business plan. Occasionally you'll want to entice users by offering a reward if they return to the game or invite a friend to play, but that's very different from taking real-world money *out* of the game and giving it back to the user. Smart designers find ways to keep their players' cash once they've got it, and instead offer other types of incentives. In a game like *Lemonade Stand,* rewards could potentially be as simple as in-game objects (such as lemons) as enticements. This might be an easy, efficient, and effective choice, but once you make this choice you have effectively created a dual currency model.

10.3 DUAL CURRENCY MODELS

Dual currency systems are common in games that ask players to spend real money to purchase in-game…anything. Most social games on Facebook have a dual currency model, in which in-game soft "engagement currencies" are used to reward players and cash-based "hard currencies" are purchased in order to give the player particular kinds of in-game advantages. This has become a standard practice on many successful free-to-play mobile games, as well. Everything from CCGs like *Blood Brothers* to RPG-style -Ville games like Kabam's *Kingdoms of Camelot* tend to use a dual currency model, as discussed.

It is important to note that not just any game with multiple types of rewards is dual currency in the way we mean here. *World of Warcraft* offers gold (and its variants), reputation, and a few other tradable currencies that only matter within the game, but because the game is purely subscription based and none of these in-game currencies can be "purchased" with real world cash, it is not considered a dual currency game. *League of Legends* offers Riot Points and Influence Points, one of which is earned, the other of which must be purchased;

this makes *League of Legends* a standard dual currency model. XP and gold feature promi-nently in their mid-session economy, but because these cannot be exchanged for real-world cash, they are not considered part of the dual currency system. *Empires and Allies* sells items based on Coins (soft) and Empire Points (hard, which convert to energy and a few other necessities). Older Zynga games like *Vampire Wars* trade in Blood (soft) and Favor Points (hard), and so on. To be considered truly a dual currency game, the game needs to distinguish between soft and hard currency.

It is common for freemium games within the in-game fiction to use one currency, usually a soft currency, which can be earned inside the game. Most then have a meta-layer on top that allows users to purchase a second type of currency, usually a hard currency, which is based on real money. It's rare to allow users to earn much of the hard currency by performing in-game tasks. (Designers don't typically want to de-incentivize sales, since it undercuts the monetization model.) Instead, an item the user might want can typically be purchased for either a particular amount of an in-game currency or a different amount of the hard currency. Commonly the best (the most powerful, the rarest, etc.) items can be purchased only using the cash-based hard currency.

10.3.1 Uses for Soft and Hard Currencies

Here are some of the common uses of soft currencies in games:

- Soft currencies should commonly be used as "engagement currency," or currency that forms the core of the reward loop for the game. We recommend setting the value for almost everything you sell in the hundreds or thousands of units of the in-game currency, then lavishly distribute rewards in ones and tens, whenever the player does something you want to encourage.

- Create alternate items that can serve as stand-ins for small denominations; for exam-ple, give out rubies worth 50 units of in-game currency or golden trophies that equate to 60 units, etc. By giving away trinket valuables, you can vary the soft currency rewards and keep players more engaged. Players now have the opportunity to collect "cash," or the basic currency, *or* see who can win the most rubies, collect the most gold trophies, or some combination therein.

- Reward users for community engagement, participating in forums, helping new users get their bearings, and the like. The greater the sense of community, the likelier your players are to stay and play, which hopefully develops into stay and pay.

- Offer soft currency as a reward to encourage daily logins. Even a brief login estab-lishes your game as a part of your player's daily routine. And the more often they enter the game, the greater your chances of "hooking" them to stick around, and perhaps spend money.

- Use soft currencies or their equivalent trinket items as part of an email lure campaign to regain lapsed users. New trinkets, especially clever or "cool" variations on what lapsed players once enjoyed, can be a positive draw to return to the game.

- Any game with user-generated content should find ways to allow users to earn soft currency from the sale of those items. All user-to-user transactions (auction house, etc.) should use the soft currency. Allowing user-to-user cash equivalent transactions will multiply your headaches exponentially.

- Any sort of in-game wagering should be done using soft currency to avoid the risks associated with violating gambling laws.

- As a rule, the user should never be able to turn soft currency into hard currency. For all the reasons discussed in earlier chapters, you don't want users pulling money out of the system, and there is no reason to undercut your monetization model by letting users gain (very much) hard currency without paying for it.

- Designers need to adjust the conversion rate between soft and hard currencies to keep the game economy balanced and healthy; this sort of economic manipulation requires as much care in virtual worlds as does monetary policy in the real world.

Hard currencies can be used in slightly different ways:

- Users can buy hard currencies with their real-world dollars. (This is the definition of a hard currency.)

- Hard currencies can often be used by a number of different games, either on the same platform or within the same publisher's family. Facebook Credits serve this function on Facebook, serving a unifying function across games; this increases the value of a currency by giving it alternate uses.

- Hard currency should be used to buy in-game soft currency, but be careful about establishing a fixed exchange rate. Phrase currency exchanges as "limited time offers" in order to always retain the right to alter the relative value of the two currencies. Depending on what your metrics teach you about your regular users, you'll want to retain a great deal of flexibility in your exchange rate.

- The most valuable items should always require hard currency to purchase in order to motivate monetization.

- If users want to buy gifts for friends, they should use hard currency. Gifting is such a popular way of monetizing users that it's usually a good revenue source. Allowing users to exchange hard currency for accelerators that allow them to gain soft currency faster tends to be popular with Western users. Where buying a sword that could beat anyone in the game might feel like cheating, buying "power points" that allow you to buy a cloak that increases XP by 5 percent creates a distance between the cash expenditure and the in-game reward. The player feels more like they've purchased an accessory to their game play and less like they bought themselves a victory.

- As a corollary to the previous point, allowing users to buy accelerators that allow them to progress more quickly through the content enables users with varying levels of spare time to enjoy the content, and more importantly, to reach a level parity with their friends. The easier it is for various players to invite in their disparate types of friends, the greater your user base and the likelier your game becomes "sticky."

- If your game sells features, like the ability to rename a character, carry more items, and keep a bigger stable of horses, allow players to spend hard currency.

- Typically third-party offer walls and similar tactics reward users with hard currency. (Else they have little value to the game designer.)

10.3.2 Additional Tips for Running a Dual Currency Game

The superb website InsideSocialGames.com ran an article several years ago that still offers excellent advice on implementing and balancing a dual currency system.* Authors Matt McAllister and Jaini Shah generously offer us their insight. Here are a few of their suggestions, with color commentary to supplement:

1. *Engage users first; monetize second.* This is a concise and salient point that designers should never forget. There's a certain type of seediness to a game that begins trying to pick your pocket before you've even seen what makes it great. We recommend, instead, getting users engaged, letting them experience (and get hooked on) the core toy of the game before they are gently introduced to the idea of spending money. There's a popular metaphor in the game designer community about not wanting to marry a stripper, because you can't have a conversation without them asking you for a dollar. While a bit crass, this may be a good mental image to keep in mind. Give your users a taste of what is exciting and awesome and different about your game, and start out by rewarding them with in-game soft currencies for their successes. Once you have them hooked, *then* hit them up for money; you'll likely keep them interested for longer.

2. *Balance your cash sinks.* Users will want to see value in both types of currency. If the game rewards them with loads of soft currency, but only really allows them to spend the hard currency, users are likely to see that the soft currency is a sham. Instead, try to ensure that both currencies are consumed and valued in the game systems at a rate that makes them both feel valuable, *at all levels of the game.* This last bit is quite important. It's easy for a game designer to mistakenly balance a game such that the in-game soft currency is valuable only for the first hour or two of the game. Thereafter all the higher level items are based on hard currency alone. This is the sort of flaw that often isn't revealed until a game is in the wild with a dedicated user base, but it is a serious issue, because it will end up causing your more advanced users to get bored and "churn out" of the game once they've put a few hours' investment into it. So balance your cash sinks so that both hard and soft currencies have and retain values across all levels of play. As long as the integration of your monetization is a gentle,

---

* http://www.insidesocialgames.com/2009/10/16/using-dual-currency-systems-for-better-revenues-and-engagement/

seamless, balanced *portion* of your game, your users will focus on the fun and not on the money.

3. *Offer multiple sources for both currencies.* Reward users with soft, in-game currencies for a variety of activities. For example, in *World of Warcraft* the player can pick up gold from slaying monsters, completing quests, selling items, crafting items and vending them to other players, playing a commodities game in the auction house, and so on. This variety keeps users from getting bored and allows the designers to have a number of subtle levers with which they can balance the in-game soft currency economy. For hard currency, the challenge has less to do with game design; you're typically not going to give much of this out in the game anyway. Instead you need to ensure that users with different spending habits and mechanisms can buy your currency. As we've discussed previously, offering credit card processing, PayPal, cell phone charges, and offer walls, and generally supporting as many different payment systems as possible are important to monetizing the greatest possible percentage of your users.

4. *Spell it out for your users.* Modern games are complicated. Even when the user interface has been simplified to a single-click mechanic, simply understanding the complexities of an in-game economy can be a daunting proposition. Consider, too, that the definition of "gamer" has become exponentially broader with the advent of social games. Billions of people have been playing electronic, online, or mobile games of any kind for only a few years. In many parts of the world, where there simply is no history with Nintendo, Atari, or even Windows, the populace is picking up cheap mobile phones that are smart enough to play games. The old-school systems are new to a great percentage of the gaming population; you can't rely on your users "getting it" on their own, because for many, the idea of playing these games at all is something new. Offer your users tooltips and other kinds of contextual help so they can understand how the game works and how the economy and currencies function. Spend real time examining how users respond to this help, and keep any assistance as concise and clear as possible. If you can, relate the lesson back to user motivation. How do the currencies allow a user to do what they want to do in the game? How will earning and spending let them heighten the fantasy at the beating heart of the game? And how best can you get your users this information without making them feel silly, stupid, or distracted from the core game?

5. *Test, measure, and optimize.* No one produces the perfect game, fresh out of the gate. It's a tragically common form of game designer hubris to assume that *this game* is different, and *this* system will be perfectly balanced without the need for constant A/B testing, analytic gathering, and tinkering. Guess what? The other guys have really smart designers on their staff, too, and they *are* out there iterating rapidly and studying the data carefully. So strategically plan how the different moving parts of your game should work, then relentlessly push your system and backend and analytics

design to allow for as much data gathering and rapid rollout of tweaks as possible. Be prepared to constantly adjust the types of currency-balancing factors we've discussed throughout the lifespan of the game if you want to maximize your success.

10.4 CLOSED AND OPEN ECONOMIES

There has long been a debate among designers about the value of "closed" versus "open" economic models for games. For the early single or session-based multiplayer games with no meta-economy, this debate mattered little. In the era of MMO development, this question became far more meaningful, as a poorly designed economy (or even a well-designed economy that users just reacted to in unexpected ways) could so seriously alter game balance as to end up breaking the game and driving users away. (*Eve Online,* for example, had so complex an economic model that various servers ended up playing very differently after only a few months. Relative levels of wealth, inflation, and the basic value of goods ended up differing hugely for different players.) In modern free-to-play mobile and social games, since the game economy is often tied to real-world currency, albeit at some level of remove, the onus on designers to understand and carefully control the economy is now even more critical to success.

What do we mean by a closed economy? If the total amount of money in the game world is fixed at a certain value or range, the game economy is closed. For the most part, this will prevent any sort of inflation. For example, in a fantasy RPG, the game could be balanced such that the amount of gold dropped by monsters when killed is perfectly balanced against the cost of various types of "gold sinks," which remove money from the world. Typically these gold sinks come in the form of a cost to heal player characters, the price of consumable items, and so on. In fact, by establishing an under-the-hood gold : health : damage formula, games were able to ensure that the amount of currency in the world always remained relatively flat.

In an open game economy, by comparison, new money can be added to the game world, either in a controlled fashion or with experimental abandon. Using the above fantasy RPG example, every new player could start with gold, each new monster that spawned could generate new gold (which would be dropped once the monster was killed), and gold sinks could be at a fixed rate that didn't change over time. Players could add money into the system using microtransactions and use the resulting hard currency to build wealth in soft currency (gold). The net result would be a system in which the total amount of gold in the world would continually increase, which would ultimately lead to game-changing inflation. Often the effects of this inflation end up manifesting in player-to-player transactions, since the rate at which individual players gain currency in the world can be controlled and predicted fairly accurately (i.e., a level 1 character can only kill level 1 monsters, which typically drop only 1 gold piece each, and so on, such that if they are only interacting with the game world, the player behavior will usually follow a well understood, level treadmill curve).

Your game economy and the relationships of different currencies on/in game mechanics is a deeply complex topic and is highly specialized to each individual game. Does your game have a crafting type of mechanic? If so, then the relative rarity of items needed to craft goods and their value in soft (or hard) currency ends up being very closely tied to inflation. If you have a game where enemies respawn in an area and drop new wealth each time, this has a real effect on how closely tied your hard currency is to the value of your soft currency. (Inflation rears its head again.) Are items that users can buy using hard currency completely aesthetic, with no functional component in your game? If so, you can probably ignore the relationship between soft and hard currency, and keep your soft currency balanced as befits your gameplay and hard currency tied only to vanity items (though this isn't likely to be as engaging as two better integrated systems). These sorts of questions and a hundred more like them need to be asked of each potential game design, long before any real implementation work is done.

The goal of this chapter was not to tell you how to set up and balance the economy for your social game. There are entire books written on the subject of game economy balance, and every game is different. Instead we hope that we've communicated how important it is to have someone on your game team who is able to think deeply about these problems and take ownership of monitoring and balancing the economy. This is exactly the sort of thing that lends itself to the study of metrics and analytic instrumentation discussed in the previous chapters, as well as in several of the interviews. An online game with an evolving user base requires constant maintenance, and almost any mobile, Facebook, web, or console game falls into this category these days. Few games are fire-and-forget, certainly not any games that require ongoing monetization to be profitable.

Indeed, many teams plan for a live support team equivalent to 50 percent of the total game development team just to monitor and adjust their in-game economy. So consider carefully your in-game economy, both those soft levers you can pull to create tight compulsion loops and those hard currency items you will use to make your money. Then plan to commit bright, dedicated people to the cause, each of whom (ideally) will have the mind of a dungeon master crossed with that of Alan Greenspan. If you build a great game economy and a great hard currency model that feels natural to users, you'll potentially have that mystical brass ring: a game that is both awesome and awesomely profitable.

10.5 ADDRESSING THE MATTER OF "HONEST" GAMEPLAY

As discussed in Chapter 9, "Virtual Goods," some feel that if a free player is persistent enough, they should have access to everything that a paying player does. Indeed, many games like *Pocket Legends* design their entire game and item system around this concept, primarily selling "accelerators" rather than items available only to the paying customer. The notion here is that this strategy makes the game feel "honest"; players won't feel cheated if they don't spend anything other than their time to gain parity with paying players. As you may have picked up from the stripper metaphor earlier, many game designers tend to be puritanical when it comes to monetization, and they equate charging money with something shady, if not downright prostitution of the game design. This core division between game purists, who don't believe that spending money should give players an advantage over other players or let them see anything a free player cannot, and those who instead are comfortable with selling unique content or selling an advantage is one of the most hotly debated topics in game design.

It is important to remember, then, that there is no single right way to address this problem.

The gaming world is changing; mostly it is expanding incredibly rapidly. Hundreds of different cultures play games across dozens of languages. Different types of players are playing different types of games, in very different social settings and delivery format. Currently many social games use hard currency for special items not available to the player any other way, the thought being that this creates rarity, desirability, and profitability. Yet many other games have thrived without selling anything that tips the balance in favor of one player over another. What matters is that a dual currency system has the capacity to cater to both points of view and to both player archetypes: those who value money over time and those who value time over money. The more you are able to indulge both types of players simultaneously, selling advantage to those who seek it while offering alternative avenues of advancement and uses for hard currency for those who don't, the broader your appeal and the greater your overall success.

10.6 INTERVIEW WITH BEN LAMM: "CONTROLLING CHAOS"

Ben Lamm has been leading the creative and marketing side of interactive entertainment projects since 2004. Ben served as a founder and CEO for Simply Interactive, an interactive advertising agency, then founded and is CEO of mobile-focused Chaotic Moon Studios in Austin, Texas, in 2010. Chaotic Moon focuses on creating a strong interactive mobile presence for major brands, while their sister company, Team Chaos, creates original games like *Elements: Broken Lands* for iOS.

Q: Can you tell us a little bit about who you are and what you do?

A: I'm Ben Lamm—CEO and co-founder of Chaotic Moon Studios and co-founder of Team Chaos.

Q: What is your company currently working on in the social and mobile space?

A: We're working on a healthy mix of projects in the mobile space that all use social in some capacity. Companies like Fox and Whole Foods see a definite benefit to being on mobile and connecting with their users both with content and social media. Between content sharing and even simple functions like signing into apps, mobile and social are starting to dovetail into a singular space. Makes sense, since a phone is naturally social to begin with. In just the last six months we have launched some of the world's largest apps including Marvel's mobile comic book reader and service, *Finding Nemo, American Idol,* Fox's Network App, *Xfactor,* and many more.

Q: What do you see as your major goals in the mobile gaming market?

A: Like anyone, we'd love to have a billion people playing our games and using our apps. I can also tell you that we just want to own it and build the best content for consumers as possible. From a development perspective, we're trying to really build titles that take advantage of the platform's unique strengths. That includes the way you interact, the way you pay for your experience, and even where and when gamers play. Mobile gaming brings a lot of interesting ways to really connect with gamers and bring them something really cool with all of the functionality that's being tossed into these devices, so making good use of that is key to our success in the space.

Q: You guys focus primarily on mobile games and apps. Why? Any interest in branching out to Facebook or console games?

A: Focusing on mobile and the app space is what we do now because, frankly, that's where there is the most opportunity to do new, interesting products that have the opportunity to touch millions of people. It's an evolving space and exciting to see how users influence the direction, especially being tied so close to people's everyday lives. A phone rarely leaves a person's side nowadays and that's an interesting challenge to develop an experience that ties organically into that personal connection. Since users are not just sitting down in front of a screen like a television, the time you have the user and the entire experience is different. These devices know so much about our habits and us. Using all this sensor data and new ways to input it is awesome and gives us a huge toolset to build great products.

The real fun is how mobile is only the beginning of this pervasive computing space and we plan on branching out to other digital platforms that evolve from where mobile and tablet are taking us. Wearable devices, new set top boxes with deeper connectivity, and even everyday hardware that ties into a mobile or tablet device offer a host of ways to evolve with users.

Facebook and console definitely are a part of our plot, but more along the lines that mobile will be a huge part in both console and Facebook's future. You've got a Facebook OS on Android and new consoles touting the way they play with mobile and tablet devices, so our efforts here at Chaotic Moon will, inevitably, end up working with both platforms in some capacity. We also have a collective of Unity developers in house, so that engine's compatibility with PS4, Vita, WiiU, etc. also makes consoles a bit easier to jump into.

Q: *What do you see as the future of gaming platforms on mobile devices? What services should developers look for when trying to choose a platform or publisher to release their game with?*

A: I think it's going to get weird, but in a good way.

Consoles are now latching onto mobile as another screen to play with, so you'll probably see a lot of twenty-four-hour games that go along with you, using the same assets as the console version and providing a way for gamers to always be playing with their favorite titles in experiences crafted as mobile complements to a larger game. On the flip side, mobile developers now have tools and engines that can push their games out to a larger audience on console and gaming hand-helds like Vita, which means there's a broader audience out there for developers to tap into and different ways to take advantage of being on different platforms. I think we're heading to a point where mobile gaming and console gaming will dovetail into just "gaming," with value coming from the constant engagement alongside the unique experiences the devices can offer. It will become more about connected experiences.

It'll be interesting to see how Android-based devices like Ouya and Nvidia's Project Shield are adopted, since they take a mobile market away from phones and plop a controller into the mix. Will that fracture the market and development efforts now that a peripheral is present? I hope not, but if enough people latch onto these platforms, there may be added value in developing for those gamers.

For developers, choosing a platform should be about getting the game into as many hands as possible, which means developing with an eye toward iOS and Android, naturally, but also considering how it could extend further outward. I'd also make that same challenge to indie devs on PC, to see how what they're building could extend out to mobile. Look at what 2K is doing with XCOM on tablet—it's the same game for PC, but the control scheme and tactical mechanics all will work on iOS with minor tweaks. They suddenly have a potential audience of millions who may never have played their game on a PC or Xbox, but are drawn in by the polish and gameplay they'd find there.

Q: *You've worked with some of the top brands in the world to bring them to life in mobile games, everything from Marvel to American Idol. You've also released new IP on mobile, like Elements. Many people have spoken of the difficulty of getting new IP recognized... Do you strive for a blend of licensed IP and new IP? What are the challenges in working with each type of game?*

A: Having a balance is great for us because it lets us partner and collaborate with some of the best brands and companies in the world. They're experts at what they do and that kind of collaboration helps us do some really amazing things when we all get in a room and discuss a plan for mobile. It's always fun to work on your own things and craft your own ideas and we're not moving away from that. If anything, the work we do with our partners on the licensed side of things helps us get inspired and pushes us with our original IP.

Original IP is always going to be tough to get onto people's radar, but mobile's such a reactive, adaptive platform for user feedback that we can be patient and really answer to what users want rather than float a game or app out there and hope for the best. Iteration and adaptation to the user is key to success with new IP and even licensed work, as well. You answer to the player with everything and mobile lowers the barrier of communication between ourselves and our players.

I believe mobile is also forcing really good content in games. Big studios are getting their ass kicked by independents for a reason. These consumers have a voice and channel to tell you how bad you suck or what they want changed. They also have the ability to socially promote your products. This puts a real focus on the games and the quality you are bringing to market. In some cases, it helps to balance the playing field because it becomes about the content.

Q: *What kind of advice do you have for smaller developers who are trying to get their game to break through the noise?*

A: Listen to your core user base and iterate the hell out of your projects. Build this community and have a channel to communicate with them. Remember that it's not just how the app functions, but how that app looks and what it can do for the platform you release it to that get you attention from the Apples and Googles who can feature your work. Build unique experiences, don't just rely on what's worked in the past or lash yourself to successful tropes that can turn a quick buck.

Q: *Where do you see the future of mobile and social gaming 5 years from now?*

A: Honestly, who can tell? We just started seeing Facebook and iOS/Android start to emerge a relatively short time ago and we're already seeing them evolve and shift. They disrupted the model so much and changed everyone into a gamer overnight in some fashion. If anything, the more engrained into culture these devices become, the more organic the evolution will be. You'll see that "magic" technology promises in smaller steps, integrating into things you wear, places you shop, media you view, all working in an accessible way that feels natural rather than having to jump through a few hoops to get things future forward. If broadband proliferates and becomes as important to households as gas and power, it'll be a much quicker path for this to happen.

CHAPTER 11

Conclusions

11.1 THE PLENTIFUL TIDE

There is no end in sight. For a moment, wherever you are, look toward the night sky. Count every star that you can possibly see unaided. The number is trivial compared to the number of people playing games in almost any given city block tonight in Hong Kong alone. Now imagine a billion smartphones. It's a number we passed on Earth sometime before you read this line. Imagine ten billion. Imagine that each is ten times more powerful than the PlayStation 4 or the most powerful computer in your office. Imagine each is a hundred times more powerful. Imagine a network of tightly carved up radio wave spectrums, all humming with the buzz of data from millions upon millions of simultaneous gamers playing together, online, mostly for free. This isn't a world of distant science fiction. It's more dazzling than either Edward Gibbon or William Gibson foresaw. And it is at hand, or very nearly so.

And this means there's no end in sight for you. Far below those stars and that ionosphere of humming data, we mortals have to work to make sense of this fast-moving market. The daily tide of gaming and business news brings fresh delights each morning. New acquisitions that change the landscape of mobile gaming are announced every few days. The technologies that let us dream up, create, balance, and maintain social and mobile games continue to improve at such an incredible rate that just keeping up with the newest tools requires a scholar's discipline and a centurion's stamina. And every few days three new social games and ten new connected mobile games appear, any one of which could very well change the landscape of the industry and the state of the art.

At the same time, the competition out there is fierce, the discussion fast and often heated. LinkedIn maintains a steady stream of threads from social game developers looking for work, mobile studios for hire in exotic sounding places, and chatter about partnerships, tools, designs, and potential new hires. Game development conferences like San Francisco's GDC in the spring and ChinaJoy in the summer are crowded with insightful lectures and panel discussions on the last year's design trends, while the lobby bars of the posh hotels in both cities create a watering hole where deal-makers can gather and discuss the wars and rumors of war that comprise industry scuttlebutt.

If you are someone who attends these sorts of conferences or participates in online discussions on these topics, we hope that reading this book has helped provide you with some new insight into at least a few elements of this highly complex and constantly evolving world. We hope our interviews with some of the players, both the old-timers and young upstarts, provoked the spark of a new idea or brought a smile to your face in remembering some of the good times from the past. If you find yourself attending one of these sorts of events in the future, feel free to look for us in those lobby bars and online discussions. Drop us a line or buy us a drink, and let us know your thoughts on what you've read here.

If you aren't currently in the business of making games, we hope that this book has helped demystify some of the arcana around this business. We've sought to engage with a few of the broad issues fundamental to this discipline, like monetization techniques and user acquisition, with enough depth to let you understand the major concerns and issues associated with the topics. These are constantly expanding currents of research and strategy that motivate new techniques (and jobs) within the industry. At the same time, we've tried to dive in and look at some of the seminal, exemplary works of the last few years in sufficient detail that they helped provide concrete case studies for how other games have addressed some of the challenges we've discussed. We hope that the interviews have given you a sense of the language used by industry professionals and the topics we spend hours discussing in those fancy hotel barrooms and air-conditioned corporate park conference rooms. The folks we've visited with are thought-leaders in this space, at least over the last few years, and the companies and products they discuss are worth watching, and in some cases served as educational points of reference; they're providing entertainment for literally hundreds of millions of people every month. They are also our friends, and we hope that in reading their thoughts you were able to get a sense of what a friendly, open community the game development industry can be. Generally most developers out there are motivated by their intellectual curiosity and interested in sharing their thoughts via friendly debate. We play one another's games and genuinely root for each other's success, even when our friends end up being our competitors.

Because it just never stops, this breakneck evolution of technology and industry, there is no way we can visit with every brilliant friend, colleague, and co-worker out there who could help shed a little more light on these topics. Nor could we ever cover every topic, at least not in the detail they deserve. There are countless fascinating elements of both social and mobile game design that will, for now, have to be left unscrutinized. But we hope that this brief missive has equipped you with enough of the tools and vocabulary that you might explore these topics further on your own (or at least helped to sharpen those tools you brought in with you). Since we recognize that the tides of time are working against us all, let's quickly go back and review what we've studied. Going chapter by chapter, let's briefly look at what we've discussed, with an eye toward timeliness and currency, calling out which bits have at least a hope of remaining valuable when the current crop of sand castles have all been washed back out to sea.

11.2 REVIEW

We started by looking backward in time, toward the history of gaming and the ways previous commercially successful products and networks made money from their users. We discussed early boxed products and even heard from one of the pioneers in the industry, his early Ziploc packaging, and his recap of what he thinks of as the "three eras of gaming." In the second chapter we learned that an asynchronous gameplay strategy based on an energy model that limits a users' turns within a particular time period is not new, but instead dates back to early computer networks called Bulletin Board Systems. We discussed the rise of the subscription model for gaming, first on early social networks like America Online, then with Massively Multiplayer Online games, the antediluvian predecessors of today's mega-hits like *World of Warcraft*.

We moved on to define what makes games social, not so much by how they play as by the uses to which they put social networks and social platforms. We highlight the need to encourage player-to-player behaviors that drive adoption of the game and lend themselves to user retention. We lean into an inclusive definition because we believe it offers a critical insight useful for shaping game features and systems designs, and because it seems to be the one thing that truly distinguishes "social" games from games that just happen to be played on a network. In later chapters we dwelt on ways to acquire new users through advertising, and formulas for evaluating the "K factor" of virality; the heart of social game design is in this definition, and will be long after Mark Zuckerberg is dust: A social game is one in which the user's interactions with other players help drive adoption of the game and help retain players, and which uses an external social platform of some type to facilitate these goals.

We also recognize that mobile games and social games are now very nearly one and the same. It is our belief that mobile and social games have converged, though the mobile networks have thus far been slow to realize the power of the social graphs stored on every one of our smartphones. *Words With Friends* was quite clearly a social game that benefitted hugely from virality, despite originally being offered only on mobile devices that made little innate use of the social graph. It is also our belief, after having made more than a few games for always-online, networked consoles, that the console services are racing toward a similar point of convergence in an effort not to be left behind. Indeed, we expect that within a year or three both Xbox LIVE and PlayStation Network will begin to feature games that make far more effective use of the social nature of the platform, as well as some of the business models currently popular with games on Facebook and mobile devices, and will look beyond their clouds to become better integrated with the other points of light in the social and mobile sky.

We moved on from throwing wide our arms to a broad and inclusive definition of mobile and social games to start exploring some of the business models common to such games. We cast a nostalgic eye over our shoulders here again and reviewed how each of the major monetization models rose to popularity over the last few decades. We also began to introduce and study different types of currencies, from those offered inside a particular game, to those which provide value across an entire network, like Facebook Credits. We observed that the price of games for gamers tends to get cheaper as the number of users increases. (This continues to be an interesting inverse to the cost for game publishers to acquire new users, which only seems to *increase* as the game becomes more popular.) As you move on from this book, we encourage you to keep in mind the question posed at the end of Chapter 3: "What business models make sense in a world of 2 billion gamers?" Be the first to figure out the answer to that question, and you'll be able to become richer than Donald Trump. But hurry. We're pretty close.

We moved on to discuss the parallel rise of social and mobile gaming, and why these games quickly became so popular, especially for developers. Many of the designers we interviewed mention their attraction to the space, and in Chapter 4 we looked at some of the reasons why this new area was so appealing. The ability to directly transmit a game to a consumer and more importantly the ability to study every intimate detail of how users interact with a game quickly became foundational elements for thinking about this type of game design, both on the web and on iOS and Android platforms. Finally we built on this key notion, discussing how to use analytics and A/B testing to ensure that you know what your users most want, and you're able to give it to them. Simply put, if you aren't instrumenting your software with features that make it easy to gather data about how your customers use your products—and why they stop using them—then you're unlikely to be able to compete very effectively with the rest of the industry.

We briefly skimmed over the technical advantages of modern distributed computing using "the cloud," and why social games of any type migrated in this direction. As bandwidth increases and Moore's law continues to wrestle with problems at a near atomic scale, this sort of network topology will become increasingly more important. Moreover, without fundamental improvements in battery technology, a development that seems unlikely in the absence of breakthroughs in the core sciences, mobile devices too will ultimately be forced to lean more on the cloud. Your smartphone's processor can get only so much better before it starts to consume your battery in just a few minutes, but it can easily send instructions to a vast cavern filled with computers in Norway, then happily display the results for you. The move to multi-threaded, parallel local processing has defined the architecture of gaming for the last five to ten years; hugely parallel processing distributed across a network will likely define future of gaming for the next ten years.

In this chapter we also began our discussion of why reducing user friction in initial user experiences is so critically important to social and mobile games. Users need no longer sit through lengthy install processes, and moreover they won't. As web and smartphone games grow in production polish and seek to provide ever-more immersive 3D experiences (previously the province of console and PC gaming), the technical challenges of keeping install footprints should be on the mind of every development team. An entire community of players, many of whom were never gamers before, have been taught that they can expect rich entertainment within seconds of first hearing about a game, and for free. And for mobile developers, who must deal with the twin problems of short-attention span and uncertain network topologies, the need to streamline the first moments of a gamer's experience forces us to very cleverly choreograph our front-end and user sign-in processes.

We stopped and peered down an interesting cul-de-sac then and considered what the rise of social and mobile gaming means for the retail sector. The prognosis is not particularly positive, and indeed retail gaming has suffered terrific year-over-year losses recently, as the market contracts to a small number of hugely profitable franchises. We discussed ways in which developing games for digital distribution could help offset some of the financial pain of the used games market, and we looked at how major retail gaming chains are beginning to respond to this threat to their bottom line. In so doing, we touched briefly on some of the new models of distribution networks, such as Kongregate, that are beginning to form that may well evolve into new, exploitable ecosystems for game developers.

Knowing that we were about to dive into the more detailed mechanics of user acquisition, we made a peremptory visit to a lexographer's library. We studied DAU and MAU, and learned about the relationship between the two. Both are as good of a general measure of the relative health of a game as any (other than the publisher's bank account!). And when we look at DAU/MAU we can begin to deduce some information about how sticky a game is. A sticky game should end up having an MAU consistently higher than its daily user value; gamers should be coming back almost every day to play. This, in turn, can advise your strategies regarding where to spend your time and money to get the greatest return. In a game with a high ratio, more advertising is likely to be effective. In a game with a much lower ratio, that money might be better spent improving the stickiness of the game. This sort of information has lasting value, because these sorts of analyses are useful for any game, on any platform, and even decades into the future. Indeed, the rise of post-launch analytics-driven game tuning is quickly becoming a mandate for success on almost all platforms. The days of ship-and-forget game development are over.

We ran through a non-exhaustive glossary of some of the most popular acronyms and slang expressions used in the industry. ("Whales!") Most of these are derived from old MMO developer jargon, but the concepts are still applicable here, and likely will continue to be so long as games are played on networked devices. Of these, perhaps the most powerful concept is that of lifetime network value (LTNV). This unwieldy little acronym is critical because it conveys the important (but hard to measure) sense that users have immense value to the developer beyond the money they directly spend on a product. This notion touches on the idea of virality, in which users have value because they may tell their friends about the game and so "infect" them with the desire to play. LTNV also captures the notion that users can be monetized in indirect ways, from offer walls to being called upon to tutor new players.

Projecting forward, one could imagine any number of innovative ways to monetize users beyond those currently in play. Remember SETI@Home, or the various protein-chain analysis screensavers that were popular around 2005? What if users could agree to devote a portion of their computing power to solving hard problems like those? Might compensation in in-game currency be a good reward for them? Could an enterprising game developer architect a system by which the idle processing cycles from millions of users were farmed out as a cloud service? Could gamers be rewarded for performing in-game actions that also helped mine bitcoins? Certainly such a thing is technically possible and could have broadly useful applications.

Midway through the chapter on terms and metrics, we discussed measurements and analytics at length. Indeed, as we harped on earlier, this is now a critical component of online games, but there is nothing inherently social about this practice. All games, software, and other user applications could benefit from this sort of calculated introspection. This concept remains critical throughout the rest of the book and appears in several of our interviews, as well. In short, networked games allow developers to harvest information about how users play their games, how they monetize, and when they stop playing. This information allows designers to tune games in response to user preferences to a degree that was simply impossible only a few decades ago. Of course, properly architected software and backend systems are key to genuinely successful fine-tuning, and the platform must support the kind of rapid iteration that allows developers to respond to the data they gather; currently this is something of a roadblock to a truly effective use of analytic data on many social networks, but this won't be the case for long. Whatever else Zynga's legacy may end up being, they have certainly taught the game development community the power of these sorts of iterative techniques.

We wrapped up the section on metrics by looking at the results of *Ravenwood Fair*'s public analytic data, which provided valuable insight into the early days of a successful social game created by one of gaming's storied designers. From our *Ravenwood Fair* study we learned how the metrics surrounding user retention are used by the current crop of successful social games to evaluate their current level of success and the health of their future development. The *Ravenwood Fair* study and the core concepts that made it successful have broad applicability to various types of games in development right now; moreover these fundamentals are sure to continue to be valuable far into the future of game development.

We waited until what may have seemed shockingly late to pose the key question, "What is a Social Network?" But we did it to support a theory that there are in fact several more burgeoning social networks than just Facebook. It is our stance that mobile devices themselves, and the currently dominant iOS and Android operating systems that make them accessible, are untapped and powerful social networks. We believe that modern connected console platforms (like Xbox LIVE and PlayStation Network) are themselves exploding with a wealth of social features. And we believe that there are a number of upcoming social networks that are interesting and may ultimately end up challenging Facebook's dominance of the market (though not likely this year). Much as Rome ruled the West, Atari once ruled the games market. Then there was Nintendo. Then Facebook. Now Apple and Android. Empires are inherently transient. No one can sit on a throne forever. As Richard Garriott reminds us in his interview, the evolution of game development technology is accelerating; there's always room for new ideas, new platforms, new markets, new leaders. Evolution rarely slows down, but it often speeds up. Don't let yourself be trapped into thinking that today's platforms are the only ones to consider. Don't believe that Flash-driven games will remain the standard for web-based games; barbarians like Unity and HTML5 are already at the gate. (And indeed both Facebook and mobile platforms have leapfrogged past the clumsy browser games that originally dominated the space.) Strive to think broadly about what makes games and networks social now and what will make them such a decade from now.

After defining social networks, we learned a bit about PopCap's seminal study on social gaming populations. Their message has often been reduced to the slightly misleading notion that "Social gamers are all 35-year-old women." This is not the point of the study, even if it were true, which it is clearly not. The broader message here is that gamers are *no longer* the relatively narrow band of adolescent (and post-adolescent) males that used to dominate the realm. The entire world now games, or at least those parts that are not concerned with the daily mechanics of survival, and even some of them. As you think about this section of the book, keep an eye toward the future; remember Mark Pincus's comment regarding thinking of games like a cocktail party that you want everyone to enjoy attending. At the same time, also keep Ryan Cleven's comment in mind. Whatever narrow subgenre you are into, digital distribution will probably allow you to connect with hundreds of thousands of people who are into it, too. As we've all learned from Wargaming.net, it turns out that even something as niche as historically accurate World War II tanks can reach a terrific market if well executed.

The world is full, but our connections make it tiny. As I write this, I'm sitting a few stories up in a hotel in Seattle, watching a throng of Penny Arcade attendees swarm about for what I'm told is now the city's largest annual convention. These conventioneers span all ages and come in all shapes, sizes, colors, and genders. They are gamers, every one, and despite their diversity, they represent only the tip-top of the most hardcore market: gamers now are of every age, ethnicity, gender, and economic background.

Once we really understood who our target users were, we dived into a discussion of how to acquire and retain them. We dusted off an old marketing and sales metaphor called the Purchase Funnel and examined how virality alters that model. Since marketing and the acquisition of new users are inexorably linked, it's important that anyone with a stake in game development understand the various tactics currently employed to attract new users. While on the surface this discussion might have appeared focused on the concerns of the moment, there are certain lessons that can be extracted for extrapolation onto future platforms, in future decades:

- Persuading disinterested users to evaluate your product for some external gain isn't likely to lead to new and loyal customers.

- In a world of ever increasing noise-to-signal ratio, simply flashing ads on a website or throwing a game onto the iTunes App store and hoping it might catch a prospective user's eye is unlikely to win many converts. Modern audiences are cynical and often immune to advertising such that the value of a random impression is low and gets lower every year. You'll need a bigger bag of tricks.

- The more targeted an enticement is, the greater chance of the user becoming someone with a significant LTNV. There's just no substitute for directing advertising to the type of person who already wants to play your game. Understanding your users is the only real way to effectively target them.

- Networks of all types and all devices will continue to improve their ability to profile users. The sorts of technologies Google has so dramatically improved in the last decade with AdWords and other types of targeting have helped to reduce the number of misdirected offers and general advertisement "spamming." Facebook and other social networks have already made use of these advances, but they will continue to improve as the user base increases. Though these techniques are still in their infancy, they already allow advertisers to target users with an impressive level of specificity. We should expect ever improving ways of reaching those users most likely to care about our particular product.

Once you've got users, you need to retain them, and we discussed various strategies for increasing stickiness in game. Almost all of these design techniques are platform agnostic, and the ability to wield them effectively is one hallmark of a great game designer. A trend we've seen used to great effect in the last five years is the adoption of RPG-style metagame loops to increase user engagement. *Call of Duty Modern Warfare* gave us all a stellar example of this in the first-person shooter space; its use of a classic XP-based RPG advancement layer atop their already compelling multiplayer layer pointed the way for hundreds of other games. Most social games now use a similar leveling system, which was once the bulwark of the *Wizardry* and *Might & Magics* of the world. Expect trends like this to continue, such that successful compulsion mechanics from diverse genres will continue to be brought into more casual games in an effort to increase stickiness. Other common techniques, like leaderboards and messages to remind users to return, are likely to improve in value only as designers learn to use them more effectively and target them more directly.

In our next section, we dove a bit deeper into the different ways to monetize games. We focused on digital download models and the various ways to get money out of users who play the basic game for free. Almost the entire publishing, gaming, and financial world believes that digital distribution will continue to erode retail sales. (However, it's unlikely that the imminent death of retail is at hand; people enjoy physically shopping and malls, and probably still will in 2050.) The specifics of much of this section, dealing with Steam, Origin, Direct2Drive, Impulse, and the like will likely be valuable for the next few years, before the particular players change, but the basic practice of selling games via direct download off the internet and directly onto mobile phones will likely continue on far into the future (barring zombie apocalypse). The specific methods of monetizing freemium games, from ad sales, to selling play time and offering rare virtual goods, are all likely to remain viable strategies.

We evaluated the best monetization approaches for classic game genres and some hybrid models that have been successful for more modern game designs. Eventually we concluded that most models *might* work for almost any genre, but that by considering carefully the specifics of what motivates your users to play your game in particular, you'll be best able to design a monetization system that can maximize your profits, while minimizing your user alienation.

And because people *do* like shopping, virtual goods are and will continue to be popular in games. In fact, as virtual worlds and online gaming continue to grow in popularity, we should expect the sale of virtual goods to continue to grow in importance. If we are to believe Richard Garriott's comments about the likelihood of more immersive "virtual realities" or take our cues from the cyberpunk fiction of the 1990s like Neil Stephenson's *Snow Crash* or Tad Williams's *Otherland*, we should expect users to become increasingly invested in their avatars. One need only watch a loved one fall prey to the addiction of

World of Warcraft on a tiny screen with a primitive input device to recognize the power of enhanced immersion in fantasy worlds. Selling virtual goods will continue to increase in popularity, and the suggestions in this chapter will broadly apply to game design for decades to come.

You cannot buy a virtual good without a virtual currency, though, so in Chapter 10 we looked at in-game currencies and the most popular of the dual currency models. While the current best practices for dealing with engagement currency and hard currencies may continue to be viable for some time, this area still feels like somewhat of a frontier. One might expect a more standardized (and decentralized) internet currency to develop. Bitcoins are a fascinating development in the digital currency space, in which currency is generated based on the value of processing power, with inflation built into the currency model. Might these become a standardized global online currency? Alternately if social networks continue to follow the "winner-takes-all" trend that Facebook currently enjoys and that Apple's iTunes lists promote, it may be that a private currency owned by a commercial interest acts as the standard. We attempted to keep our discussion here practical and fairly general in the hopes that it might be broadly applicable to game designers and developers in the coming years. Beyond that, we encourage any budding students of economics and/or futurists out there to write in and tell us what they expect to see from virtual monetary policy in the coming decades. Who will be the first Alan Greenspan of a virtual country?

11.3 A FOND FAREWELL TO FRIENDS

It never stops. The constellations keep changing, and there's a new tide coming in every morning. But we've done as much analysis of this exciting space as is prudent at this juncture. You should read this book, then move forward and think further; we need to get back to making games. So take up your oars, centurion, but keep an eye on the stars. Gather those brilliant, dedicated engineers, designers, artists, and financiers and pile them into your boat. There is room for many more bright points in the firmament. Head out with tonight's tide, and keep a lookout. There be dragons out there, and sea monsters, but also enchanted isles filled with doubloons. They are yours for the taking. And send us a message in a bottle describing your journey; maybe we'll meet up on some distant shore to share a cold one and continue this debate on game design.

Until then,

—**tf**
July 7, 2013

Index

Note: Page numbers followed by *f* indicate figures.

nted in the United States
Baker & Taylor Publisher Services